momofuku

momofuku

david chang and peter meehan

PHOTOGRAPHS BY GABRIELE STABILE

CLARKSON POTTER/PUBLISHERS | NEW YORK

Published in the United States by Clarkson Potter/Publishers, an imprint
of the Crown Publishing Group, a division of Random House, Inc., New York.
www.crownpublishing.com
www.clarksonpotter.com

CLARKSON POTTER is a trademark and POTTER with colophon
is a registered trademark of Random House, Inc.

Photographs on pages 16, 17, 23, 24, 25, and 107 courtesy of the author.
Photographs on pages 28, 30, 115, and 118 reprinted courtesy of Swee Phuah.
Image on page 246 reprinted courtesy of Yoshikazu Tsuno/AFP/Getty Images.

Library of Congress Cataloging-in-Publication Data is available upon request.

ISBN 978-0-307-45195-8

Printed in China

Design by Marysarah Quinn

10 9 8 7 6 5 4

First Edition

to josh, quint, and kara

I have been ten days in this temple
and my heart is restless.
The scarlet thread of lust at my feet
has reached up long.
If someday you come looking for me,
I will be in a shop that sells fine seafood,
a good drinking place,
or a brothel.

—Ikkyu, fifteenth-century Zen Buddhist high priest

Despite a lack of natural ability, I did have the one
element necessary to all early creativity: naïveté, that
fabulous quality that keeps you from knowing just
how unsuited you are for what you are about to do.

—Steve Martin, *Born Standing Up*

contents

introduction

What is Momofuku? That's a tough one.

Momofuku is a restaurant group based in the East Village in New York City. The Momofuku restaurants are irrefutably casual places with music blaring at all hours of the day, with the kitchens opened and exposed, with backless stools to sit on, and with framed John McEnroe Nike ads passing as decor. Momofuku is the anti-restaurant.

Momofuku, the name, is Japanese; David Chang, the owner and head chef, is Korean American; the food eludes easy, or really any, classification. There is a focus on good technique, on seasonality and sustainability, on intelligent and informed creativity. But it is deliciousness by any means that they're really going for. Chang has called it "bad pseudo-fusion cuisine," by which I take him to mean that anyone who needs to ask probably wouldn't understand. Using a quote from Wolfgang Puck to describe the restaurant's cooking, he's made the argument that Momofuku tries to serve delicious "American" food. Seems like the most useful descriptor to me. Where else would labne and ssämjang and Sichuan peppercorns and poached rhubarb all end up in the same kitchen?

For people living in or attuned to the bubble world that is the post-millennial restaurant scene in America, Momofuku is a kinetic, hype-generating buzz magnet the likes of which has rarely, if ever, been seen. And few chefs, now or before, have gotten the golden shower of awards, attention, and praise that Chang has, especially at his age, especially while unapologetically pursuing a path that so aggressively flaunts convention.

Momofuku is, from the inside looking out, like a gang, or maybe a pirate crew. A way of life lived under a flag with an orange peach on it instead of a Jolly Roger. A collective, but not some idyllic hippie thing; instead a group of humble, talented, and dedicated people working as a whole to make their restaurants better every day, to revisit and re-create their menus, to always, always be pushing ahead. Complacency and contentedness are scarce commodities at Momofuku.

And me? I hated Momofuku Noodle Bar the first time I went there. Hated it.

It was late 2003. I was new to my job reviewing cheap restaurants for the *New York Times;* I was more enthralled with the ideal of authenticity than I am now, six years later. But if those were my problems, those were

Momofuku's problems, too: it took the place a while to shake off the newness and settle into a groove, for Chang and Joaquin Baca to loosen themselves from the conceptual shackles they'd opened with, to just start cooking whatever they wanted instead of laboring under the constraints of being a "noodle bar"—propagandist-in-chief Chang's way of not calling his ramen shop a ramen shop—and becoming Noodle Bar as it exists today.

And did they change it. My editor urged me to go back and check the place out about eight months into its life. And though I didn't think I'd like it any more than I had the first time around, that's what the job was all about. And that second meal at Noodle Bar just killed me. It was so fucking good, and not in some lightbulby way, but because it was gutsy. It was honest. It was delicious, that least descriptive of all food words, but it was and it was so in a way that made me want more.

After I reviewed Momofuku, I started eating there regularly, going every Saturday at noon, before the lines formed and the crowds crowded. (Chang still puzzles at the little groups that assemble outside his restaurants in the minutes before they flip over the open sign, protesting that they should go home and order some Chinese food if they're hungry. But he's like that.)

Mark Bittman, who wrote *How to Cook Everything* and was my lord and master before he helped me land the gig at the *Times,* was my regular lunch companion. Eventually he introduced me to Chang. We said hi and that was about it.

Then, one night in Brooklyn a few weeks later, I was at a club called Warsaw seeing The Hold Steady when I felt this meaty hand slap me on the back. I turned around and there was Chang, probably as toasted as I was, with a beer extended toward me and the question, which he yelled over the music, "Are we going to pretend like we don't know each other?"

We're the same age, Chang and I, and we were standing there at the same show, and he had a cold beer in his hand. I took it. That's how we got to knowing each other.

We'd grab a beer every once in a while in the months after that, bitch

about whatever, eat cheap Chinese or Korean food. At some point Dave asked me to help him write this book. I didn't see how I could say no.

It was those flavors. That pop. The fucking pork buns. The way Chang and company put together combinations that read like muddy dead ends—Brussels sprouts and kimchi, really?—but slapped me awake every time I ate them. Who wouldn't want to know how to make this stuff? Who wouldn't want to have the recipes for this food that was upending the hegemony and balance of the New York restaurant world? Who wouldn't jump at the chance to work with the kitchen there, to try and ferret out what they were doing to make the food so goddamn good?

There was also the unlikely story of Momofuku's genesis, evolution, and ascension. It's been told many times, by many good writers—in *New York, GQ, The New Yorker,* and everywhere—but it was a chance to help Chang tell it himself. Who'd pass on that?

So here it is. The story of how Momofuku happened, or at least Chang's version of it. It starts in the early years of the twenty-first century, with Dave finding his way into the kitchen, and then out of it, and then into a former chicken-wing joint, where he opens a ramen shop.

After that he opens a burrito shop that turns into something else entirely. Along the way he picks up a band of coconspirators, his chefs and chefs de cuisine, and he meets friendly science-minded chefs and meatmen who help him along the way.

It ends, at least in terms of this book, in March 2008, with the opening menu at Ko, his third restaurant. Ko, which has since been honored with all manner of stars and awards and has propelled Dave onto the international stage (at least in the food world), is actually in the space that was once a five-for-a-dollar chicken-wing spot. Go figure.

There are also the recipes for a bunch of the dishes, lots of Momofuku "classics"—or at least that's what they feel like. The menus at the Momofuku restaurants change almost daily, so these are, for the most part, dishes that

persisted, that wouldn't leave the menus without an unpleasant bout of kicking and screaming.

There are epic dishes—the bo ssäm you should plan on making for your next Super Bowl party, the rib-eye recipe to end all rib-eye recipes, the masterpiece of minutiae that is the Ko egg dish. But there are also dozens of almost insanely simple recipes that will change your approach to everyday cooking (or at least they did mine): the scores of easy pickles that keep in the fridge for weeks; ginger-scallion sauce, which was synonymous for me with summertime lunch while working on this book; the octo vin and the fish sauce vinaigrette that are as good over plain rice or cubed tofu as they are used as directed in these recipes. I have converted more than one Brussels sprout hater with Tien Ho's Vietnamese-inflected Brussels sprout recipe in the Ssäm Bar chapter.

There is no attempt herein to answer the how/why conundrum of Momofuku. Of how these restaurants run by this Dave Chang character have succeeded so phenomenally, of why Momofuku went from a plywood-walled diamond in the rough to an undeniable and seemingly unstoppable force in the world of restaurants. Or how or why Dave, when there were so many more likely candidates, turned into an award-mongering poster boy for modern chefdom. Dave is thirty-one and he doesn't know, so why press the point?

I'm sure there are some clues and signposts between these covers. But this isn't an autopsy and there's plenty more to come in the Momofuku story. Maybe the answer lies ahead, but Chang and I both suspect that whatever twists and turns will follow, none will be as improbable as the tale told here.

PFM

2009

noodle bar

noodle bar

Koreans are notorious noodle eaters.

I am no exception.

I grew up eating noodles. Chinese noodles, Korean noodles, all kinds of noodles in all kinds of places: in Los Angeles, in Seoul, in Virginia. My dad had it perfectly timed with one place near our house in Alexandria, Virginia: he'd call before we drove over to it so that bowls of *jjajangmyun*—wheat noodles in a black bean sauce—would be hot and waiting on the table as soon as we walked in. I remember being transfixed by the guy making noodles—the way he'd weave and slap a ball of dough into a ropy pile—then being struck by the sting of the white onions and vinegar served with *jjajangmyun*. On nights when it was just him and me, he'd make me eat sea cucumber along with the noodles, and the weirdness of eating them would be offset by the warm afterglow of pride that came with making him happy.

And when I was fending for myself as a teenager and, later, in college, there was only one answer to hunger if I didn't have the time or money to go out for some fried chicken: Sapporo Ichiban Original Flavor instant ramen, the kind that comes in the red packet. That was what I ate, sometimes to the exclusion of almost everything else, until I got into Nong Shim's Gourmet Spicy Shin Bowl noodle soup, which comes in a styrofoam bowl, à la Cup Noodles, making it that much easier to prepare.

As I got older, noodles became a hobby. I noted the difference in preparation and flavoring from restaurant to restaurant. It was innocent enough. My dad had warned me away from giving serious thought to working in a kitchen. He was a busboy at an Irish bar when he and my mom first immigrated here. Though he graduated from busboy to restaurant owner during the years he was getting settled, he'd sold his restaurants and gone into the golf business by the time I was a kid. He didn't see any point in my following in those footsteps.

After high school, I went to Trinity College in Hartford, Connecticut, and spent four years majoring in religion. I spent a year abroad in London back when there was just a single outpost of Wagamama. It served affordable, tasty bowls of ramen for 10 to 11 quid and I ate there regularly. I spent a bunch of the rest of my time daydreaming about writing a screenplay that told the story of the *Bhagavad-Gita* through the lens of the Civil War with Robert E. Lee in the hero's role.

After school, I worked a couple of jobs where I pushed paper and sat at a

desk. But I knew there was no way that path was going to pay off. Without a clear idea of what I wanted to do, I parlayed my useless liberal arts degree into a gig teaching English at a school in Wakayama, two hours southeast of Osaka. I decided I'd teach English by day, eat noodles the rest of the time, and maybe at some point figure out what I was going to do with myself.

I lived a few train stops away from the school in a little town called Izumi-Tottori. There wasn't much there: a maki roll place, a sushi place, a dumpling house, and a ramen shop. The ramen shop was near the train station, and it was always busy, always bustling. It was like the town pub, where everybody went to drink and talk shit about each other. The place served tonkotsu-style ramen—it's the porkiest ramen broth you can get, with the pork fat emulsi-fied into the broth—and there were bowls of hard-boiled eggs everywhere that customers helped themselves to while they waited for their soup.

Rather than try to force my way into the conversation, I'd sit there—first at this place, and later at any ramen or noodle shop I could get a seat in—by

This was the view out my back window in Izumi-Tottori. I'd spend hours watching these hundred-year-old people picking rice.

myself, shrouded in the sound of slurping noodles and the racket of the kitchen turning out bowl after bowl of soup, and just watch the place work. Watch what people ate. Watch how they ate. Try to figure out this ramen thing for myself.

But let's take a break from navel-gazing and get a few things down about what ramen is and isn't.

At the end of the day, ramen is not much different from any Asian noodle soup. It's a broth with noodles in it. And while ramen is now Japanese, the Japanese got it from the Chinese. Lo mein is ramen's Chinese precursor. (If you pronounce ramen properly, "ra-myun," you'll hear that they practically have the same name.) It has this mystique—the movie *Tampopo* did a lot to raise its profile—but it's soup with noodles in it, topped with stuff. That's it. I love ramen, but the sanctimony that's often attached to it is a bit too much.

As I've pieced it together, the Japanese started making these lo mein–style noodle soups around the turn of the nineteenth century. As would have been the case in China, the broth could be chicken or beef or seafood or pork; toppings, when added, varied. In the early 1900s, a style of ramen started to become common in Tokyo. Its components were pork broth, boiled noodles, sliced roast pork, scallions, and bamboo shoots. Over time, that became the template, the standard, the definition of ramen.

As ramen grew in popularity, it spread to other regions and islands and it began to evolve. Cooks who opened ramen shops put their stamp on the soups they made. *Shoyu ramen*—ramen with a heavy dose of soy sauce added to the broth—seems inevitable when you look back on it. *Shio ramen*—with salt in place of shoyu (and a totally different, cleaner, lighter taste)—followed. Certain styles became synonymous with the places from which they sprung: the Hokkaido Prefecture, for example, is the home of miso ramen.

The most important development in the story of the popularization of ramen—and probably one of the most important events in the history of food—occurred in 1958, when Momofuku Ando, a middle-aged tinkerer, invented instant ramen and unleashed it on the world. His invention introduced millions of people to the world of ramen, myself included.

By the eighties, every ramen shop in Japan had its own distinctive style: rigorous ordering rules, lines that wrapped around the block, how they sliced their pork, how much fat they added to their soup. (There is a type of ramen called *abura ramen,* which means "fat" ramen: hot noodles tossed in hot pork fat seasoned with things like crushed sesame seeds, soy sauce, scallions, and bonito. It can be so rich it can make you sick. I love it.) Like pizza or barbecue in America, every shop has its own fanatical following. (And, like pizza or barbecue, everyone's favorite ramen shop tends to be the one they grew up with, regardless of its faults.) I wanted to try all of them. I spent an unhealthy amount of my free time during my stay in Japan eating at ramen shops.

I learned the vocabulary: *omori* portions had extra noodles. *Menma* was the name for bamboo shoots. The soy sauce used to season and flavor the soups in Tokyo wasn't just soy, but *taré*—a combination of soy, mirin, and sake, often boiled with chicken bones, that has its roots in the yakitori tradition.

I filled up notebooks with notes on ramen and noodle places and, loser (literally) that I am, lost track of all of them over the years. Some industrious night, well before I opened Momofuku and before my notebooks disappeared, I decided I'd type all my notes into the computer. I only did it for one place, for Taishoken, the birthplace of *tsukemen*—the style of serving the noodles, hot or cold, on a plate and the broth in a bowl next to it for dunking.

. . .

This was the street outside my apartment. The ramen shop was just up the block.

Notes from October 20, 2003

Went early Sunday to Taishoken @ Higeshikebukuro, supposed to be the best or top 3 ramen shop in all of Tokyo. Left at 10:30, got there at 11:00 a.m., doors open at 11—waited 1 hour 45 minutes to get around the corner. . . . Unbelievable that by the time I get to the entrance, the line is even longer. There must be at least 300 people in line.

The place is so small: 6–7 people eat at the bar, 6 people eat at 2 tables, 2 tables outside of door seat 6. A fucking dump. 1 guy taking orders from everyone in line, about 20 people at a time. Amazing ordering system . . . you sit down, and your food is there.

3–4 cooks, 1 guy cooking noodles, 1 guy cooling noodles for *tsukemen/morisoba,* another guy prepping mise en place, another guy finishing plates, and what appears to be Mr. Yamagashi, famed owner/chef, cooking noodles and handing out the broth. Everyone has towels wrapped around their heads and is wearing rain boots.

1) soy sauce is placed in bowl, then stock
2) gigantic helping of noodles
3) toppings are placed
4) finished with a touch of stock

Size is outrageously big, biggest bowl ever?—cuts of char siu—not from belly, are ½ inch thick—butt?

Toppings: scallions, hard-boiled egg, *menma*—it seems that they cook their *menma* in their own manner, I'm not sure if it's dried and then rehydrated—a piece of fish cake, and nori

I'm figuring that the soy sauce contains vinegar and chile pepper. The stock I see contains bones, carrots, onions, konbu, dried sardines, and mackerel.

First slurp of soup: surprisingly sharp with white pepper, spicy chile, and a kick of vinegar. After 2–3 minutes, cannot notice heat.

Noodles not made there?

One can tell that they've been doing this for a while, serious business back there in the kitchen. Must go back and try regular ramen, not *omori* size. Flavors are great, not too oily, etc.

Reason for success is flavor is so different.

At the time, I knew I wasn't going to be holding forth on the conjugation of basic English verbs for Japanese kids for the rest of my life. I decided I wanted to work in a ramen shop. To learn ramen for real. My timid efforts to do so during the time I lived in Izumi-Tottori were fruitless. My Japanese was bad, I had no training, and I had no business working in a kitchen.

It was the via negativa way of figuring out I wanted to do with my life: I didn't know what I wanted, but I knew what I didn't want. I couldn't stand wearing a suit or navigating office politics. I wouldn't have to deal with either in a kitchen. I couldn't imagine striving to get promoted to associate regional manager. I could imagine that learning to cook and striving to get better at it would be rewarding—I'd been a successful golfer and football player as a kid, and the physicality of kitchen work seemed similar to me in that it was repetitious and rewarded some people's efforts more than others. I knew I wasn't going to become an academic and I couldn't stand office work, so maybe I could pour myself into cooking, to see how far it would take me—maybe, if I worked hard, I'd go back to Japan, to a ramen shop, where I'd be the guy in the rain boots hollering orders. I wanted to see how far I could go. (Though I now know that I had no idea how deep the rabbit hole is.)

I decided if I were serious, I'd need to go to culinary school first. So I closed up shop and moved back to the States, where I enrolled in the French Culinary Institute in New York City. I was going to become a cook. Then I'd go back to Japan and they'd have to hire me.

FCI was quick—six months in and out. I learned enough to get into a kitchen and get yelled at constantly about how little I knew or did right. I started off at Mercer Kitchen, one of the restaurants owned by Jean-Georges Vongerichten, a good starting place for me. I got to work the line, to do some real cooking.

While I was working at Mercer, I caught up one night with Marc Salafia, a friend from college, and he told me he was going to work at Tom Colicchio's new restaurant, Craft. Craft was massively hyped at the time. Colicchio's clean flavors and American/French cooking at Gramercy Tavern had earned him a cult following in New York—I was a huge fan—and this was his first post-Gramercy venture. After talking to Marc about Craft, I knew it was the place I wanted to work. I put in a call to the chef de cuisine, Marco Canora, who told me he didn't have room or a need for my services "unless I wanted to answer the phones."

So on my days off from Mercer Kitchen, I answered phones at Craft.

Craft's conceit was simple: an all à la carte menu, with sides, proteins, starches, and sauces all offered separately. That meant that every item had to be cooked perfectly and that all the products had to be top quality—there was no extra dash of a delicious sauce to help along a slightly overcooked piece of meat, no imperfect polenta made passable in the presence of a perfectly braised lamb shank. Everything had to be right. The glimpse I got into the kitchen life there—the dedication of the cooks, the talent, the quality of the ingredients—kept me answering the phones and bothering Marco every single day for a chance to peel carrots and clean mushrooms.

I don't mean to slight the Mercer, but I felt that I would be better served honing my fundamentals under the tutelage of some truly amazing cooks. The crew at Craft was unbelievable: Marco Canora, Karen DeMasco, Jonathan Benno, Damon Wise, Ahktar Nawab, James Tracey, Mack Kern, Dukie, Dan Sauer, Liz Chapman, Ed Higgins—all of them have gone on to become chefs of their own restaurants, chefs of note in their own right.

My determination paid off. I found a way into the kitchen by working for free in the mornings: chopping mirepoix, cleaning morels, doing menial but essential tasks. I loved it. To make ends meet, I quit my job at the Mercer and answered phones full-time for the first month Craft was open. When they opened for lunch, I graduated to paid kitchen slave and, eventually, to cook. I learned about ingredients. I learned about technique. I learned how to work for—or at least how to avoid pissing off—a demanding chef. I learned a lot at Craft.

But I was still a noodle eater. I hit all of the relatively few ramen spots in the city and, in a bit of daydreaming, would regularly write letters, have a friend translate them into Japanese, and mail them off to ramen shops in Tokyo that I'd heard of or eaten at. I knew my chances were slim, but I didn't stop trying.

I never got a single response.

Toward the end of my second year at Craft, a friend of my father's caught wind of my situation and passed along word that he could set me up with a kitchen job in a Tokyo ramen shop if I was interested. He even had a place for me to stay.

Me, in a ramen shop in Tokyo. I didn't ask which one or where or what kind of ramen it served. All I wanted to do was go.

The one stumbling block: I didn't feel ready to leave Craft and I didn't feel great about leaving a place and a group of people who had taught me so much and still had more to teach me. But I needed to go to Tokyo.

I was freaked out about giving my notice to Marco. One afternoon, I caught him coming back from jury duty, gave three months' notice, started to explain about ramen, and . . . he didn't need to hear it. Everyone in that kitchen knew I was obsessed and understood what it meant to go to Japan and learn about ramen for real.

When I finally got to Tokyo, the situation I found myself in was stranger than anything I could have anticipated.

I was to live and work in a converted office building in the Kudan-shita district of Tokyo. On the ground floor there was an *izakaya,* or Japanese pub, and a *ramenya,* or ramen shop. In Japan, a *ramenya* serves ramen and almost nothing else. The seventh and top floor was home to a born-again Christian church run by Koreans. The floors between were split between anonymous offices for salarymen and a sort of halfway house for wayward middle-aged men who had fallen out of step with Japanese society. It seemed like many had spent some time on the streets on their way to this place—an odd group to be thrown in with, for sure, but I was thankful that most of them spoke more English than I did Japanese. At night, my room was faintly illuminated red and yellow at night by the McDonald's across the street.

The *ramenya* downstairs was where I was going to make my bones. I was ready to wash dishes, ready to slice scallions for months, ready to do whatever it took. The setting was strange and it didn't seem likely that I'd ended up in the best ramen kitchen ever, but I was ready for the challenge.

Or at least that's what I thought until my first day in the kitchen.

The restaurant's ramen was middling. Okay, maybe, but not better than that. Still, I was here in Japan, in a kitchen, going to work. It's common to work your way up from a weak kitchen to a strong one, I told myself, so I planned to keep my head down and take what I could from the arrangement.

But I could barely take it at all. The problem was the chef, a gray-haired ghost of a man, wrinkled in the way that often begs a description like "wizened" but in his case was closer to withered. He lived in the building on the floor below me. I'd spotted him the first night I was there: wandering through the hallway in saggy, sallow-looking briefs, his concave chest laboring to puff on cigarettes that I would find out were a permanent fixture of his waking life.

When I introduced myself to him in the kitchen on my first day of work, his outfit wasn't much different. I assume he owned shirts but I rarely if ever saw him wearing one. In the kitchen he added the accessory of greasy folded-over newsprint (he preferred newsprint to towels) tucked into his apron strings or, if he was being more careless than usual, into the elastic waistband of his not-so-tighty not-so-whities.

Even if I could have figured out how to make it work in a pants-optional kitchen, there were too many other things going against the place: the shortcuts in the kitchen meant I wouldn't be learning as much as I could. During my time at Craft, I'd worked with the best ingredients. Here, the ingredients were substandard to begin with and the chef had some issue with refrigerators, which meant that the meat for the soup would sometimes sit out for hours, seeping blood on the counters and the floor and steeping in the toxic cloud of cheap cigarette smoke that followed him everywhere.

I am not a quitter, so I stuck it out as long as I could—which was days, not weeks. But I couldn't stand to be there. I thought long and hard about my decision and finally resolved that even if it meant going back to New York and begging my way back into Craft, I had to quit. When I told the chef, he looked at me vacantly, like I was hard to see, and toddled off. I doubt he noticed my absence.

After the ramen shop, I wiggled my way into some work at the izakaya. It wasn't mind-blowing stuff and it wasn't ramen, but anything was better than that old man's kitchen.

My father's acquaintance who'd arranged to get me to Japan generously set out to find me another opportunity and, much to my surprise—I thought I'd deep-fry kara-age at the izakaya, eat as much ramen as I could, and when I'd blown through the money I brought with me, head back to New York—he did, at a soba shop. Out of politeness I didn't refuse the connec-

tion, but I didn't uproot my life to cook soba. But soba are noodles, too, I told myself, so I went to Mei-dae-mae, a residential neighborhood, to meet Akio Hosoda at his restaurant, Soba-ya Fuyu-Rin.

Akio and his restaurant were everything I could have hoped for. The soba shop was on the first floor of his tidy two-story home. The restaurant was simple, elegant, sparse without being minimalist, calm, and serene. Akio and Yuki, his wife, were the only people who worked there and were the only people who had ever worked there. (I have no idea what promises were made or lies constructed to convince Akio to let me train with him, but I am thankful for them all the same.)

I had imagined myself in a busy kitchen having order after order yelled at me, needing to wear rain boots to protect myself from the waves of noodle water and ramen broth that would swell like a tide during service. In contrast, I never, during my time there, saw the restaurant serve more than ten or fifteen diners in a day. In reality, the slow, steady, controlled pace—and Akio's ability to constantly, constantly be perfecting and honing and refining and fine-tuning every single thing he did—was a monumentally important lesson for me. Akio had been making soba for so long he could have gone on autopilot and still turned out excellent food. But in his kitchen I saw ritual—grinding the flour, mixing the dough, rolling the dough, slicing the noodles, making the taré, every last boring bit of prep work—treated as something important, vital, necessary. There were no shortcuts in Akio's kitchen or, I'm guessing, in Akio's world.

He was silent when other chefs I'd cooked for would have been loud. He used amazing ingredients as a matter of course and only talked to me about their provenance when I pestered him. His technique was flawless, but there was no showiness to it: things were done

Me with Sous-chef Nakamura at the New York Grill at the Park Hyatt Hotel in Tokyo.

one way, the right way. For weeks, we worked on my noodle dough mixing technique, even though none of my noodles ever ended up in a customer's bowl. When I graduated to slicing noodles, he made me shred reams of newsprint before I was allowed to cut a single noodle. He did not seek praise or the limelight, just enough customers each day to allow him to keep practicing his craft.

I studied under Akio, helping with menial preparations, washing dishes and watching, quietly, for months. Then one day, a friend, Herman Mao, a young architect who had recently graduated from Washington University, came by for a meal. He talked with Akio during his dinner, and at some point he let it slip that I was hoping to open a ramen shop back in New York.

For most chefs, the daydreams of their helpers are a distant concern if they're a concern at all. To Akio, the idea that I was at his restaurant dithering in soba when my real goals were tied to a completely different noodle was tantamount to treason.

Akio sat me down that night for the first and only man-to-man talk we ever had and told me, "It's either soba or not. Soba or nothing."

He wanted to hear that soba was my life. But it wasn't. I couched my phrases and evaded the best that I could with my remedial Japanese, but the fact was I was not dedicating my life to soba. "No, no, no," he said. "You're either soba or you're not."

Apparently I wasn't. About a week later, he took me out to his childhood *ramenya* where I remember the ramen sucked. We had a couple beers. Ceremonious and gracious to the end, he gave me a rolling pin as a parting gift.

The subtext was as obvious to me as it was hard for him to disguise: for someone like Akio, who had worked by himself for decades and knew, in his bones, everything about soba, explaining things to some kid who wasn't dead serious about it was just too much work. I was a waste of time, a pain in his ass, and he didn't want me around anymore. It was the end of my *stage* at Soba-ya Fuyu-Rin.

I still had a place to stay and, thanks to the good graces and good connections of Tom and Marco, I lucked into a great situation at the Park Hyatt Hotel, where I worked at the New York Grill, a steakhouse, and then at Kozue, a kaiseki restaurant.

The New York Grill has, in retrospect, had an enormous influence on my life—it was the first time I saw sous vide cooking, which made it possible for one guy to cook four hundred proteins a night perfectly and by himself. It was also the first place I saw Japanese ingredients used to replicate American flavors, an idea that stuck with me.

Kozue was equally eye-opening. I remember watching one cook brush the salt and sugar cure off a slab of pork belly, then absolutely burn the belly meat over an open flame. Charred beyond belief. I was like, "What the fuck is he doing?" Then he plunged it into ice water and rubbed off the charcoal-burnt blackness. I thought it was the dumbest thing I'd ever seen—until I tasted it. After they burnt it, they braised it in dashi along with some daikon. It was so good, and that charring process had given the dish an amazing smoky flavor. I knew I'd be stealing that move somewhere down the line.

I visited Akio once before I left because his food was so good. Though I've had other soba—lots of other soba—it's next to impossible for it to be as good as Akio's. He could coax water, buckwheat flour, and wheat flour into

something more than the sum of those ingredients. There was no way to write a recipe or to possibly replicate what he was doing.

I missed America. I knew that when I got back to New York, I wanted to cook in a real kitchen again, but I didn't know what style of cuisine or restaurant. I made a lot of late-night phone calls to my old crew at Craft, who had plenty of ideas and connections for me.

Through them, I had the opportunity to work as a fish butcher at Sushi Yasuda, one of New York's best sushi restaurants, but I didn't want to go back to America and work in a Japanese restaurant. (Though if I were to learn sushi today, I would definitely want to work for Chef Yasuda. The guy's amazing.)

I was looking for a place that would be a challenge, a place where I could improve and prove myself. I'm sure that if wd~50 had been open at the time, I would have wanted to work there. It came down to working for Alex Lee at Restaurant Daniel or Andrew Carmellini at Café Boulud, restaurants owned by the chef Daniel Boulud, a New York legend who had come up through the old-world French *stagiaire* system working for titans like Roger Vergé, Georges Blanc, and Michel Guérard. They were (and are) two of the best restaurants in the city, bastions of a kind of fine dining that's an endangered breed. If you wanted to learn from and cook with the best in New York, those were the kitchens to be in.

I had seen the kitchen at Daniel—a grand space staffed by a small army—but my trail at Café Boulud helped make the decision. The kitchen was cramped and uncomfortable, the cooks were badasses, the pressure was unbelievable: kitchen as crucible. My gig there started a couple days after my trail through the kitchen and within a week of when I flew back from Tokyo.

I had jet lag the day I started there, and I felt as if I still had jet lag when I left. It was the hardest fucking job I've ever had. I couldn't get to work early enough—no matter how I early I got there, I was already behind when I walked through the door.

The kitchen was like the Special Forces: Bertrand Chemel, Scott Quis, Tien Ho, Luke Olstrom, Rich Torrici, Ron Rosselli, Mike Oliver, Ryan Skeen, Matt Greco, Amy Eubanks. There was this ferocious work ethic: get it done and make it the best. Chip-on-your-shoulder cooking. We set out to outcook Restaurant Daniel with a fraction of the staff and inferior equipment, every night. It was the best restaurant crew in New York.

I worked the back garde-manger station, doing cold preparations like terrines and charcuterie and a lot of the canapés that would start the meal. I worked as hard as I could, but I got my ass handed to me nightly. I was struggling, and I wasn't cooking that well. I had come with a recommendation from the Craft crew, but I felt like a bust free agent—like I was taking up space on the roster with a middling batting average and no chance of helping the team make the postseason.

That didn't stop me from working as hard as I could, but the stress was eating away at me. Why was I weighing out twenty-five different spices for a Moroccan-themed rub that would go on a hamachi I wouldn't be cooking—and I wouldn't cook anyway, because I like hamachi raw? Who was I proving something to? What was the point? Why didn't I stop pretending and just go make noodles?

After I'd been at Café about five months, my mother got sick, and I was on the phone to Virginia whenever I wasn't at the restaurant, a mediator between aunts and uncles and my parents over an issue with the family business. It all got to be too much, and my family needed me back down south. One of my biggest regrets is not finishing my year under Carmellini. When you take a job in a good restaurant, you commit to working for a minimum amount of time, an assurance that the time they invest in getting you up to speed isn't a waste. I was the worst-case scenario—a cook they'd built up, leaving just as I was getting to the point where I wasn't an albatross. Carmellini was totally understanding and didn't blacklist me or bitch me out for bailing on him, but I still regret leaving.

After I got down to Virginia, my mom's health improved and the family business was dealt with. That's when I started laying the plans to open my own noodle restaurant—looking into the money I'd need, where I could afford to open it, how little space I could get by with. I made ramen and *onsen tamago* (a kind of slow-poached egg I'd learned about in Japan) and rice cakes at home to keep myself amused. I still hadn't ever cooked ramen professionally, but I'd eaten as much as I could, and I knew what I liked to eat and how to cook it. My dad and his friends agreed to help me get the start-up money I needed, and I headed back to New York.

I knew I'd call it Momofuku, which translates from Japanese as "lucky peach." That's where the logo came from. It's also an indirect nod to Mr. Ando: I owed him for a thousand meals-in-minutes and besides, it's a fucking killer name. Maybe the best first name ever. And then there's the homonymous quality. The restaurant was, for me, a fuck-you to so many things. Me—a Korean American—making Japanese ramen was ridiculous on its face. Me—a passable but not much better cook—opening up a restaurant while my peers, guys I worked with who were so much more talented than me, were still toiling under other regimes, paying their dues, learning. It is no accident that Momofuku sounds like motherfucker.

I found a space. It was cheap and small, a former chicken wingery on First Avenue in the East Village. My plan was simple and traditional: an open kitchen, to save space rather than to tie into or set any trends, lined with as many stools as we could squeeze in. After looking at design options, I went with plywood everywhere: it was cheapest. Plenty of great ramen shops in Japan are total fucking dumps. I aspired to the same.

The concept of Noodle Bar was "to serve food made with integrity at an affordable price." That line was in the business plan. My decision to do it was influenced by my burnout/realization of my limitations at Café Boulud, by the saturation of the fine dining market in the city in 2003–2004, and by the fact that the great *ramenya*s of Tokyo prove that food doesn't have to be served in a fine dining setting to be good.

My biggest fear, once I pitted myself against the world and got myself in a good bit of debt, was that I would have to open Momofuku alone. And it nearly turned into a reality. Everyone I tried to hire said no or backed out: the list of cooks I talked to went on and on. Some didn't want to leave cushy spots they'd fought for and won. Others didn't want to come boil noodles with me. Some were trying to get in on the ground floor of any number of good new restaurants opening around the city then—Per Se, Cru Masa, Hearth, Café Gray—and others were trying to open their own places.

I asked every cook I liked and half-liked before moving on to pestering friends of friends with no cooking experience. No one wanted in. Marco Canora thought I was nuts. I remember how he'd chuckle, saying "Dave Chang: an army of one," in this officious tone and then crack up. It got to the point where I figured all I needed was one person to share the workload with.

Around that time, my brother's buddy who worked at the Cheesecake Factory told me that they hired all their employees from monster.com. I'd never met anyone in any kitchen who got a job that way—and I didn't really want chain-restaurant-quality help—but I was beyond desperate. Months of free ads on Craigslist had yielded nothing, so I paid $375 for a thirty-day ad on monster.com. It turned out to be the best money I ever spent.

A guy who had done some cooking down in Sante Fe and wanted to work in New York sent his résumé over. (It was then and still remains the case that most chefs and restaurateurs in New York cannot bring themselves to give a shit about a résumé filled with restaurants that are outside NYC, but I didn't have the luxury at the time.) We talked, and he told me that the few *stages* he had scored at restaurants here weren't getting him any traction. He was pissed off and frustrated. We had something in common.

He came by the space while it was still a construction site. We went and had some beers over at Lucy's on Avenue A, and we put the same kind of shit on the jukebox—I think it was the combination of the Velvet Underground's

"Heroin" and a few glasses of Wild Turkey that really sealed the deal. Joaquin Baca—Quino—became my partner and co-chef at Noodle Bar.

Quino and I opened Noodle Bar alone. We had only known each other a few days, and we'd spent most of that time trying to turn the chicken-wing dive into a restaurant where we wanted to spend the rest of our foreseeable waking hours. We spent our days and nights scrubbing and fixing and scrubbing and fixing, all the while trying not to run out of money before we opened.

Between the countless hours of cleaning the stink out of everything and rotating Guns & Roses' "Lies" and Modest Mouse's "The Moon and Antarctica" in and out of an old Sony boom box, Quino told me he had dated a stripper at some point in his past.

His story got me thinking that if we could somehow lure the women from this clandestine Japanese strip club in Midtown I knew about to the restaurant, we'd be set. Get hot Japanese girls to eat at Momofuku, and everyone else would follow: that was my marketing strategy. The funniest fucking thing is that it made sense to us at the time. The night before we opened for friends-and-family dinners, Quino and I blew most of Noodle Bar's nearly negligible cash cushion on a night on the town.

Getting into this place isn't a problem if they know you. The club itself is very small, about the size of a large suburban living room. The walls are lined with floppy black leather couches. No dancing poles, no champagne room.

It's unspeakably dank: this was back when you could still smoke cigarettes in New York, or at least you could still smoke them there. Everyone did. We waited at the small bar next to the DJ booth and drank Suntory, because when you drink whiskey at a seedy secret Japanese club, you drink Suntory.

Our plan was to give cards to all the dancers. I think it's the first and last time either of us hoped that telling girls we were chefs would get us somewhere. We didn't have much to blow, about $800, but that was okay with us. We were there on business.

There was an $80 all-you-can-drink cover charge to get in, and as in most strip clubs there were rules: here you had to get dances. Every night there was a house stripper who'd come around. At some point, it becomes so expensive it doesn't even matter; you're drunk 'cause they keep sending you Suntory, and the dancers want champagne—bottles are like $350—plus you're spending $20 per dance . . .

And then a man appears out of the darkness and says, "Mr. Chang, your hour is finished. Would you like another hour?"

Of course we did. Opening a restaurant is the worst feeling in the world. When you open a restaurant, you live it, you sleep it. You always have sawdust on your clothes. You can't shower the smell of the place off you.

And we were there despite not having properly outfitted our kitchen—we'd bought everything from K-Mart, borrowed Quino's girlfriend's stand mixer, convinced ourselves we didn't need more than we had. ("We're a noodle bar. What would we need all that shit for?") We dug deep for another hour. We knew we wanted that, even if we didn't know how to operate a cash register or anything about taxes, how to do payroll, or how to get anybody to work with us.

You couldn't find two individuals who had less business opening a restaurant than us. But that was the night before we opened the door, and that's not what we were thinking about.

A couple mornings later, in late July, when we were about to open for real for the first time, I ran to Craft to ask Tom for help with some paperwork, and when I came back, an inspector from the Department of Health was there. We had to pass an inspection minutes before we would have the chance to make our first dollar. I went straight to the bathroom and tried not to be sick. Quino still makes fun of me for pretending that they didn't hear me give up the goods when I did. We both knew how thin the door on the bathroom was.

Noodles
Ramen – shredded pork 7
Momofuku Ramen – Berkshire pork, poached egg, kamaboko 12
Ginger Scallion Noodles – steamed rice noodles 8
Bi Bim Neng Myun – cold spicy noodles, pork, pear, egg 9

– All ramen garnished w/ menma, scallions, seasonal greens and nori.

Extras
Poached Egg 1
Sweet Summer Corn 3
Miso Butter 1

Etc.
Chicken & Egg – chicken, poached egg, rice 10
Pork Buns – pork belly, steamed bread, pickled cucumber, scallions 5
Pan-Fried Pork Dumplings – pork and Chinese chives 5
Edamame 5

Pickles
Spicy Radishes 3
Cucumbers 2

Soft Drinks
Coke, Diet Coke 10 oz 2
Poland Spring 16 oz 1

Beer
Pabst Blue Ribbon 12oz 3
Orion 12oz 5

Sake
Junmai Ginjo
Junmai Dai-Ginjo

– Cash Only
– Let us know if you have any food allergies.

Then there was the holy-shit moment. Three beautiful Japanese women strolled in. We couldn't believe it. They sat down, had some ramen, and we didn't comp their meal. I don't think those girls ever pay for anything. I know they didn't look happy. They were some of our first customers. And they never came back.

The opening menu at Noodle Bar had ten items, with a lot of ingredients doing double or triple duty: this was back before we were even making kimchi. We served dumplings and edamame because we were a noodle bar and I thought we had to—maybe we weren't the most authentic place, but it was a Japanese-inspired noodle restaurant all the same—and once upon a time, we even had as many as three vegetarian-friendly things on the menu.

After the strippers came and went and the first wave of curious locals started to ebb, we were dead slow for a few weeks. Scary slow. Going out of business slow.

Thank God our friends started coming—kitchen guys we used to work with, guys in the business. Tony DiSalvo and Greg Brainin, Jean-Georges's right-hand men, started coming by on the late side very early on. After they made us a regular stop on their after-work rounds, a whole bunch of other kitchen crews started coming in.

A month after we opened, Liz Chapman (who I met at Craft, and who is now Liz Benno) arranged for the Per Se crew to take over Noodle Bar on the night before their review came out in the Wednesday food section of the *New York Times*. Jonathan Benno, Thomas Keller's chef de cuisine at Per Se, was a mentor to me at Craft. And here he was, in my restaurant, eating my food on the night his got four stars—the highest rating the paper gives, one of the hardest accolades to come by in our business. That night it seemed like every cook and chef in New York was at Momofuku noshing on buns and beer. That support from the Craft crew—from Benno and Marco and the guys I'd come up under—and from other cooks made those first slow months that much more bearable and made the dim future seem less bleak.

I think a lot of them came because the beer was cheap and cold and because Momofuku was like a freak show: let's watch these guys go up in a ball of fire. I know that's what my friends were saying, "Check it out, man, Chang's running a restaurant. He has no idea what he's doing."

They were right: I didn't. We bought what we figured were enough dishes for us to get through service and then would wash them all in a Hercu-

lean push at the end of the night. I'd come in at 8 a.m. to do the prep work and work lunch service by myself (cooking, waiting, bussing). Quino came in at one. I knocked off at some point during dinner and left everything to him—and he stayed and washed all the dishes by himself, usually until about two in the morning. Six hours later, I'd be back.

People could see we were working our asses off, and the food was slowly getting better. Eventually reviews and write-ups started trickling in: Joe Dziemianowicz in the *Daily News* (Momofuku was, in his estimation, worth a trip from anywhere "in the borough," a step up from the lowest rating, "in the hood") and from Robin Raisfeld and Rob Patronite, who wrote some nice things about us in *New York* magazine. I don't know what triggered it—it might have been that write-up in *New York*—but there was one Saturday early on when Noodle Bar did $800 in sales at lunch. It was an unthinkable amount for us at the time. And I was there alone. It was the worst day ever.

After a couple months of killing ourselves, and within a couple days of that Saturday that almost did me in, Quino and I started trying to hire servers and to get more cooks. I put an ad in the paper, but it was still the case that almost nobody wanted to work with us. So we tapped Quino's linguistic abilities and put an ad in *El Diario*, the Spanish-language newspaper of record in New York City. That first ad landed us a guy who had worked at Menchanko-Tei, a ramen restaurant uptown, and we were convinced he was going to be the best hire ever. He had his own kitchen chopsticks and decent knife skills, and he taught us how to make large quantities of rice properly. We finally had a few people around to help handle the load.

All the bloggers could talk about was my temper and how I'd lose it on people. One of the first posts about Momofuku on one of those Internet food chat rooms, where people will write a searing condemnation of a restaurant fifteen minutes after it opens, was a screed about me. I wore my hat as low as possible and tried not to make eye contact with the customers eighteen inches away from me. I looked at the board and got the food out. If it wasn't right, I would yell. I would tell the cooks how much they sucked, in pornographic detail. I didn't care what anyone thought of me. I was doing the books, making bank deposits, going to the Greenmarket, slicing scallions in the morning, working service all day. I had a lot more to worry about than what customers thought. I just kept pushing and pushing everyone. All I knew was how to crack the whip like it had been cracked on me at Craft and

Café Boulud. Barely anybody lasted with us for more than a week.

One morning, I walked in and found our new dishwasher mixing hand soap with bleach in the mop tub. It drove me crazy—it makes no sense as a way to wash floors—and I had told him so many times before. So this morning, a couple weeks after we'd actually got the skeleton of a kitchen crew together, there he was, standing over the bucket with a bottle of bleach in one hand and a bottle of hand soap in the other. I lost it.

The cook from Menchanko-Tei watched me blow up. Then he quit. And he told me in no uncertain terms that I was never going to find employees who would work the way I wanted them to work, that our management style sucked, that we had to stop this bullshit fraternity-style hazing process, and that we should just close the restaurant.

I fired four other people that day. He was probably right.

Finally, in December, we made a great hire: Scott Garfinkel, who had worked in a few really good kitchens: Ilo, Palladin, and Barbuto. Kevin Pemoulie, who had been at Craftbar—the second restaurant in the Craft empire—came on board shortly after. Pedro Dominguez, king of a.m. prep and pickle making and keeping good dudes from quitting even when I acted like an asshole, joined the team. We had a nucleus, finally.

We were doing better, but we weren't doing great. Quino and I weren't paying ourselves. After a few months in the pressure cooker that was that restaurant (twenty-seven diners and two or three cooks as well as servers in a 600-square-foot space, plus more cooks downstairs in the cramped basement prep kitchen), we were miserable.

At least most of the time. But right around then, on one of our nights off—we closed on Sundays for a while—we were all out at dinner, eating a pretty casual meal, burgers and beers, and making merry at a place that had a great reputation . . . and then the bill came: $400. That was a Eureka moment. We were sitting there, talking pretty low-level shit about how much better we could cook than this place. But it was packed. Critically adored. Obviously profitable. What the hell were we doing wrong?

Shortly after the New Year, Quino and I were out on the stoop next to the restaurant having a cigarette, and we just decided to screw it all. We had zero money. We were straining to do this "noodle bar" concept, limiting ourselves in the kitchen, limiting what we could cook, and constantly hearing about "authenticity" and how we didn't embody it. We felt that we *had* to serve gyoza, because everybody likes to eat dumplings at Asian restaurants. We were listening to too much outside advice.

We figured we had nothing to lose—and we didn't. So we decided to start cooking whatever we wanted, to start using the Green-

market like we really should, and, most important, to try to stay in business for one calendar year. "Undersell, overdeliver" became our slogan. If we were going to go out of business anyway, we wanted to go out on our best face.

And when we did start expanding the boundaries of what we served—bowls of tripe, fried veal sweetbreads, all kinds of shellfish, headcheese, a Korean-inspired burrito, and, as the Greenmarket started to blow up in the spring, more riffs on local vegetables—something happened. People started coming to the restaurant more often. We were full a lot. After a while, a little crowd of people waiting outside became the norm. (I always felt bad for the neighborhood folks who had supported us during the early going on those nights.) Insolvency wasn't as immediate a threat. All of a sudden, the press began paying an undue amount of attention to us.

Momofuku was becoming something more than a shitty noodle bar. It was taking on a life of its own. We started attracting better cooks and waiters and we found people who could handle the business end of the restaurant. Noodle Bar was slowly turning into a success.

By summer, we were packed. I was getting interviewed and getting on television and spending less and less time in the kitchen. I was slowly

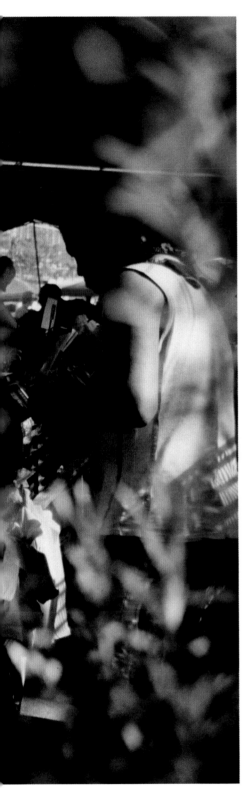

walking down the path to becoming the sort of chef I had made fun of only a year before—the noncooking variety. The other guys cooked their asses off, and I learned that being a chef demands much more than just being in the kitchen yelling at people, even if that was what I'd rather be doing.

By our second fall, the one-year point we never thought we'd reach in January, things were bordering on the surreal. I was nominated for some big awards—the same awards Andrew Carmellini had won and Marco Canora had unjustifiably been passed over for. None of it made sense to me. But we had money to pay everybody and a restaurant full of customers from the moment we opened until the moment we closed every day.

I don't think it could have happened if we had been more successful at the get-go. The way we operate now is because of all that ridiculous shit we went through on the way.

momofuku ramen

Ramen = broth + noodles + meat + toppings and garnishes. It's that simple and that complex, because the variations are endless.

Ramen broth is usually made with pig bones and seaweed. Most places add seafood. We add bacon.

The noodles are most often freshly made alkaline noodles (see page 48), though within that subcategory of noodles there are a billion variations. For a long time, we served the fresh flour-and-water lo mein noodles you can buy at most Asian grocery stores. Now we make our own.

The meat is usually pork. Belly is the best. The toppings and garnishes can vary, but nori, bamboo shoots, eggs, and scallions are all commonplace.

Here's how we put together a bowl of our Momofuku ramen. Scale this up—double or triple or more—as desired to feed the number in your crew. And don't freak out if you can't find fish cakes or bamboo shoots: Everyone says ramen is rigid; that it has to be one exact thing. It isn't, and it doesn't. Yes, this is what we put into our ramen, but the most important thing is that you make it delicious, not that you make it exact: bean sprouts, chicken, tofu—there's a world of stuff you can put in the broth. Make it taste good.

First, get everything ready. The broth should be hot, just shy of boiling. Taste it one last time and make any adjustments (taré for depth? salt for roundness? mirin for sweetness? water to dilute it?). The large pot of boiling water for the noodles should be well salted. Any meat you are adding should be hot. Nori should be cut into squares, scallions and fish cakes sliced, bamboo shoots stewed, seasonal vegetables prepared, eggs cooked. Have a strainer (or colander, whatever, something to drain the noodles in), ladle, chopsticks, and spoon (or measuring cup, if you're that anal) at the ready. Bonus points for heating up your ramen bowls (which should comfortably hold about 3 cups) in a low oven. If you're attempting to make more than a few portions at a time, you may want to enlist a helper.

Next, boil the noodles according to the recipe you've used or according to the manufacturer's instructions. Portion them out into your ramen bowls. Top with hot broth.

Dress the soup: Arrange the meat (shoulder and belly) and other garnishes (scallions, bamboo shoots, fish cake, vegetables) around the edges of each bowl. Plop the egg, if using, into the middle of the bowl. Finish by tucking a couple pieces of nori about one-third of the way into one side of the soup, so they lean against the side of the bowl and stand up above the rim. Serve hot.

2 cups Ramen Broth (page 40)

Taré (page 42), kosher salt, and/or mirin if needed

5 to 6 ounces fresh ramen noodles (see page 48—but trust me, you don't need to make these)

2 to 3 slices Pork Belly (page 50)

½ cup Pork Shoulder for Ramen (page 51)

Two 3-by-3-inch sheets nori (cut from larger sheets)

¼ cup thinly sliced scallions (greens and whites)

2 thin slices store-bought fish cake

4 or 5 pieces Bamboo Shoots (page 54)

¼ cup Seasonal Vegetables (page 54)

1 Slow-Poached Egg (page 52)

ramen broth MAKES 5 QUARTS

This makes enough broth for about 10 portions of ramen, more than you'll need for one sitting. But it freezes nicely and you'll see it in a lot of the recipes in this chapter. Making less seems like a waste of time when you've got a pot on the stove.

"Meaty pork bones" should be just that: pork bones with some meat on them. Neck bones are the best, but they'll be hard to find. Bones from the shoulder or leg are very good. Ribs can be used to supplement a supply of other more desirable bones, but used alone, they will yield an anemic broth.

Note that the konbu and shiitakes can all be used for other purposes after contributing their flavors to the broth. See Grilled Octopus Salad (page 105) and Pickled Shiitakes (page 173).

Two 3-by-6-inch pieces konbu

6 quarts water

2 cups dried shiitakes, rinsed

4 pounds chicken, either a whole bird or legs

5 pounds meaty pork bones

1 pound smoky bacon, preferably Benton's (see page 147)

1 bunch scallions

1 medium onion, cut in half

2 large carrots, peeled and roughly chopped

Taré (page 42), preferably, or kosher salt, soy sauce, and mirin

1. Rinse the konbu under running water, then combine it with the water in an 8-quart stockpot. Bring the water to a simmer over high heat and turn off the heat. Let steep for 10 minutes.

2. Remove the konbu from the pot and add the shiitakes. Turn the heat back up to high and bring the water to a boil, then turn the heat down so the liquid simmers gently. Simmer for 30 minutes, until the mushrooms are plumped and rehydrated and have lent the broth their color and aroma.

3. Heat the oven to 400°F.

4. Remove the mushrooms from the pot with a spider or slotted spoon. Add the chicken to the pot. Keep the liquid at a gentle simmer, with bubbles lazily and occasionally breaking the surface. Skim and discard any froth, foam, or fat that rises to the surface of the broth while the chicken is simmering, and replenish the water as necessary to keep the chicken covered. After about 1 hour, test the chicken: the meat should pull away from the bones easily. If it doesn't, simmer until that's the case and then remove the chicken from the pot with a spider or slotted spoon.

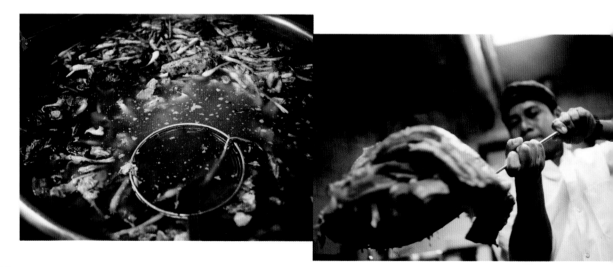

5. While the chicken is simmering, put the pork bones on a baking sheet or in a roasting pan and slide them into the oven to brown for an hour; turn them over after about 30 minutes to ensure even browning.

6. Remove the chicken from the pot and add the roasted bones to the broth, along with the bacon. Adjust the heat as necessary to keep the broth at a steady simmer; skim the scum and replenish the water as needed. After 45 minutes, fish out the bacon and discard it. Then gently simmer the pork bones for 6 to 7 hours—as much time as your schedule allows. Stop adding water to replenish the pot after hour 5 or so.

7. Add the scallions, onion, and carrots to the pot and simmer for the final 45 minutes.

8. Remove and discard the spent bones and vegetables. Pass the broth through a strainer lined with cheesecloth. You can use the broth at this point, or, if you're making it in advance and want to save on storage space, you can do what we do: return it to the pot, and reduce it by half over high heat, then portion out the concentrated broth into containers. It keeps for a couple of days in the refrigerator and up to a few months in the freezer. When you want to use it, dilute it with an equal measure of water and reheat it on the stove.

9. In either case, finish the broth by seasoning it to taste with taré. Some days the salt of the bacon, or the seaweed, or whatever, comes out more than others. Only your taste buds can guide you as to the right amount of seasoning; start with 2 or 3 tablespoons per quart. Taste it and get it right. I like it so it's not quite too salty but almost. Very seasoned. Under-seasoned broth is a crime.

taré MAKES ABOUT 2½ CUPS

The meaning of the term *taré* isn't consistent up and down Japan, but in Tokyo, where I learned about it, it is essentially Japanese barbecue sauce. At yakitori restaurants, places where they grill skewers of chicken over clean-burning bincho-tan charcoal, they brush the chicken with a slick of taré just as it finishes cooking. One of the coolest taré-making systems I've ever seen was at a yakitori joint in Japan where there was a channel underneath the grill funneling all the chicken drippings into a stone jar full of taré that was constantly being infused with grilled chicken drippings. (I imagine they replenished it with fresh soy, mirin, and sake the next day, boiled it, and returned it to its station.)

But in addition to its place of honor in the yakitori tradition, taré is the main seasoning—the primary "salt" component—in ramen shops, at least in Tokyo. *Ramenyas* have their own formulas for broth and their own recipes for taré. Broths are usually easy to figure out, because there's always a big pot bubbling away in plain view, with apples or leeks or whatever secret-ish ingredients a shop adds to it, but taré recipes are more mysterious because you rarely see them being made. Some places add dried scallops, others leave out the chicken bones.

Ours is robust if simple, and it's a good way to put chicken trimmings or bones to use. Most ramen shops add the taré to the bowl when the soup is being assembled to be served, but that always struck me as a Russian roulette way of seasoning a soup—too much, too little, too easy to screw up. So we season our broth with it beforehand, tasting carefully with each addition to strike the right balance.

2 to 3 chicken backs, or the bones and their immediately attendant flesh and skin reserved from butchering 1 chicken

1 cup sake

1 cup mirin

2 cups usukuchi (light soy sauce)

Freshly ground black pepper

1. Heat the oven to 450°F.

2. Cut chicken back into 3 pieces, split rib cages in half, and separate thigh from leg bones. (More surface area = more browning area = deeper better flavor, as long as you don't burn the bones.)

3. Spread the bones out in a wide (12- to 14-inch) ovenproof sauté pan or skillet and put it in the oven for 45 minutes to 1 hour: check on the bones after about 40 minutes to make sure they're just browning, not burning. You want deeply browned bones, and you want the *fond*—the fatty liquid caramelizing on the bottom of the pan—to be very dark but not black-ened. (A fleck of black here and there, or at the edges of the pool, is fine, but charred *fond* is useless; it will only add bitterness and should be discarded.) Watch as the bones color, and pull them out when they're perfectly browned.

4. When the bones are browned, remove the pan from the oven and put it on a stovetop. Pour a splash of the sake onto the pan and put the pan over a burner and turn the heat to medium-high. Once the sake starts to bubble, scrape the *fond* up off the bottom of the pan.

5. Once the fond is free from the bottom of the pan, add the remaining sake, mirin, and soy to the pan and turn the heat under it to high. Bring the liquid to a boil, then lower the heat so that it barely simmers. Cook for 1 hour. It will reduce somewhat, the flavors will meld, and the taré will thicken ever so slightly.

6. Strain the bones out of the taré and season the liquid with 5 or 6 turns of black pepper. The taré can be used right away or cooled and then stored, covered, in the refrigerator for 3 or 4 days.

dashi

Ramen broth is traditionally built on a foundation of dashi, the seaweed-and-dried fish broth that is the cornerstone of Japanese cooking. It's amazing stuff: smoky, a little fishy, loaded with natural MSG.

But when we first opened Noodle Bar and for years afterward, it was impossible for me to find katsuo-bushi (the traditional dried fish flakes) of a quality I was happy with. (I've mellowed on that point over the years.) So I got to thinking about how else to get that smoky flavor, that meaty MSG that katsuo-bushi adds. And what's the smoky meat most common to American kitchens and cooking? One you can get a good-quality version of almost anywhere? Bacon.

So that was the thought process that prompted my substituting bacon for katsuo-bushi in the Momofuku ramen broth and, later, in the dashi we use. The results are awesome. Bacon dashi smells almost exactly like traditional dashi but the flavor is completely different—smoky but not fishy.

Even if bacon dashi is my favorite, and traditional dashi is a close second, there's no reason in the world not to have a jar of instant dashi powder on hand: it's cheap, it has some flavor, and it really is instant. Sometimes it's a lifesaver.

traditional dashi MAKES 2 QUARTS

Stir ¼ cup miso into this, throw in some tofu and/or mushrooms or shredded nori or whatever you've got around, and you've got miso soup. Katsuo-bushi is dried smoked bonito; it's available shredded in bags at every Japanese market on the planet.

One 3-by-6-inch piece konbu

8 cups water

2 handfuls of katsuo-bushi
(see headnote)

1. Rinse the konbu under running water, then combine it with the water in a medium saucepan. Bring the water to a simmer over medium heat and turn off the stove. Let steep for 10 minutes.

2. Remove the pan from the heat and add the katsuo-bushi. Cover and let steep for 7 minutes.

3. Strain the dashi (discard the katsuo-bushi; if you like, keep the konbu to use as directed on page 40) and use immediately, or cover and refrigerate for up to a couple days.

bacon dashi

I can't overstate the significance of bacon dashi to us at Momofuku. It's not the dashi itself—though it is delicious—but the thought process that went into it. The successful transposition of bacon from Tennessee for Japanese dried and smoked fish was an important early success for us, and it continues to be a driving inspiration of how we cook.

We respect tradition and we revere many traditional flavor profiles, but we do not subscribe to the idea that there's one set of blueprints that everyone should follow. I think that in the questioning of basic assumptions—about how we cook and why we cook with what we do—is when a lot of the coolest cooking happens.

You can use this anywhere you'd use regular dashi. We like to pour it, hot, over shaved raw or blanched or pickled vegetables (usually a mix) and shaved raw mushrooms (like porcini or lobster mushrooms) in a small bowl, for an elegant first-course/amuse-bouche-type thing. And it's excellent with clams; see the recipe on page 102.

1. Rinse the konbu under running water, then combine it with the water in a medium saucepan. Bring the water to a simmer over medium heat and turn off the stove. Let steep for 10 minutes.

2. Remove the konbu from the pot and add the bacon. Bring to a boil, then turn the heat down so the water simmers gently. Simmer for 30 minutes.

3. Strain the bacon from the dashi, and chill the broth until the fat separates and hardens into a solid cap on top of it. Remove and discard the fat and use the dashi or store it. Bacon dashi will keep, covered, for a few days in the refrigerator.

Two 3-by-6-inch pieces konbu

8 cups water

½ pound smoky bacon, preferably Benton's (see page 147)

noodles

Of all the challenges making ramen poses, getting the noodles right might be the toughest. It was for us at Noodle Bar.

Ramen noodles are traditionally fresh flour-and-water noodles made with alkaline salts (sodium carbonate and potassium carbonate, mixed and sold as "*kansui*" in some Asian supermarkets). They are firm and chewy and, because of the way the salts and flour interact, an oxidized yellowish color that makes them look as if they're made with eggs, though they aren't and shouldn't be. Some ramen shops—especially shops that are part of a chain—make their own using a noodle machine that works kind of like those doughnut machines at Krispy Kreme: dough in one end, noodles (or doughnuts) out the other. Fewer shops make them by hand, and most purchase their noodles.

For the first few years Noodle Bar was open, we bought our noodles—lo mein, not ramen, and not made with alkaline salts—from Canton Noodle Company, an amazing family-owned noodle-making operation down on Mott Street in Chinatown. Canton would be a third-generation business, except that the third generation, the kids my age, isn't in the noodle business—they're all doctors or Indian chiefs or whatever. So it's Grandma and

Grandpa and a couple of uncles who make the noodles—covered in flour, pushing around huge amounts of dough through industrial-sized noodle mixers and kneaders and cutters.

They're about as friendly and genuine as people get, and the funny thing is, with kids who are future leaders of tomorrow and with their own considerable holding of Chinatown real estate, they have no reason to still be making noodles. They always say they're going to close up shop and take it easy, but they're still at it today.

Our first problem with the lo mein we were buying was our problem: boiling them to shit and back, which we did for months. We were as guilty of overcooking our noodles as people said we were. (It's more of a challenge at an understaffed and tiny restaurant than it should be at home, but don't hesitate to test a noodle every minute or so to familiarize yourself with the arc of doneness any kind of noodle travels.)

Once we got the noodle-cooking thing down, the difference between our lo mein and traditional ramen noodles started becoming more of an issue, especially for me. We needed chewier, firmer noodles—the two qualities those alkaline salts add. But the folks at Canton were not down with changing their program. They said alkaline salts would ruin their machines, that their previous attempts at kansui-noodle making hadn't been great, that they would do it if that was the only style of noodle they made, but that they couldn't because they made so many lo mein noodles. In short, they said no.

So I relented on my demands that they experiment with alkaline salts, and we turned our attention to getting the lo mein right. We lengthened the kneading time and added more passes through the roller, trying to get the lo mein to cook and taste like ramen. After three years of tinkering (and listening to people bitch about Noodle Bar's noodles), it became clear that I was never going to be quite satisfied with the lo mein. At that point, we might have bought the same ramen noodles used at almost every other ramen shop in the city, but then we would have had the same product as everyone else, and that's not what we wanted.

It was a bummer, but we moved on from Canton and started buying ramen noodles from a supplier, George Kao, who helped us get noodles manufactured to our specs. We also started researching what we'd need to do to make our own. Harold McGee, whose book *On Food and Cooking* should be on your shelf or your nightstand or your kitchen counter (if it isn't, you should probably put this book down and go and purchase it posthaste), helped us put the pieces together. A reading from the Book of Harold:

> Salted white noodles arose in northern China and are now most widely known in their Japanese version, udon. Yellow noodles, which are made with alkaline salts, appear to have originated in southeast China sometime before 1600, and then spread with Chinese migrants to Indonesia, Malaysia, and Thailand. The yellowness of the traditional noodles (modern ones are sometimes colored with egg yolks) is caused by phenolic compounds in the flour called flavones, which are normally colorless but become yellow in alkaline conditions. The flavones are especially concentrated in the bran and germ, so less refined flours develop a deeper color. Because they're based on harder wheats, southern yellow noodles have a firmer texture than white salted noodles, and alkalinity (pH 9–11, the equivalent of old egg whites) increases this firmness. The alkaline salts (sodium and potassium carbonate at 0.5–1% of noodle weight) also cause the noodles to take longer to cook and absorb more water, and they contribute a characteristic aroma and taste. . . . *Ra-men* noodles are light yellow and somewhat stiff, and are made from hard wheat flour, water, and alkaline salts (*kansui*).

With that knowledge, Harold's guidance, and the hard work of Christina Tosi, Momofuku's pastry chef/everything expert/sole bastion of sanity, we developed the recipe for alkaline noodles on page 48, the recipe for the noodles we use at Noodle Bar. We've found that if your noodles are really oxidizing—that your flavones are overreacting to their alkaline environment and coloring the noodles to a gray-green—a pinch of citric acid (like the amount of cocaine a movie cop would taste off the tip of his switchblade to confirm that the bust was going to stick) will help.

But, and this is a big but, I really don't think you need to track down alkaline salts or kansui and make these noodles. Finding the ingredients is a pain in the ass. Of course, if you want to do it, do it, kudos to you. Otherwise, substitute any other homemade pasta you like, or fresh lo mein, which you can buy in any half-respectable Asian food store or supermarket (a superstocked Japanese grocery might have fresh ramen noodles if you're lucky), or even rice noodles, which are really great at holding their shape and texture in a bowl of hot soup.

alkaline noodles (aka ramen) MAKES 6 TO 8 PORTIONS OF NOODLES

Using a precise amount of alkaline salts is important when making these noodles, hence the metric measurements. If you've got a scale, use it. For information on where to score alkaline salts, see page 294.

5⅓ cups (800 grams) bread flour or "00" pasta flour, plus additional flour for rolling out the noodles

1⅓ cups (300 grams) water, at room temperature, or more if needed

2 teaspoons (7.2 grams) sodium carbonate

Scant ¼ teaspoon (0.8 gram) potassium carbonate

1. Combine the flour, water, sodium carbonate, and potassium carbonate in the bowl of a stand mixer outfitted with the dough hook. Knead on medium-low speed for 10 minutes; the dough should come together into a ball after just a couple minutes—if it doesn't, add additional water by the tablespoon until it does. After 10 minutes of kneading, you should have fairly elastic, smooth dough on your hands. Wrap the dough in plastic and put it in the refrigerator to rest for 30 minutes.

2. Set up a pasta machine on your counter or work surface. Cut off a ball of dough about 1 cup in size, and keep the rest of the dough wrapped and in the refrigerator. Dust the ball of dough with flour and use a rolling pin to help flatten it out into a rectangular shape that will go through your pasta machine. Roll the pasta through twice on the widest setting, then reduce the width by a setting or two with each pass through the machine, dusting the dough with flour as necessary to keep it from sticking to itself or the machine, until the dough is as thin as the machine can roll it. Cut the noodles using the narrowest cutter for your machine, then use a scale to divide the noodles into 6-ounce bundles. (If you don't have a scale, a 6-ounce bundle of noodles will probably be slightly larger than 1 cup. Consider buying a scale.) Wrap individual bundles in plastic wrap. Repeat for the remaining dough. You can hold the noodles in the refrigerator for up to a day or so, or freeze them if you're going to use them down the road.

3. Cook the noodles in a large pot of salted water at a rolling boil for about 5 minutes, until tender but still toothsome (slightly longer if they were frozen). Drain well and deploy as directed.

Our Momofuku ramen is garnished with two types of pork: sliced pork belly and pulled shoulder meat. Pork belly and shoulder are two of the cheapest and most flavorful pieces of the hog, discounting all the goodness you can wring out of the head and the tail.

When we opened we were braising our pork in a mixture of pork stock and soy. It was slow and time-consuming, and the results weren't ideal. It was an accident that spurred us down a new path: One day I put a pan of bellies into the oven and accidentally cranked it to 500°F. After about an hour, I stumbled across my mistake.

The good: the belly was a beautiful golden brown. The bad: it had rendered out about half its weight in fat. In a restaurant, turning a 10-pound pork belly into a 5-pound pork belly is not good for the bottom line; at home, it's less of a concern. I chose to look at the upside—I certainly wasn't going to waste that pork—and to call what I was doing confit. I turned the heat down to 200°F or so and let the belly mellow out in its pork fat bath until it was tender and ready to go.

The results were good. Easy. And quick, in that it didn't require much shepherding. The high-heat/low-heat method became our de facto way for cooking belly for buns, ramen, everything.

If there was a downside, it was the sheer volume of pork fat we were generating, but we dealt with that by cooking everything in pork fat: we doused our kimchi stew with it to add body and temper the spicy heat, we confited chicken legs in it, we deep-fried in it. Pork fat is amazing, versatile stuff. And while newspapers and the like made a lot out of how "pork-centric" our restaurant was early on—and we are pork-centric, I don't reject the label—it was really more a function of using up what we were producing as a by-product, not some crusade on behalf of the pig.

pork belly for ramen, pork buns & just about anything else

MAKES ENOUGH PORK FOR 6 TO 8 BOWLS OF RAMEN OR ABOUT 12 PORK BUNS

The best part of this belly, besides the unctuous, fatty meat itself, which we use in two of our most popular dishes at the restaurants—ramen and pork buns—is the layer that settles at the bottom of the pan after you chill it. Most cooks who are familiar with it know it from making duck confit, and they know it's liquid gold (or jellied gold, if you want to get technical). We label containers of it "pork jelly." I add it to broths, to taré, to vegetable sautés—anything that would benefit from a hit of meaty flavor and the glossier mouthfeel the gelatin adds.

To harvest it, decant the fat and juices from the pan you cooked the belly in into a glass measuring cup or other clear container. Let it cool until the fat separates from the meat juices, which will settle to the bottom. Pour or scoop off the fat and reserve it for cooking. Save the juices, which will turn to a ready-to-use meat jelly after a couple of hours in the fridge. The meat jelly will keep for 1 week in the refrigerator or indefinitely in the freezer.

We get pork belly without the skin. If you can only find skin-on belly, don't fret. If the meat is cold and your knife is sharp, the skin is a cinch to slice off. And you can save it to make the Chicharrón (page 231) we serve as a first bite at Momofuku Ko.

One 3-pound slab skinless pork belly

¼ cup kosher salt

¼ cup sugar

1. Nestle the belly into a roasting pan or other oven-safe vessel that holds it snugly. Mix together the salt and sugar in a small bowl and rub the mix all over the meat; discard any excess salt-and-sugar mixture. Cover the container with plastic wrap and put it into the fridge for at least 6 hours, but no longer than 24.

2. Heat the oven to 450°F.

3. Discard any liquid that accumulated in the container. Put the belly in the oven, fat side up, and cook for 1 hour, basting it with the rendered fat at the halfway point, until it's an appetizing golden brown.

4. Turn the oven temperature down to 250°F and cook for another 1 hour to 1 hour 15 minutes, until the belly is tender—it shouldn't be falling apart, but it should have a down pillow–like yield to a firm finger poke. Remove the pan from the oven and transfer the belly to a plate. Decant the fat and the meat juices from the pan and reserve (see the headnote). Allow the belly to cool slightly.

5. When it's cool enough to handle, wrap the belly in plastic wrap or aluminum foil and put it in the fridge until it's thoroughly chilled and firm. (You can skip this step if you're pressed for time, but the only way to get neat, nice-looking slices is to chill the belly thoroughly before slicing it.)

6. Cut the pork belly into ½-inch-thick slices that are about 2 inches long. Warm them for serving in a pan over medium heat, just for a minute or two, until they are jiggly soft and heated through. Use at once.

pork shoulder for ramen

MAKES ABOUT 3 CUPS, ENOUGH FOR ABOUT 6 BOWLS OF RAMEN

Multiply this recipe as needed. A 10-pound shoulder—a whole shoulder, the size we typically cook—takes three times the seasoning as a 3-pounder but the same amount of time to cook.

1. Put the pork shoulder into a roasting pan or other oven-safe vessel that holds it snugly. Mix together the salt and sugar in a small bowl and rub the mix all over the meat; discard any excess salt-and-sugar mixture. Cover the container with plastic wrap and put it into the fridge for at least 6 hours, but no longer than 24.

2. Heat the oven to 250°F.

3. Discard any liquid that accumulated in the container. Put the shoulder in the oven and cook for 6 hours, basting it with the rendered fat and pan juices every hour. Take it out of the oven and let it rest for 30 minutes.

4. Shred the meat, pulling it into ropy strands using two forks, as you would pulled pork. If you need to hold the pork for a day or so, add some of the rendered fat from the pan to the shredded meat to keep it moist and store it, tightly covered, in the refrigerator. Reheat it in a low oven (250° or 300°F) before using.

One 3-pound piece boneless pork shoulder

¼ cup kosher salt

¼ cup sugar

slow-poached eggs

MAKES AS MANY AS YOU CHOOSE TO COOK

We started making slow-poached eggs at Noodle Bar because we didn't want to serve hard-boiled eggs in our soup like every other ramen operation in town. (And poaching eggs for each and every bowl of ramen we served would have been a nightmare.) So we slow-poach a few dozen eggs before each service, then crack the cooked eggs out of their shells into the broth. Easy. I've never seen another place that uses this kind of egg for ramen.

And I can't tell you how often customers ooh when a cook cracks a cooked egg out of what looks like an uncooked intact eggshell. I can tell you it's not that difficult a trick and also that I oohed when I saw this style of egg for the first time. I was at a movie theater in the Shinjuku neighborhood of Tokyo where they played bad U.S. movies at a discount price. I was settling down to take in the artistry of *Formula 51* with Samuel L. Jackson ("Nice Wheels. Dirty Deals. And One Mean Mother in a Kilt.") when the woman next to me pulled out a bowl of what looked like take-out sukiyaki-don and what I assumed to be a raw egg. It was hardcore. When she cracked it, a poached egg came out. She poked the egg with her chopsticks, and out oozed the yolk.

I thought the crazy Japanese had altered the egg with technology, but after asking around, I found out that slow-poaching is a time-tested and trusted technique in Japan. (The story I was told is that old ladies would bring baskets of eggs with them to the natural hot springs that are all around Japan—hot springs and public bathing are important national pastimes—and while they were there, the hot spring water cooked the eggs at a constant temperature of around 60°C or 141°F.) The technique produces eggs that, because they've been slowly coaxed into cookedness, are creamier and more unctuous than regular poached eggs. (In a pinch, you can substitute traditionally poached eggs for slow-poached eggs in our recipes.)

A few things to note: The bigger the pot, the better this technique will work. This is because a pot of hot water is hotter at the bottom (from the heating element) and coolest on the surface (from which the heat is escaping). Using the biggest possible pot gives you the greatest volume of water at the right temperature and therefore the greatest certainty of success. That same concern about the heat of the water is the reason you need to use something to keep the eggs from sitting on the bottom of the pot—they need to be suspended in the water, in a zone where it's easiest to ensure they're cooking at the right temperature. To that end, if your stove really cranks and you're having a tough time getting the water to a low enough temperature, you can make a doughnut out of aluminum foil and put it between the pot and the burner (at as low a heat as possible) to help diffuse the burner's heat.

1. Fill your biggest, deepest pot with water and put it on the stove over the lowest possible heat.

Large eggs, as many as you like

2. Use something to keep the eggs from sitting on the bottom of the pot, where the temperature will be highest. If you've got a cake rack or a steamer rack, use it. If not, improvise: a doughnut of aluminum foil or a few chopsticks scattered helter skelter across the bottom of the pan will usually do the trick, but you know what you've got lying around. Be resourceful.

3. Use an instant-read thermometer to monitor the temperature in the pot—if it's too hot, add cold water or an ice cube. Once the water is between 140° and 145°F, add the eggs to the pot. Let them bathe for 40 to 45 minutes, checking the temperature regularly with the thermometer or by sticking your finger in the water (it should be the temperature of a very hot bath) and moderating it as needed.

4. You can use the eggs immediately or store them in the refrigerator for up to 24 hours. (If you're planning on storing them, chill them until cold in an ice-water bath.) If you refrigerate the eggs, warm them under piping-hot tap water for 1 minute before using.

5. To serve the eggs, crack them one at a time into a small saucer. The thin white will not and should not be firm or solid; tip the dish to pour off and discard the loosest part of the white, then slide the egg onto the dish it's destined for.

fried slow-poached eggs

Slow-poached eggs make for fried eggs with perfectly runny yolks and creamy whites, bookended by crispy brown sides. They're shaped like hard-boiled eggs that have been lightly run over by a car. Heat a dash of oil in a skillet until nearly smoking. Crack open the egg, discard the loosest of the thin white, and slide the egg into the pan. Sear for 45 seconds on the first side, then flip the egg over and repeat on the other side. Sprinkle with salt and deploy.

ramen toppings

Face it: as important as the broth and noodles and taré are to ramen, it's the meat and toppings that most people focus on. Eggs and meat take a little work, but three of the most common garnishes (scallions, nori, and fish cakes) require almost no effort on the part of the cook other than a little cutting. Here we go.

nori

Stick a sheet in the bowl, halfway submerged and pinned between the noodles and the bowl, and you're done. If you want to complicate things, hold the nori over the open flame of a burner on your stove (apologies to those cooking on electric stoves) for just a couple of seconds—it will instantly become more aromatic and a little less brittle—and then add to the soup.

bamboo shoots (aka menma)
MAKES ENOUGH FOR 6 BOWLS OF RAMEN

One 12-ounce can sliced bamboo shoots

Splashes of grapeseed and Asian sesame oils

Splash of usukuchi (light soy sauce)

1 Pickled Chile (page 68), if you've got it, seeded and chopped

Salt, possibly

Drain the bamboo shoots in a colander and rinse them well under running water. Put them in a small saucepan with the oils, soy, and chile, if you have it, and stew them over low heat for 20 to 30 minutes, stirring occasionally, until tender. Taste them, and season with salt if needed. Set aside until ready to use, or refrigerate for 3 or 4 days; reheat them before adding to soup.

fish cakes (aka naruto)

Fish cakes, pressed protein creations derived from pollock or haddock or other mild-to-flavorless fish, are there to add color and texture. You can sometimes find them in the freezer case at Japanese markets; if not, omit them. Defrost the frozen fish cakes and cut them into ⅛-inch-thin slices.

seasonal vegetables

In the spring and early summer, use English or shelling peas, right out of the pod and raw if they're tender and good eating. If they're tougher, blanch them for 10 seconds in a large pot of salted water at a rolling boil, then immediately chill them in an ice water bath. Figure on about 2 tablespoons of shucked peas per bowl, or about ½ pound of peas in the pot from the market for 4 servings.

In the late summer, corn is the way to go. Shuck the ears and cut the kernels from the cobs. One ear of corn is enough for 2 portions of ramen.

Most of the rest of the year we use collard greens. To make enough for 6 or so bowls of soup, do this:

Cut the sturdy center rib and the stem from 1 bunch collards. Wash and drain the leaves, then coarsely chop them. Put a piece of bacon in a wide skillet (that can later be covered) and get it cooking over medium-high heat. Once it's begun to really render some fat into the pan, add the collard leaves, tossing well to coat them in the fat. Add a large pinch of kosher salt and cook, stirring, for a few minutes, until the collards start to give up some of their liquid and shrink a little. Add 1 tablespoon soy sauce, 1 tablespoon sherry vinegar, 1 tablespoon brown sugar (white is fine if you don't have brown), and 1 cup water (or Ramen Broth, page 40). Throw a lid on the pan, reduce the heat to medium-low, and simmer the collards, stirring them once in a while, for about 40 minutes, until tender. Keep at room temperature until ready to use.

ginger scallion noodles

Our ginger scallion noodles are an homage to/out-and-out rip-off of one of the greatest dishes in New York City: the $4.95 plate of ginger scallion noodles at Great New York Noodletown down on the Bowery in Chinatown.

Ginger scallion sauce is one of the greatest sauces or condiments ever. Ever. It's definitely a mother sauce at Momofuku, something that we use over and over and over again. If you have ginger scallion sauce in the fridge, you will never go hungry: stir 6 tablespoons into a bowl of hot noodles—lo mein, rice noodles, Shanghai thick noodles—and you're in business. Or serve over a bowl of rice topped with a fried egg. Or with grilled meat or any kind of seafood. Or almost anything.

At Noodle Bar, we add a few vegetables to the Noodletown dish to appease the vegetarians, add a little sherry vinegar to the sauce to cut the fat, and leave off the squirt of hoisin sauce that Noodletown finishes the noodles with. (Not because it's a bad idea or anything, just that we've got hoisin in our pork buns, and too much hoisin in a meal can be too much of a good thing. Feel free to add it back.)

The dish goes something like this: boil 6 ounces of ramen noodles, drain, toss with 6 tablespoons Ginger Scallion Sauce (below); top the bowl with ¼ cup each of Bamboo Shoots (page 54); Quick-Pickled Cucumbers (page 65); pan-roasted cauliflower (a little oil in a hot wide pan, 8 or so minutes over high heat, stirring occasionally, until the florets are dotted with brown and tender all the way through; season with salt); a pile of sliced scallions; and a sheet of toasted nori. But that's because we've always got all that stuff on hand. Improvise to your needs, but know that you need ginger scallion sauce on your noodles, in your fridge, and in your life. For real.

ginger scallion sauce

MAKES ABOUT 3 CUPS

Mix together the scallions, ginger, oil, soy, vinegar, and salt in a bowl. Taste and check for salt, adding more if needed. Though it's best after 15 or 20 minutes of sitting, ginger scallion sauce is good from the minute it's stirred together up to a day or two in the fridge. Use as directed, or apply as needed.

2½ cups thinly sliced scallions (greens and whites; from 1 to 2 large bunches)

½ cup finely minced peeled fresh ginger

¼ cup grapeseed or other neutral oil

1½ teaspoons usukuchi (light soy sauce)

¾ teaspoon sherry vinegar

¾ teaspoon kosher salt, or more to taste

roasted rice cakes SERVES 4

Korean kids are raised on them like cows on corn: *dok,* or rice cakes, fill up the soup bowl and fill out the plate. *Dok boki*—the classic dish of rice cakes in spicy bibim sauce that is the inspiration for this dish—was a weeknight staple at the Chang house.

But my fondest memories of eating rice cakes at home come from the rare, rare occasions when my grandfather would venture into the kitchen. Dok are the only thing I ever remember him cooking. I'd sit at the kitchen counter and watch him heat up some oil in a Teflon pan, roast long sticks of dok until they were crisp and brown, pour a little soy sauce on them, and feed them to me straight out of the pan as an afternoon snack. They were immeasurably better than the boiled dok I got in restaurants or from my mom, but my grandfather was the only person I ever knew to cook them like that.

When I lived in Korea as a teenager, I found that vendors selling dok on the sidewalks of Seoul were as commonplace as dirty-water hot dog stands on the streets of New York. I'd eat them all the time: big, steaming (totally unsanitary unwashed plastic) bowls of boiled dok and sliced fish cakes sloshed with a spicy sauce. My favorite spots boiled up the dok in a pot with a package of instant ramen, so you'd get ramen and rice cakes at the same time.

After I got to Japan—where they call dok *mochi*—I finally saw them crisped and browned again. In Japan, they grill them at street-side stalls and serve piping-hot bags of deep-fried square-shaped mochi at baseball games, like they do peanuts at games here. That's when I put it together that my grandfather's way of cooking the rice cakes—browning them so they got crisp and blackened—wasn't Korean. He must have picked it up when he went to Waseda University in Tokyo between the first and second world wars.

I equate the difference between boiled dok and grilled, griddled, or fried rice cakes to the difference between boiled and grilled hot dogs. Each has its place, but that char, that extra bit of flavor and texture you get from the direct heat, does a lot for dok, just as it does for hot dogs. As such, this isn't straight-up dok boki, but rather a take on it that substitutes the superior flavor and texture of crisp browned dok for the more traditional boiled rice cakes. And it's *way* fucking better.

1. Make the sauce: Combine the mirin and ramen broth in a saucepan large enough to accommodate the rice cakes later and put it on the stove over high heat. Boil to reduce until lightly thickened, 2 to 3 minutes. Add the red dragon sauce, turn the heat down to medium, and reduce the sauce to a glossy consistency, 6 to 7 minutes. Stir in the roasted onions. Cover and keep warm over very low heat until the rice cakes are ready.

2. While the sauce is reducing, heat a large (at least 12-inch) cast-iron skillet (make sure it's wiped really clean, because the white cakes will pick up any schmutz from the pan) over medium-high heat until hot. Add the oil to the pan, and just when it's about to smoke, add the rice cakes. They should sizzle when they hit the oil, at which point you can drop the heat down to medium. Sear the rice cakes for about 3 minutes per side, until

¼ cup mirin

¼ cup Ramen Broth (page 40)

½ cup Korean Red Dragon Sauce (page 60)

¼ cup Roasted Onions (page 61)

2 tablespoons grapeseed or other neutral oil

6 long rice cake sticks (see note, page 60)

1 tablespoon sesame seeds

½ cup sliced scallions (greens and whites)

RECIPE CONTINUES

they're a light golden brown: you want to brown them, but don't overdo it, or they will dry out. Transfer the rice cakes to a cutting board and cut them into fifths.

3. Bring the sauce back up to a boil and toss the rice cakes in it just for a few seconds, until they're evenly coated. Sprinkle them with the sesame seeds and toss again, then divide the sauced rice cakes among bowls. Garnish each serving with a few large pinches of sliced scallions and serve hot.

NOTE: Rice cakes are made by beating the hell out of cooked rice and then molding the very glutinous, thick results into shapes. We mainly use sliced rice cakes (the oblong coin-shaped disks) in soups and the long sticks or cylinders for other dishes. Cut into shorter lengths, they have a gnocchi-like appeal; charred until brown, they take on an amazing crisp texture and a smoky, deep flavor.

Rice cakes are sold frozen and they keep in the freezer for months. You can buy them at any Korean (or Japanese) grocery store.

korean red dragon sauce
MAKES ABOUT 1¼ CUPS

½ cup water

½ cup sugar

¾ cup ssämjang (fermented bean and chile sauce), or more to taste

2 tablespoons usukuchi (light soy sauce), or more to taste

1 teaspoon sherry vinegar, or more to taste

1 teaspoon Asian sesame oil, or more to taste

Bring the water and sugar to a boil in a small saucepan, stirring until the sugar dissolves. Remove from the heat and let cool for a few minutes, then stir in the ssämjang to dissolve it. Stir in the soy, vinegar, and sesame and taste the sauce: no one flavor should stand out, but all should be present and accounted for. Adjust as necessary.

roasted onions

MAKES ABOUT 1 CUP

Onions roasted like this will keep for a week or more in the fridge, so it's fine to make them well ahead of time. And there's really almost nothing that they don't make better—eggs, a roast beef sandwich, you name it. That said, you could also halve this recipe and make half a cup.

1. Heat the oil in a 12-inch cast-iron skillet over medium-high heat for 1 to 1½ minutes, until it's very, very hot but not smoking. Add the onions to the pan—they will be piled up high, probably to the rim—and let them cook undisturbed for 2 to 3 minutes.

2. Carefully toss the onions and, while doing so, season them with the salt. Now you've got 50 or so minutes of onion cookery ahead of you, and given all the eccentricities of pans and heat sources and the variables of moisture in the onions, etc., the best I can do is tell you what you're doing and what you're looking for:

2 tablespoons grapeseed or other neutral oil

6 onions, thinly sliced (about 8 very loosely packed cups)

Large pinch of kosher salt

    a. For the first 15 minutes or so, you want the onions at the bottom of the pan to be slowly but steadily taking on color as they sweat out their liquid. The onions above them are helping this happen by virtue of their weight, gently pressing down the onions below. Do not press down on the onions with a spatula or jack up the heat to try and accelerate this process. Just turn the whole pile of onions over on itself every 3 or 4 minutes during the early going to help distribute the tasty, caramelizing juice the onions are oozing throughout the pile.

    b. After the mass of onions in the pan has significantly reduced in volume—the onions are softer and suppler and have fallen considerably—it's time to turn the heat to medium-low and ride this baby out for as long as it takes, stirring and turning the onions every 10 minutes or so and making sure that they don't start to stick or burn at any point. This is the part that matters, when the onions soften and sweeten without drying out. Remember: slow and steady wins this race.

    c. After 50 minutes or so, you're going to be about there. The onions will have shrunk from a pile that threatened mutiny to the stovetop to a huddled mass that doesn't even cover the floor of the pan. They will have a definite sweetness, a deep roasted flavor, and a texture that's just this side of mushy. Use them straightaway, or let them cool and then store, tightly covered, in the refrigerator for up to a week or longer.

kimchi stew rice cakes & shredded pork SERVES 4

When I was growing up, my mother made kimchi stew a lot: Korean moms usually do. It always had cubes of soft tofu disintegrating in it and was often based on a quick anchovy stock—a primal, primitive relation to dashi made with dried anchovies boiled in water until the water tasted like boiled dried anchovies. Sometimes she'd use Memmi, Kikkoman's bottled "noodle soup base," a soy-and-bonito extract concoction that's popular with hurried moms and that you should probably avoid. Sometimes she garnished it with the true head-to-tail pork, Spam. And she always made it with kimchi that was so fridge-stinkingly fermented it had to be rinsed off before it went into the pot. That last touch is just so Korean: squeezing one more use out of a vegetable that has aged past even its fermented prime.

So this is not a traditional take on *kimchi jigae,* but a Momofuku take on it. Instead of using a light seafood stock or light beef stock—another common traditional approach—we juice up the overall body of the stew by making it with our ramen broth. (A classic French veal broth would be cool too.) Instead of using garbage kimchi from the back of the fridge, we use the same kimchi we serve on our pickle plate and in other dishes—kimchi that's just two weeks old, right at the first stages of its fermentation, still bright and fresh and with some texture to it. Instead of tempering the spice by rinsing off the kimchi, we do it by adding sweetness in the form of mirin and roasted onions. And we kick out the soft tofu normally used with the dish and swap in sliced rice cakes, which add body and depth and contrast.

The result is a smoldering bowl of spice and pork—perfect for a hangover or a cold that needs a kick in the ass.

1. Heat the grapeseed oil in a soup pot over medium heat. After giving it a minute or so, add the roasted onions and cook, stirring regularly, for a minute or two, until warmed through.

2. Add the radish and cabbage kimchis and broth, turn the heat up to medium-high, and let the flavors mingle and integrate for 5 to 6 minutes after the broth comes to a simmer. Skim off any impurities.

3. Add the meat to the pot and stir to incorporate and warm it through. Add the mirin and a few grinds of black pepper. Taste the soup, and add salt if needed, but that's rarely the case with this soup, because kimchi itself is salty. The sweetness of mirin can tame the sourness of super-fermented kimchi, so add more mirin if you feel you need to reel in the kimchi flavor. When the mix is right, add the rice cakes to the pot.

4. Once the rice cakes are warmed through—probably no more than 30 seconds (they'll keep cooking as the soup sits, so there's no need to boil the hell out of them)—portion the soup into bowls. Top each with lots of sliced scallions, then lots of julienned carrots, and serve with the rice on the side.

¼ cup grapeseed or other neutral oil

Roasted Onions (page 61)

4 cups Radish Kimchi (page 75)

4 cups Napa Cabbage Kimchi (page 74)

8 cups Ramen Broth (page 40)

Pork Shoulder for Ramen (page 51)

6 tablespoons mirin, or more to taste

Freshly ground black pepper

Kosher salt, if needed

1 cup sliced rice cakes (see note, page 60)

Heaping 1 cup sliced scallions (greens and whites)

Heaping 1 cup very finely julienned carrots

4 cups cooked Short-Grain Rice (page 279)

pickles

In cooking school, students are taught there are five cooking techniques: sautéing, frying, dry methods like roasting, wet methods like steaming or boiling, and combination methods like braising. At least that's the French perspective on things. I consider pickling to be a sixth technique that anyone who spends any time in the kitchen should be comfortable with. Seriously. At Momofuku, we serve pickles as a course on their own and use them as garnishes or as ingredients in many of our dishes.

Pickling is practical and doesn't need to be complicated. Lots of cooks equate pickling with canning (which is simple but time-consuming), but pickling can be as easy as making a brine, pouring it over chopped vegetables packed into a container, and waiting the right amount of time to eat them. You can do that, right? Sometimes it's even easier: the salt pickles barely require a recipe. And although kimchi is one of the more involved pickling processes, if you reduce it to its basic steps—salt the vegetable, mix up a spicy marinade to soak it in, and wait a week or two—it's not difficult.

You know how you see scallops at the fish market and think to yourself, I could sauté those with butter? Or see steaks at the butcher and think about throwing them on the grill? When I'm at the farmers' market, I see bushels and baskets of potential pickles: cauliflower, radishes, cucumbers, fennel. Almost anything. There are fewer vegetables and fruits that don't take to pickling than those that do, so get pickling. Now. As soon as you do, you'll wonder what took you so long.

quick salt pickles

A recipe almost seems excessive for these types of quickly made salt-and-sugar pickles, because the technique for making them is so simple: Sprinkle some thinly sliced vegetables with a 3:1 mix of sugar to kosher salt and toss. Ten to 20 minutes later, they're ready to eat. The resulting pickles have a fresh snap.

quick salt pickles, master recipe
MAKES ABOUT 2 CUPS

Halve or double the recipe as needed.

1. Combine the vegetable with the sugar and salt in a small mixing bowl and toss to coat with the sugar and salt. Let sit for 5 to 10 minutes.
2. Taste: if the pickles are too sweet or too salty, put them into a colander, rinse off the seasoning, and dry in a kitchen towel. Taste again and add more sugar or salt as needed. Serve after 5 to 10 minutes, or refrigerate for up to 4 hours.

Vegetable, prepared as indicated

1 tablespoon sugar, or more to taste

1 teaspoon kosher salt, or more to taste

quick-pickled cucumbers: 2 meaty Kirby cucumbers, cut into ⅛-inch-thick disks.

quick-pickled radishes: 1 bunch radishes (breakfast radishes, icicle radishes, and the like), well scrubbed and cut into thin wedges through the root end.

quick-pickled daikon: 1 large or 3 small daikon radishes, peeled and cut into very, very thin slices.

vinegar pickles

The best advice I can give to help ease you into the world of pickles is this: Pick up a sackful of pickle-able produce at your market on an afternoon or evening when you've got an hour or so to dedicate to stocking your larder. Line up a series of sealable quart containers on your countertop (Mason jars are great; at the restaurant we use sturdy lidded plastic containers like you might get a quart of soup in from a take-out joint). Trim the vegetables, pack each kind tightly in its own container, and brew up a big batch of brine. Fill each container with brine, cover the containers, and put them in the fridge to cure.

vinegar pickles, master recipe
MAKES 1 QUART

1 cup water, piping hot from the tap

½ cup rice wine vinegar

6 tablespoons sugar

2¼ teaspoons kosher salt

Vegetable or fruit, prepared as indicated

1. Combine the water, vinegar, sugar, and salt in a mixing bowl and stir until the sugar dissolves.
2. Pack the prepared vegetables into a quart container. Pour the brine over the vegetables, cover, and refrigerate. You can eat the pickles immediately, but they will taste better after they've had time to sit—3 to 4 days at a minimum, a week for optimum flavor. Most of these pickles will keep for at least a month, except where noted, though we typically go through them in a week or so after they've had a chance to sit and mature.

pickled apples or asian pears: 3 apples (choose a firm-fleshed variety, like Mutsu) or 2 Asian pears, peeled, cored, and sliced just a hair less than ¼ inch thick. These will be ready to eat after an hour in the brine and should be eaten the day you prepare them.

pickled beets: About 2 pounds beets, preferably smaller beets (bigger beets tend toward woodiness, though they're better than no beets at all), peeled, halved if they're not tiny, and cut into very, very thin disks or half-moons.

pickled cantaloupe, watermelon, or other melon:
Cut the flesh of 1 cantaloupe or 1 baby watermelon or other melon into large chunks—single-bite size, but not too small. Cool the brine before pouring it over the fruit. These will be ready to serve in an hour and are best eaten within 24 hours.

VARIATIONS CONTINUE

pickled carrots: 2 pounds baby carrots (as in infant or dwarf, not the whittled and bagged supermarket variety), scrubbed, peeled, and trimmed. If you can buy carrots with the tops, leave ½ inch of the tops attached and clean them well; it makes for a better presentation. The carrots we get from Satur Farms on Long Island are 5 to 6 inches long and slender—perfect for our purposes. For larger (but still small) carrots, cut them lengthwise into halves or thirds—they should be a size that's comfortable to pick up and snack on, though they don't need to be bite-sized.

pickled cauliflower: Cut the florets from 1 head of cauliflower, separating them into one-bite pieces.

pickled celery: 1 bunch celery, tops and bottoms trimmed, fibrous strands (particularly from the outside stalks) peeled or stripped away, and cut into ¼-inch slices on the bias.

pickled cherries: I cribbed this recipe from Bertrand Chemel, who was the sous-chef at Café Boulud while I was there. It demonstrates how using something that so often gets thrown away can make food more delicious. The cherry pits add a flavor that is subtle, a little like vanilla or almond. Pit 2 pints washed cherries, reserving the pits, and halve the cherries. Roughly crack the cherry pits in a mortar and pestle (or put them under a kitchen towel and crack them with a mallet or hammer) and wrap in a cheesecloth sachet. Omit the salt from the brine; combine the water, vinegar, sugar, and sachet in a saucepan and bring to a boil before pouring it over the cherries. Cool and then refrigerate.

pickled chiles: 4 cups Thai bird's-eye chiles or other small (no longer than 2 inches) fresh hot chiles. Yes, that's a lot of chiles, but they will last until the apocalypse. We slice them after they've been pickled and add them to a wide range of dishes. Be sure to wash your hands after handling the chiles, especially once they're pickled, or don't blame me for the consequences.

pickled crosnes: 4 cups (about 2 pounds) crosnes, well scrubbed. Crosnes are a corkscrew-looking tuber. They're more common in China, Japan, and France than they are here, but they're starting to make inroads. Flavorwise, they're not dissimilar to sunchokes—crunchy, crisp, like a cross between an apple and a potato. If you see them, buy them, and put them up in this brine. They're a good snack and a good addition to a salad or dish that needs crunch, like the Roasted Mushroom Salad on page 157. Bring the brine to a boil before pouring over the crosnes. Cool and then refrigerate. Optional: Add 1 teaspoon of shichimi togarashi (Japanese 7-spice powder) to the brine.

pickled fennel: 2 to 4 fennel bulbs, depending on size. Cut each bulb in half (all cuts are made on the root-to-stalk axis), cut out the core, cut the halves in half, and slice the fennel into thin strips, less than ⅛ inch thick. Optional: Add 1 teaspoon coriander seeds to the brine with the pickles.

pickled napa cabbage: Remove the greener outer layer leaves from the head of cabbage and discard them. Use the next couple of layers—16 to 20 of the bigger leaves—for this pickle. Make a triangular incision into each of the cabbage leaves to cut out the large, tough white rib and discard it. Combine the water, vinegar, sugar, and salt in a pickling container, stir until the sugar dissolves, and gently pack the leaves into the container. Cover and refrigerate.

pickled ramps: 2 pounds ramps, scrubbed, whiskers trimmed. Small ramps with narrow leaves that fit comfortably into your pickling container can be left whole. Those with large broad leaves—more common later in the ramp season—should be trimmed: leave 1 inch of green and reserve the trimmings for another use, like scrambling up with some eggs. Bring the brine to a boil before pouring over the ramps. Cool and then refrigerate. Optional: Add 1 teaspoon shichimi togarashi (Japanese 7-spice powder), 1 teaspoon kochukaru, and 1 tablespoon whole white peppercorns to the brine. Note that if you want to keep pickled ramps for more than about a month, it's best to separate the green leaves from the whites and pickle them separately. Use the pickled greens first (or don't pickle them, and use them in a different preparation) and then the whites (the greens will turn soft after about a month, the whites will keep for a few months).

pickled sunchokes: 2 pounds sunchokes (also called Jerusalem artichokes), peeled and cut into ⅛-inch-thick batons. Bring the brine to a boil before pouring it over the sunchokes. Optional: Add 1 teaspoon shichimi togarashi (Japanese 7-spice powder) to the brine.

pickled tokyo turnips: 4 cups (typically about 2 bunches) Tokyo turnips. Tokyo turnips are diminutive turnips that look like something out of Super Mario Brothers; we use them in our pickle plates and they're pictured on page 276 as part of a soup-and-rice course at Ko. Scrub them well and trim their tops so there's just ¼ inch or so of green still attached to the turnips.

STRETCHING THE PICKLE: When the pickles are gone, the brine's left, and if you're at all creative in the kitchen, you can find a way to put it to use. We use shiitake and pear pickling liquids to season the dipping sauce for our somen, and the chili-garlic-ginger-goodness sludge from the bottom of a container of kimchi could be swapped for pureed kimchi in recipes like the Fuji Apple Salad on page 162. Our friend Don Lee at PDT, a bar near the restaurants, has made cocktails with the brine from our pickled ramps.

pickled mustard seeds
MAKES ABOUT 1 CUP

Pickled mustard seeds are a preparation I straight up copped from years at Craft. They've been a staple of Tom Colicchio's cooking for years and with good reason—they have an intriguing texture, a discernible but not overwhelming flavor, and a glossy, elegant appearance because of all the pectin they exude into the pickling liquid they're cooked in.

1 cup yellow mustard seeds

1½ cups water

1½ cups rice wine vinegar

½ cup sugar

1 tablespoon kosher salt

Combine the mustard seeds, water, vinegar, sugar, and salt in a small saucepan and bring to the gentlest of simmers over low heat. Cook the mustard seeds, stirring often, until they're plump and tender, about 45 minutes. If the seeds look to be drying out, add water as needed to the pot to keep them barely submerged. Cool and store in a covered container in the refrigerator. Pickled mustard seeds will keep for months.

pickled watermelon rind
MAKES 1 QUART

These are a little different from the other vinegar pickles, as the watermelon rinds take to a sweeter pickling medium and require some cooking to tenderize them. Pickled watermelon rinds are good on their own or as part of a pickle plate. The best dish we ever made with them was a take on *frisée aux lardons:* frisée, pickled watermelon rinds, Benton's bacon lardons, a poached egg, and a vinaigrette that incorporated some of the pickling liquid and some of the bacon fat.

Rind of ½ medium watermelon, including ½ inch red flesh

1 cup rice wine vinegar

½ cup water

1 cup sugar

1 tablespoon plus ¾ teaspoon kosher salt

1 whole star anise

1 thumb-sized knob of fresh ginger, peeled

1. Cut the watermelon rind into 1-inch-thick slices. Carefully slice the skin off each slice, and cut the slices into 1-inch chunks.
2. Combine the vinegar, water, sugar, salt, star anise, and ginger in a saucepan and bring to a boil, stirring to dissolve the sugar. Add the watermelon rind and boil for 1 minute, then carefully transfer to a quart container. Cool and then refrigerate. These pickles are ready to eat in a couple of hours and will keep for about a week and a half—they start to lose flavor and get too soft after that.

soy sauce pickles

Shiitake mushrooms are what we typically pickle in the shoyuzuke, or soy sauce pickles, style: shiitakes are meaty and tasty, and they really soak up and showcase the vinegar-soy solution well.

pickled shiitakes
MAKES A GENEROUS QUART

Making ramen broth in the quantities we do generates an enormous amount of leftover—but not flavorless—shiitakes. One morning I came in and found Scott Garfinkel snacking on a bowl of the simmered shiitakes he'd taken from the broth and then pickled in soy sauce. They were so good we added them to the pickle plate immediately, and, like Scott, they've been a part of Noodle Bar ever since.

1. Steep the shiitakes in boiling water (or really hot tap water) in a medium mixing bowl until softened, about 15 minutes.

2. Lift the shiitakes from the steeping water, trim off and discard their stems, and cut the caps into ⅛-inch-thick slices. Reserve 2 cups of the steeping liquid, and pass it through a fine-mesh strainer to remove any sand or debris.

3. Combine the reserved steeping liquid, the sugar, soy sauce, vinegar, ginger, and sliced shiitakes in a saucepan. Turn the heat to medium, bring to a simmer, and simmer gently (bubbles should lazily rise up to the surface), stirring occasionally, for 30 minutes. Let cool.

4. Discard the ginger, and pack the shiitakes (and as much of the liquid as necessary to cover them) into a quart container. These pickles are ready to eat immediately and will keep, refrigerated, for at least 1 month.

4 loosely packed cups (about ⅓ ounce) dried shiitake mushrooms (or use spent shiitake caps from the Ramen Broth on page 40)

1 cup sugar

1 cup usukuchi (light soy sauce)

1 cup sherry vinegar

Two 3-inch knobs of fresh ginger, peeled

kimchi: fermented pickles

Kimchi is a fermented pickle, like sauerkraut, and the fermentation process is key to its flavor. It's elemental in Korean food and in Momofuku food, and you can make it with almost anything. In northern Virginia, where I grew up, my mom and my grandmother made it with blue crabs (which was totally gross, in case you're wondering). But some kind of seafood is often added to kimchi to help kick-start the fermentation process. Raw oysters are common as are squid, shrimp, or yellow croaker. We use the jarred salted shrimp that look like krill and have a strong but still appealing and sweet shrimp aroma. A little goes a long way, and a 500-gram jar will last even an avid kimchi maker a while, so take the time and hunt one down.

The amount of salt in kimchi stops almost every kind of food-borne nastiness from working except for lactic acid bacteria, and once that bacteria starts to produce lactic acid, the pH of the whole thing drops, and nothing grows that's going to cause spoilage. My friend Dave Arnold, The Smartest Person Alive and a food-science genius, explained that to me, and he also says that using sea salt or any naturally evaporated salt will help the pickles keep and stay firmer longer because of the trace amounts of impurities you can't taste, like magnesium and calcium.

At Momofuku, we make three types of kimchi: Napa cabbage (*paechu*), radish (from long white Korean mu radishes or, failing that, Japanese daikon), and Kirby cucumber (*oi*). Our recipe has changed some since I learned it from my mom, who learned it from her mom. I add more sugar than they would. We let the fermentation happen in the refrigerator instead of starting the kimchi at room temperature and then moving it into the fridge when it starts to get funky. At the restaurant, we let the kimchi ferment for only a couple of weeks, instead of allowing it to get really stinky and soft. There's a point, after about two weeks, where the bacteria that are fermenting the kimchi start producing CO_2 and the kimchi takes on a prickly mouthfeel, like the feeling of letting the bubbles in a soft drink pop on your tongue. It's right around then that I like it best.

1 small to medium head Napa cabbage, discolored or loose outer leaves discarded

2 tablespoons kosher or coarse sea salt

½ cup plus 2 tablespoons sugar

20 garlic cloves, minced

20 slices peeled fresh ginger, minced

½ cup kochukaru (Korean chile powder)

¼ cup fish sauce

¼ cup usukuchi (light soy sauce)

2 teaspoons jarred salted shrimp

½ cup 1-inch pieces scallions (greens and whites)

½ cup julienned carrots

napa cabbage kimchi (aka paechu kimchi)
MAKES 1 TO 1½ QUARTS

This is the kimchi we use most often in our cooking and in our restaurants.

1. Cut the cabbage lengthwise in half, then cut the halves crosswise into 1-inch-wide pieces. Toss the cabbage with the salt and 2 tablespoons of the sugar in a bowl. Let sit overnight in the refrigerator.
2. Combine the garlic, ginger, kochukaru, fish sauce, soy sauce, shrimp, and remaining ½ cup sugar in a large bowl. If it is very thick, add water ⅓ cup at a time until the brine is just thicker than a creamy salad dressing but no longer a sludge. Stir in the scallions and carrots.
3. Drain the cabbage and add it to the brine. Cover and refrigerate. Though the kimchi will be tasty after 24 hours, it will be better in a week and at its prime in 2 weeks. It will still be good for another couple weeks after that, though it will grow incrementally stronger and funkier.

radish kimchi (aka kakdugi): Radish kimchi is most often used in soups, like Kimchi Stew (page 63), but it's good for snacking on as part of a pickle plate. Substitute 3 medium mu or daikon radishes, peeled, any discolored portions trimmed away, and cut into ½-inch chunks, for the cabbage.

cucumber kimchi (aka oi kimchi)
MAKES ABOUT 1 QUART

This recipe is at the intersection of the ease of quick pickling and the full-on flavor of a long-fermented kimchi. It's best in the summer, when Kirby cucumbers, flavorful and sturdy, are in season and there are hot dogs around to put them on.

1. Toss the cucumbers with 1½ teaspoons of the sugar and ¼ teaspoon of the salt in a bowl. Let stand for about 10 minutes, until they've given up some of their juice and softened lightly.

2. Combine the remaining 2 tablespoons sugar and 1¼ teaspoons of salt with the kochukaru, ginger, garlic, fish sauce, soy sauce, and dried shrimp in a medium bowl. Toss in the carrot, scallion, onion, and drained cucumbers. Toss well, and let sit for 15 minutes and serve or store. Cucumber kimchi keeps in the fridge for up to a couple weeks, getting a little softer and stinkier with each passing day.

1 pound Kirby cucumbers, halved lengthwise and cut into ½-inch-wide spears

2½ tablespoons sugar

1½ teaspoons kosher salt

1½ tablespoons kochukaru (Korean chile powder)

1½ tablespoons thinly sliced strips peeled fresh ginger

4 garlic cloves, thinly sliced

1 tablespoon fish sauce

1 tablespoon usukuchi (light soy sauce)

½ teaspoon jarred salted shrimp (optional)

1 small carrot, cut into 2-inch matchsticks

1 scallion (green and white), cut into 2-inch matchsticks

¼ small onion, thinly sliced

momofuku pork buns SERVES 1

It's weird to be "famous" for something. Can you imagine being Neil Diamond and having to sing "Cracklin' Rosie" every time you get onstage for the rest of your life? Neither can I. But if Momofuku is "famous" for something, it's these steamed pork buns. Are they good? They are. Are they something that sprang from our collective imagination like Athena out of Zeus's forehead? Hell no. They're just our take on a pretty common Asian food formula: steamed bread + tasty meat = good eating.

And they were an eleventh-hour addition to the menu. Almost a mistake. No one thought they were a good idea or that anyone would want to eat pork belly sandwiches.

I got into the whole steamed bread thing when I stayed in Beijing. I ate *char siu bao*—steamed buns stuffed with dark, sweet roast pork—morning, noon, and night from vendors on the street who did nothing but satisfy that city's voracious appetite for steamed buns. When I lived in Tokyo, I'd pick up a *niku-man*—the Japanese version, with a milder-flavored filling—every time I passed the local convenience store. They're like the 7-Eleven hot dogs of Tokyo, with an appeal not unlike that of the soft meatiness of White Castle hamburgers.

And in the early days of my relationship with Oriental Garden—the restaurant in Manhattan's Chinatown where I've eaten more meals than anywhere else on the planet—I'd always order the Peking duck, which the restaurant serves with folded-over steamed buns with fluted edges, an inauthentic improvement on the more common accompaniment of scallion pancakes. *Char siu bao* and *niku-man* were influential, but the Peking duck service at Oriental Garden was the most important, if only because it was here in the city and I could go back and study what made their buns so good— and also because the owner of the restaurant was willing to help me out, at least after a point.

After I'd eaten his Peking duck about a million times, I asked Mr. Choy, the owner (whom I now call Uncle Choy, because he's the Chinese uncle I never had), to show me how to make the steamed buns. For as many times as I had eaten steamed buns, I had never thought about making them, but with Noodle Bar about to open, I had the menu on my mind. He laughed and put me off for weeks before finally relenting. (He likes to remind me that I am the *kung-fu*—the student, the seeker, the workman—and he is the *si-fu*—the master.) But instead of taking me back into the kitchen, he handed me a scrap of paper with an address, the name John on it, and a note scribbled in Chinese that I couldn't read.

Have you ever seen the blaxploitation martial arts movie *The Last Dragon* from the eighties, where the dude is in constant search for some type of master who can provide some wisdom, and in the end it turns out to be a hoax—the master's place is a fortune cookie factory? Probably not. But that's how I felt when the place I was sent to learn the secret of steamed bread turned out to be May May Foods, a local company that supplied dozens of New York restaurants with premade dim sum items, including buns, for decades before it closed in 2007. The guy there, John, showed me the dead-simple process: a little mixing, a little steaming, and presto! buns. It turns out they are made from a simple white bread dough, *mantou* (not so different from, say, Wonder Bread), that is steamed instead of baked.

But when I saw the flour everywhere and tried to imagine that mess in our tiny, already overcrowded kitchen, I immediately placed an order. We didn't have the space to attempt them then, and we continued to buy them from Chinatown bakeries even after May May closed.

If you have that option—a Chinese bakery or restaurant where you can easily buy them, or even a well-stocked freezer section at a local Chinese grocery store—I encourage you to exercise it without any pangs of guilt. How many sandwich shops bake their own bread? Right. Don't kill yourself. But don't be put off by the idea of making them either. They're easy and they freeze perfectly.

Here's the recipe for our pork buns, which you can increase ad infinitum to make more to share.

1 Steamed Bun (opposite)

About 1 tablespoon hoisin sauce

3 or 4 slices Quick-Pickled Cucumbers (page 65)

3 thick slices Pork Belly (page 50)

1 scant tablespoon thinly sliced scallion (green and white)

Sriracha, for serving

1. Heat the bun in a steamer on the stovetop. It should be hot to the touch, which will take almost no time with just-made buns and 2 to 3 minutes with frozen buns.

2. Grab the bun from the steamer and flop it open on a plate. Slather the inside with the hoisin sauce, using a pastry brush or the back of a spoon. Arrange the pickles on one side of the fold in the bun and the slices of pork belly on the other. Scatter the belly and pickles with sliced scallion, fold closed, and voilà: pork bun. Serve with sriracha.

steamed buns

MAKES 50 BUNS

Okay, fifty buns is a lot of buns. But the buns keep in the freezer for months and months without losing any quality, and if you cut the recipe down any more than this, there's barely enough stuff in the bowl of the mixer for the dough hook to pick up. So clear out a couple of hours and some space in the freezer and get to work.

1. Combine the yeast and water in the bowl of a stand mixer outfitted with the dough hook. Add the flour, sugar, milk powder, salt, baking powder, baking soda, and fat and mix on the lowest speed possible, just above a stir, for 8 to 10 minutes. The dough should gather together into a neat, not-too-tacky ball on the hook. When it does, lightly oil a medium mixing bowl, put the dough in it, and cover the bowl with a dry kitchen towel. Put it in a turned-off oven with a pilot light or other warmish place and let rise until the dough doubles in bulk, about 1 hour 15 minutes.
2. Punch the dough down and turn it out onto a clean work surface. Using a bench scraper or a knife, divide the dough in half, then divide each half into 5 equal pieces. Gently roll the pieces into logs, then cut each log into 5 pieces, making 50 pieces total. They should be about the size of a Ping-Pong ball and weigh about 25 grams, or a smidge under an ounce. Roll each piece into a ball. Cover the armada of little dough balls with a draping of plastic wrap and allow them to rest and rise for 30 minutes.
3. Meanwhile, cut out fifty 4-inch squares of parchment paper. Coat a chopstick with whatever fat you're working with.
4. Flatten one ball with the palm of your hand, then use a rolling pin to roll it out into a 4-inch-long oval. Lay the greased chopstick across the middle of the oval and fold the oval over onto itself to form the bun shape. Withdraw the chopstick, leaving the bun folded, and put the bun on a square of parchment paper. Stick it back under the plastic wrap (or a dry kitchen towel) and form the rest of the buns. Let the buns rest for 30 to 45 minutes: they will rise a little.
5. Set up a steamer on the stove. Working in batches so you don't crowd the steamer, steam the buns on the parchment squares for 10 minutes. Remove the parchment. You can use the buns immediately (reheat them for a minute or so in the steamer if necessary) or allow to cool completely, then seal in plastic freezer bags and freeze for up to a few months. Reheat frozen buns in a stovetop steamer for 2 to 3 minutes, until puffy, soft, and warmed all the way through.

1 tablespoon plus 1 teaspoon active dry yeast

1½ cups water, at room temperature

4¼ cups bread flour

6 tablespoons sugar

3 tablespoons nonfat dry milk powder

1 tablespoon kosher salt

Rounded ½ teaspoon baking powder

½ teaspoon baking soda

⅓ cup rendered pork fat or vegetable shortening, at room temperature, plus more for shaping the buns, as needed

chicken & egg SERVES 4

Momofuku's "Chicken and Egg" was inspired by a rendition of *oyako-don* (*oyako* means "mother and child," referring to the hen and its egg) that I ate at a yakitori house in the Kappabashi district of Tokyo. A pile of rice filled the bowl. It was brushed with a taré that was smoky, salty, and very sweet and on top of it sat a pile of scallions, an egg, and a single boneless chicken leg grilled over *bincho-tan* charcoal, with crisp, dark skin and just-cooked flesh that was delicate but had an amazing char-grilled flavor. Italian sea salt crowned the chicken, and a plate of *oshinko*—the Japanese name for a plate of mixed pickles—rode shotgun.

Over a couple weeks of meals at crappy Japanese restaurants with lackluster *oyako-dons* when we were first building Noodle Bar, Quino had heard me talk about the *oyako-don* enough that we decided we'd mess around with the dish for the Momofuku menu. We took my memories of that smoky yakitori chicken-and-rice dish and used them as a kind of guiding light for the flavor we were looking for: a smoki-ness unlike that of American barbecue—more subtle, more restrained, but no less affecting.

Smokiness is a flavor that is not often heralded in Japanese cuisine, but it's omnipresent: dashi, the cornerstone of Japanese cooking, is made with smoked dried fish. And the further you delve, the more you find it. While I was training with Akio at Soba-ya Fuyu-Rin, I learned his secret taré method that imbued his soup broths with such a supersmoky flavor: he would heat two steel rods until they were blacksmith hot, as red as swords ready to be shaped, and then plunge them in a batch of taré, scorching the sauce and giving it an unreal smoky flavor.

Back in the East Village, we didn't have the money to buy *bincho-tan* or a grill, so we had to get creative about achieving the flavor we were looking for. After a bit of screwing around—Quino, Texan that he is, demanded we switch from apple wood to mesquite, and he was right about that—we settled on a three-step method that does what we wanted it to: we cold-smoke the chicken, confit it in pork fat (as I mentioned earlier, the restaurant produced gallons of the stuff, and this was a way to use some), and then crisp it on the griddle under a bacon press. The confit process yields two rewards: pork-chicken fat that has a definite smokiness to it—meaning we could use that to add more subtle smokiness to any other dish we wanted; and the gelatinous goodness that collected at the bottom of the pans, the kitchen equivalent of gold—there's almost nothing you can't stir that stuff into and improve it. (For more on that, see page 50.) It's also the perfect way to produce supremely tender, juicy, deeply smoky chicken that requires little last-minute cooking.

I guess you could call it one of Momofuku's axioms: to cook a product to the point where it just needs to be reheated, to minimize à la minute preparation without ruining the integrity of the dish. That idea also works at home. You can make the chicken days ahead of time and—on the night you want to serve it—free it from the fat it's been cooked in, make some rice and eggs, brown the chicken, and you're good to go.

8 cups lukewarm water

1 cup plus 1 tablespoon sugar

1 cup plus 1 teaspoon kosher salt

4 boneless chicken legs

2 strips smoky bacon, preferably Benton's (see page 147), if not cold-smoking the chicken

5 cups rendered pork or duck fat or grapeseed or other neutral oil, or more if needed

2 Kirby cucumbers

4 cups cooked Short-Grain Rice (page 279)

4 Slow-Poached Eggs (page 52) or regular poached eggs

½ cup sliced scallions (greens and whites)

1. Combine the water, 1 cup of the sugar, and 1 cup of the salt in a large container with a lid or a plastic freezer bag large enough to accommodate the brine and chicken and stir until the salt and sugar have dissolved. Add the chicken, cover or seal, and refrigerate for at least 1 hour, no more than 6.

2. Remove the chicken from the brine and discard the brine. Cold-smoke the chicken as directed on the facing page. (If you do not have the resources to cold-smoke chicken, just add the optional bacon to the pot in the next step. It won't be the same, but it will be close.)

3. Heat the oven to 180°F.

4. Pack the chicken legs snugly into a pot or other oven-safe vessel—the shape doesn't matter so much, but the less extra space there is, the less fat will be required to submerge the chicken. (If you did not smoke the chicken, tuck the bacon in with it.) Heat the pork fat until warm and liquefied and pour it over the chicken to cover. Put the chicken in the oven and cook for 50 minutes. Remove the pot from the oven and cool to room temperature.

5. Put the chicken in the refrigerator to thoroughly chill it in the fat. The chicken can be prepared through this step a week or more in advance.

6. When you're ready to serve the dish, heat the chicken confit in its pot, in a low oven (around 200°F) or on the stovetop just until the fat liquefies.

7. While you're waiting, make a quick cucumber pickle: Slice the cucumbers into coins a little less than ⅛ inch thick. Toss with the remaining 1 tablespoon sugar and 1 teaspoon salt in a small bowl and allow to sit until ready to use.

8. Remove the chicken from the fat with a slotted spoon and put it on a cutting board or large plate; set the pot aside. Heat a 12-inch cast-iron skillet over medium-high heat for a minute or two, until the pan is hot (hold your hand over the center of the pan—it should feel hot from an inch or so away). Add the chicken legs skin side down (use two pans if too crowded), and brown them deeply, 3 to 4 minutes, on the skin side only, using a bacon press or a small heavy skillet to weigh them down while cooking. Transfer the browned legs to a cutting board.

9. Portion the rice among four deep soup bowls. Use the back of a spoon to create a shallow divot in the middle of each bowl of rice and slide an egg into it. Divide the cucumber pickles among the bowls, nestling them together into a little mound. Slice the chicken legs into ½-inch-thick slices, and fan one sliced chicken leg around the egg in each bowl. Sprinkle with the scallions and serve.

10. After dinner, rewarm the confit pot and decant the clear, golden fat into a clean container; pour the juices—i.e., all the non-fat contents of the pan—into another small container. Store both in the refrigerator: the fat will last for months; the meat jelly about a week.

Cold-smoking meat is a go-to move in the Momofuku kitchen. Here's a way to do it on a kettle grill, the kind most people have at home.

Put two large handfuls of wood chips, preferably mesquite, in a large mixing bowl and add water to cover. Put a chimney starter on a heat-proof surface. Dump four handfuls charcoal, preferably hardwood lump, in the chimney starter, put crumpled newspaper in the bottom of the chimney, and light the paper.

Open up the vents in the lid and the bottom of the grill. Remove the top grill rack and wash it well

with soapy water. Put a disposable aluminum roasting pan on the bottom rack (or in the bottom of the grill). Grab the wood chips from the water, shake them off, and scatter them in an even layer in the pan.

When the charcoal is glowing red and covered with ash, about 20 minutes, scatter a few coals over the wood chips in the aluminum pan—you want enough heat so that the wood chips will smolder, but not so much that there's going to be a fire or all that much heat produced. Put the top rack back in the grill, and put your brined meat on the grate.

Put the lid on the grill. After a couple of minutes, stick an instant-read thermometer through the vent in the top of the grill: it should be between 80° and 120°F, and there should be smoke rising out of the grill. If it's too hot, lift up the lid and sneak out a coal or two; if there's no smoke and no heat at all, add a few more coals, but don't overdo it. Cold-smoke the meat for 45 minutes, adding more wood chips or coals along the way if you run out of smoke. Deploy in the kitchen as directed. (Note that chicken prepared this way is cold-smoked but not cooked, and so it is not ready to eat.)

cold-smoking

chicken wings SERVES 4 TO 8

This is the world's longest recipe for chicken wings. Sorry. But they're very, very good chicken wings.

20 chicken wings, with wing tips attached (about 4½ pounds)

8 cups lukewarm water

1 cup sugar

1 cup kosher salt

2 strips smoky bacon, preferably Benton's (see page 147), if not cold-smoking the chicken

¼ cup vegetable oil

5 cups rendered pork or duck fat or grapeseed or other neutral oil, or more if needed

1 cup mirin

1 cup sake

1 cup usukuchi (light soy sauce)

Freshly ground black pepper

6 medium garlic cloves, thinly sliced

5 to 6 Pickled Chiles (page 68), seeded and ribs removed

1 bunch scallions, thinly sliced (greens and whites)

1. Cut the tips off the wings and save them to make the broth you need to sauce the wings. Cut the wings apart at the elbow joint.

2. Combine the water, sugar, and salt in a large container with a lid or a plastic freezer bag large enough to accommodate the brine and wings and stir until the sugar and salt have dissolved. Add the chicken wings, cover or seal, and refrigerate for at least 1 hour, no more than 6.

3. Remove the chicken from the brine and discard the brine. Cold-smoke the chicken as directed on page 85. (If you do not have the resources to cold-smoke chicken, just add the optional bacon to the pot in the next step. It won't be the same, but it will be close.)

4. Heat the oven to 180°F.

5. Pack the wings snugly into a pot or other oven-safe vessel—the shape doesn't matter so much, but the less extra space there is, the less fat will be required to submerge the chicken. (If you did not smoke the chicken, tuck the bacon in with it.) Heat the pork fat until warm and liquefied and pour it over the chicken to cover. Put the chicken in the oven and cook for 30 minutes. Remove the pot from the oven and cool to room temperature. Put the chicken wings in the refrigerator to thoroughly chill them in the fat. The chicken can be prepared through this step up to a week in advance.

6. While the wings are confiting, make taré: Put the wing tips in a wide sauté pan or skillet and brown over medium-high heat, stirring occasionally, for 10 to 15 minutes, until they're deeply colored. Add the mirin, sake, and soy sauce and use a spatula or wooden spoon to scrape up any meaty bits stuck to the pan. Bring the liquid to a boil, then drop the heat so it simmers and cook for 40 minutes. Remove from the heat and pass the liquid through a strainer; discard the spent wingtips. Season the broth with 5 to 6 turns of black pepper. Let cool, then refrigerate until ready to use.

7. When you're ready to serve the wings, heat the chicken confit in its pot, in a low oven (around 200°F) or on the stovetop just until the fat liquefies. Remove the wings from the fat with a slotted spoon and drain on paper towels; set the pot aside.

8. Heat a 12-inch cast-iron skillet over medium-high heat for a minute or two, until the pan is hot (hold your hand over the center of the pan—it should feel hot from an inch or so away). Add the wings, working in batches so as not to crowd the pan, and brown them deeply, 3 to 4 minutes

on each side, using a bacon press or a small heavy skillet to weigh them down while cooking.

9. While the wings are browning, make the sauce: Heat a couple tablespoons of the confit fat in a wide skillet or sauté pan over medium heat. After a minute, add the garlic and cook, stirring, until softened and aromatic, 2 to 3 minutes. Add half the taré (reserve the rest for another use), turn the heat up high, and let it simmer with the garlic for 8 to 10 minutes—about as long as it should take the wings to get good and browned.

10. When the wings are ready, add them and the pickled chiles to the sauce in the pan, working in batches as necessary, and toss the wings to coat. Turn them out into a serving bowl. Garnish with the scallions and serve hot. Strain and save the confit fat in a covered container in the refrigerator. It keeps forever and only gets more delicious.

fried chicken SERVES 2 TO 4

I love, love, love, love, love fried chicken. I order it like a side dish at restaurants or when I get takeout. I will eat the worst fried chicken and love it.

We came up with this dish at the new Noodle Bar, once we had moved up the block. We tried different methods. Buttermilk soaking—the traditional southern way—was okay, but it didn't amplify the natural flavor of the chicken, which took a long time to cook in the fryer. Kevin and Scott experimented with some batters and coatings, all of which were tasty, but none of which was right.

We were using a crazy expensive and delicious chicken—the breed name is poulet rouge—and I wanted to strip away as much excess flavoring as possible. That's when we settled on this method: steam the chicken first, just until it's cooked, then use the fryer just to crisp and brown the outside. We came around to that method in part because of the new kitchen and the new Noodle Bar. At the original Noodle Bar we had just about the worst equipment on the planet: one oven in the basement in which everything was roasted and one tiny countertop fryer that fit maybe two chicken legs at a time. At the new Noodle Bar we have a fancy oven that allows us to cook the chicken at 160°F in a steam-filled chamber and also a big deep fryer in which we could probably fry an entire baby pig.

But it isn't just a gear-driven approach: frying the chicken this way means the chicken spends less time in the oil, so it has a really clean flavor, and because of the sugar in the brine, it browns deeply—quickly. Take it out, chop it up, douse it in octo vin, and there it is: fried chicken dinner.

1. Combine the water, sugar, and salt in a large container with a lid or a large freezer bag, and stir until the sugar and salt dissolve. Add the chicken to the brine, cover or seal, and refrigerate for at least 1 hour and no more than 6.

2. Set up a steamer on the stove. Drain the chicken and discard the brine. Put the chicken in the steamer basket (if you are using a stacking Chinese-style bamboo steamer, put the legs in the bottom level and the breast on the top). Turn the heat to medium and set the lid of the steamer ever so slightly ajar. Steam the chicken for 40 minutes, then remove it from the steamer and put it on a cooling rack to cool. Chill it in the refrigerator, preferably on the rack, for at least 2 hours or overnight.

3. Take the chicken out of the refrigerator at least 30 minutes before you fry it.

4. In a deep skillet, heat enough oil for the chicken to be submerged to 375°F. Fry the chicken in batches, turning once, until the skin is deep brown and crisp, 6 to 8 minutes. Remove to a paper towel–lined plate to drain.

5. Cut the chicken into a few pieces: cut the wing from the breast, cut the breast in half, cut through the knee to separate the thigh from the drumstick. Put in a large bowl, toss with the vinaigrette, and serve hot.

4 cups lukewarm water

½ cup sugar

½ cup kosher salt

One 3- to 3½-pound chicken, cut into 4 pieces (2 legs, 2 breast halves with wings attached)

4 cups grapeseed or other neutral cooking oil

Octo Vinaigrette (page 107)

pan-roasted asparagus poached egg
& miso butter SERVES 4

I love miso ramen. I ate a lot of it in the Sapporo region, where it was invented, when I was living in Japan. In many places, they'd finish it with a huge knob of butter and some canned corn as a garnish—totally ghetto, totally delicious. Daydreaming about that miso ramen got me to thinking about making a miso compound butter, which I'd never seen anywhere else. Butter + miso worked like crazy on those bowls of soup, so I mixed up a batch, adding more and more miso as I went. The end result was nutty and creamy, and it just tasted good—so good I licked it off my fingers, like cake frosting.

Quino was messing around with the miso butter one day and found that when he mixed it with an egg it tasted like carbonara—the fermented, salty tang of miso standing in for the pig. One day, I was trying to make a beurre monté based on sherry vinegar and the miso butter instead of water and plain butter. I mixed it with an egg and realized it tasted like hollandaise sauce—not so literally, but in a similar appealing fat-on-fat sort of way. We saw it had potential, and we put this dish together, to look like an asparagus-and-fried-egg dish you'd see at any rustico Italian market-driven restaurant in New York, but with the idea that nothing really prepared you for the flavor combination you get from that not-quite-hollandaise.

½ cup shiro (white) miso

8 tablespoons (1 stick) unsalted butter, at room temperature, plus more if needed

½ pound thin to medium asparagus

Kosher salt

2 teaspoons sherry vinegar

4 Slow-Poached Eggs (page 52) or regular poached eggs

Freshly ground black pepper

NOTE: If you have reason to make a larger quantity of miso butter—and there are many, because miso butter has a weeks-long shelf life and makes just about anything more delicious—mix together larger quantities of butter and miso in a stand mixer fitted with the paddle attachment.

1. Make the miso butter: Combine the miso with 5 tablespoons of the butter in a small bowl and beat with a wooden spoon until well mixed; the butter should be one color, not a streaky mess. Reserve until needed; you can refrigerate it, well wrapped, for up to a few weeks.

2. Snap off the woodier bottom inch or so of each asparagus stalk. Use a vegetable peeler to shave away the tougher outer layer from each stalk, but don't get carried away: you probably won't need to peel the stalks more than 2 or so inches up from the trimmed end.

3. Heat the remaining 3 tablespoons butter in a wide skillet over medium-high heat. Line a plate with paper towels for draining the asparagus. When the butter sends up the first wisp of smoke, put the asparagus in the pan. (Do not overcrowd the pan; cook in batches if necessary, draining each one, and refreshing the butter if the butter from the first batch smells scorched.) When the asparagus start to take on some color, 2 to 3 minutes, season them with a generous pinch of salt and turn the heat down to medium. Turn them with a spoon or spatula so they can color on the second side, another few minutes. When the asparagus are nicely browned and tender (but not exactly soft), transfer them to the paper towels to drain.

RECIPE CONTINUES

4. While the asparagus are cooking, heat the sherry vinegar in a small saucepan over medium heat. After half a minute, add the miso butter, turn the heat to low, and stir to warm it through. When the butter has loosened slightly—it should still have a certain viscosity to it and shouldn't be melted—remove the pan from the burner and put it in a warm spot.

5. Season the cooked asparagus with another pinch of salt if needed. Smear a quarter of the warmed miso butter into a thickish puddle in the middle of each plate. Divide the asparagus among the plates and top each with an egg. Finish each dish with a few turns of black pepper, and serve at once.

roasted sweet summer corn miso butter, bacon
& roasted onions SERVES 4

When the first summer rolled around at the old Noodle Bar, and asparagus were done and corn came into season, we decided we'd make a succotash with our miso butter. Then we got lazy and cut out the lima beans and such, so we had just corn, bacon, onions, and the miso butter. It turned out to be one of our most popular dishes ever. It will never go back on the menu, though, because the summer we ran that dish, it was like we were a corn restaurant that just happened to sling some noodles on the side.

Later on, Kevin Pemoulie devised an even more ingenious corn-and-miso combo: grilled cobs, dusted with kochukaru (Korean red pepper flakes) and frozen miso butter shaved with a Microplane—a Momofuku *elote* (the Mexican corn prep of grilled corn with mayonnaise, chile pepper, cheese, and lime). We've never put that *elote* on the menu for fear that we'd turn into Café Habana—a café in NoLita that probably grills more corn than Iowa grows over the course of a year—but that shouldn't stop you from trying it at home should you be so inclined.

This is excellent as a summer side dish/starter/small plate, but you can turn it into a main course by topping each portion with a few shrimp (use the method from the grits dish on page 110) or a poached or fried egg.

1. Make the miso butter: Combine the miso with the butter in a small bowl and beat with a wooden spoon until well mixed; the butter should be one color, not a streaky mess. Reserve until needed.

2. Heat a 10- to 12-inch cast-iron skillet over medium heat for a minute or so, until very warm. Add the bacon and cook, stirring occasionally, until it shrinks to about half its original size and browns but does not overly crisp, about 4 minutes. Remove the bacon with a slotted spoon and drain it on paper towels. Drain the bacon fat from the pan (reserve it for another use if you like) and return the pan to the stove.

3. Turn the heat to high and add the oil to the pan. When the oil smokes, add the corn to the pan. Sauté, agitating the pan or stirring the corn with a spoon, until it turns bright yellow and just a few of the kernels start to brown, 3 to 4 minutes. (If the corn makes a popping noise like popcorn when it hits the pan, ease the heat back down to medium-high.)

4. Add the bacon and roasted onions to the pan and stir to combine. Add the broth, miso butter, a tiny pinch of salt, and 7 or 8 turns of black pepper. Glaze the corn with the butter and broth by tossing it in the pan (potentially messy) or stirring (safer) until the butter has melted, the corn is glossy with the sauce, and there's no broth pooled in the bottom of the pan, just a minute or two.

5. Transfer the corn to serving bowls, scatter with the sliced scallions, and serve hot or warm.

2 heaping tablespoons shiro (white) miso

2 tablespoons unsalted butter, at room temperature

6 slices smoky bacon, preferably Benton's (see page 147), cut crosswise into 1- to 1½-inch-long batons (1 cup)

1 tablespoon grapeseed or other neutral oil

4 cups corn kernels (cut from 4 to 5 cobs)

Heaping ¼ cup Roasted Onions (page 61)

½ cup Ramen Broth (page 40)

Kosher salt and freshly ground black pepper

1 cup sliced scallions (greens and whites)

brussels sprouts kimchi puree & bacon SERVES 4

I remember walking through the Greenmarket one day after we opened and thinking, "What the fuck would I do with Brussels sprouts?" We weren't busy then and we weren't working with much market produce.

Months later, when Brussels sprouts came back into season, we were letting the Greenmarket dictate a portion of our menu. I took their reappearance as sort of a challenge—we did stuff with almost everything that has a big season near us, so what would we do with Brussels sprouts? How were we gonna get people to eat Brussels sprouts without using bacon and chestnuts, like every other New American market-driven restaurant in the city?

They're just baby cabbages, I told myself. Being Korean, I thought, "Let's make kimchi out of them." That didn't work out so well. The centers were hard and raw when we tried pickling them whole, and shredding and pickling the sprouts just made for a soggy mess. So I knew we'd have to create a dish around them.

It didn't take me long to come around to the bacon thing—I usually do. We decided to roast them off—I love the dark sweetness and faint bitterness of well-charred Brussels sprouts—and toss them in some pureed kimchi, like a sauce, because Brussels sprouts, stinky little fuckers that they are, take really well to the funkiness of kimchi. Added in some bacon, 'cause bacon and Brussels sprouts just go together. It was good, but it looked not good. So we put a big bright pile of julienned carrots on top to give it some color, and away we went.

1 pound Brussels sprouts

¼ pound smoky bacon, preferably Benton's (see page 147), cut into 1- to 1½-inch-long batons

1 cup Napa Cabbage Kimchi (page 74), pureed

2 tablespoons unsalted butter

Kosher salt and freshly ground black pepper

1 cup julienned carrots

1. Preheat the oven to 400°F.

2. Remove and discard the loose outer leaves from the sprouts, and cut the sprouts in half through the core.

3. Put the bacon in a wide oven-safe sauté pan or skillet and cook over medium heat, stirring occasionally, until just about crisp, 5 minutes or so. With a slotted spoon, transfer the bacon to a paper towel–lined plate and reserve.

4. Drain off most of the fat from the pan and add the sprouts, cut side down. Raise the heat to medium-high and sear until the sprouts begin to sizzle. Put the skillet in the oven and roast until the sprouts are deeply browned, 8 minutes or so, then shake the pan to redistribute them. Pull the pan from the oven when the sprouts are bright green and fairly tender (taste one to check), 10 to 15 minutes more.

5. Return the pan to the stovetop over medium heat and stir in the butter, bacon, and salt and pepper to taste. Toss the sprouts to coat them.

6. Divide the kimchi among four shallow bowls. Use the back of a spoon to spread the kimchi out so it covers the bottom of the bowls. Divide the sprouts among the bowls, arranging them in a tidy pile on top of the kimchi. Garnish each with a pile of carrot julienne and serve.

cherry tomato salad soft tofu & shiso SERVES 4

I was at some event talking with Jean-Georges Vongerichten, one of the greatest chefs alive, when he told me this was the best dish we'd ever come up with. Not the frozen foie gras at Ko (more about that later), not anything like that—this was the one that made him think, "Why didn't I think of this first?" That's insanely high praise.

But, smart man that he is, he honed in on something there: this salad is the mission of Noodle Bar in a single dish. The first year we did it, there were amazing tomatoes at the market pretty much all summer. That's uncommon in New York— usually it takes until late August for tomatoes to get really good. Confronted with that abundance, we asked ourselves what to do with them. Basil, sea salt, and olive oil were the first things in my mind, the flavors I associated with tomatoes like those. But since we didn't want Noodle Bar to turn into the sort of "pan-Asian" restaurant that has pizza and bibimbap on the menu, we started to riff on it, to take its flavor profile and twist it to our needs.

Tofu, we realized, could do the same thing mozzarella does in a traditional caprese salad: moderate the acidity of the tomatoes, lend the dish some creaminess, and make it more substantial. Shiso and basil are like long-lost cousins: they have totally different flavors, though they share a sort of mintiness, but they're used in a lot of the same ways. And the touch of sesame oil in the vinaigrette echoes the nuttiness of good olive oil.

The result? A world away from an Italian salad, but a riff on a combination and approach to showcasing tomatoes we knew would work.

One 12-ounce block silken tofu, drained

2 pints (1¼ to 1½ pounds) mixed cherry tomatoes

¼ cup sherry vinegar

1 tablespoon usukuchi (light soy sauce)

1 teaspoon Asian sesame oil

½ cup grapeseed or other neutral oil

Kosher salt and freshly ground black pepper

6 shiso leaves, stacked atop one another, rolled into a tight cigar, and thinly sliced crosswise

1. With your knife blade parallel to the cutting board, cut the block of tofu in half. Using a 2- to 2½-inch ring mold (or a narrow straight-sided glass), cut cylinders of tofu out of each slab. Carefully turn each cylinder on its side and slice it in half, yielding 8 rounds of tofu. (Save the tofu scraps for another use.)

2. Bring a large saucepan of salted water to a boil. Prepare an ice bath in a large mixing bowl. Cut a tiny X or slash into the bottom of about two-thirds of the tomatoes. Drop them, in batches, into the boiling water, and after 10 seconds, remove them with a slotted spoon and transfer them to the ice bath to cool. Slip the skins off the blanched tomatoes, put them in a bowl, and refrigerate for 10 minutes.

3. Meanwhile, cut the remaining cherry tomatoes in half.

4. Stir together the vinegar, soy sauce, and sesame and grapeseed oils in a large mixing bowl. Add all the tomatoes and toss to coat.

5. To serve, place 2 slices of tofu in each of four shallow serving bowls, and sprinkle with a pinch of salt. Top each portion with about a cup of dressed tomatoes, season with a pinch of salt and a few turns of freshly ground black pepper, and garnish, generously, with the shiso chiffonade.

No matter how happy we are with a dish, the kitchen ethos at Momofuku dictates that it can always be tweaked or altered or interpreted differently. Made better. It's the only way to keep cooking interesting. If you wanted to get really esoteric about it, you could say it's an approach rooted in Japanese *kaizen*—that every day you work to make yourself do better. And the way that frequently plays out on the plate is when we reengineer and reimagine our own dishes. This tomato salad was Tomato Salad 1.0.

During the first summer at Ssäm Bar, Tien, Tim, and Co. did their own take on the salad: chilled peeled cherry tomatoes, firm tofu cut into small croutons and deep-fried until crisp, a similar vinaigrette, and opal basil—the purple basil you see in Thai restaurants—to finish: Version 2.0

Back at the new Noodle Bar, Kevin, Scott, and Jo got rid of the tofu and shiso and added shredded romaine and candied bacon: Tomato Salad Version 3.0

Our first summer at Ko yielded Version 4.0: peeled cherry tomatoes marinated in smoked taré for the "vinaigrette" (all the tomatoes were chilled, one was frozen for texture); made-to-order yuba, or tofu skin, in place of the soft tofu; and shiso to finish.

peas with horseradish SERVES 4

Early on, we did a lot of our supplementary shopping at the local bodegas. (Even today, I'm really happy as a cook when I realize we need something we don't have but there's a 24-hour deli two blocks away stocked with five brands of everything.) I was in one getting stuff—I think Kewpie Mayonnaise, which you can find at a surprising number of East Village bodegas—and while I was waiting in line, I just was staring at this bag of wasabi peas near the checkout. It was June; peas were in season.

Back in the early days, in the worst, most-clichéd *High Fidelity*–dork sort of way, we were always making lists: top five best dishes you've ever eaten, top five worst dishes of all time, etc. Wasabi mashed potatoes was usually number one on the ten worst dishes list. It always made the list. (I hold a personal grudge against Cat Cora and a professional grudge against the American *Iron Chef* show because Cat Cora "beat" Alex Lee—a titan, an idol of mine, and a profoundly talented cook who kept Restaurant Daniel at the head of the New York pack for years—with wasabi mashed potatoes on her menu. That show is dead to me.)

Anyway, back to the deli: I'm spacing out while staring at these wasabi peas, which people *love,* and I don't get. They're just dried peas covered in horseradish oil applied with some kind of space-age polymer. So I get to thinking: fresh horseradish is a great ingredient, it has a great flavor. (It's also cheap and it lasts forever.) That was it: peas with horseradish. Done. We made it and added radishes for crunch and texture and color—if you can find them, watermelon radishes make this dish look really good.

Remember that "cooked" sugar snap peas should be almost raw. All you're doing here is warming them through and coating them with the butter. Snow and sugar snap peas both work and the radishes are optional but nice, seeing as they complement the bite of the freshly grated horseradish. You could make this dish with frozen snow peas in a pinch, but it will lack some of the pertness of fresh peas. Whatever you do, do not substitute jarred horseradish for fresh: it will turn the dish into a wet mess.

1. Bring the broth to a boil in a wide sauté pan over high heat and boil until reduced by about half, about 5 minutes.

2. Meanwhile, toss the radishes with a couple of pinches of salt and let them sit.

3. Once the broth has reduced, add the snap or snow peas and cook, stirring frequently, until they are bright green, 2 to 3 minutes. Add the soy sauce and turn the heat down to medium. Add the butter and cook, stirring and spooning the pan juices over the vegetables, until the butter has melted and the peas are glazed.

4. Add the radishes, a pinch of salt, and a few turns of fresh black pepper. Stir once, then put in a warmed bowl, scatter the horseradish over the peas, and serve at once.

1 cup Ramen Broth (page 40)

3 small red radishes, trimmed and sliced into paper-thin coins

Kosher salt

1 pound sugar snap peas or snow peas (pull the strings off either kind)

1 tablespoon usukuchi (light soy sauce)

3 tablespoons unsalted butter

Freshly ground black pepper

¼ cup freshly grated horseradish

pan-roasted bouchot mussels with os SERVES 4

Mussels were a menu mainstay at Noodle Bar for a year or more of the early going. They were most often billed by themselves: "pan-roasted bouchot mussels." Sometimes the menu went into more detail: "with fermented bean sauce," or "w/OS," which stood for "with Oriental sauce," my name for this generic pan-Asian seafood sauce I came up with. I enjoy appropriating the out-of-date and borderline-racist term *Oriental* whenever I get the chance. But I was one of the few Orientals working in the kitchen at Noodle Bar, and the rest of the round-eye crew wasn't happy with the name. So we kept it under wraps. Since we're here alone together, let's call it what it is: Oriental sauce.

We put it on our favorite mussels, which come from just off Hardwood Island in Maine, where they raise "bouchot" mussels. The bouchot style dictates that the mussels are raised on thick wooden posts plunged into the sea floor. Because of their perch, bouchot mussels spend a little time above water when the tide is out; the resulting mussels harbor little to no sediment and are more flavorful, firm, and meaty than rope-raised mussels, which spend all their lives feeding in deep water.

If you can't find bouchot mussels, rope-raised Prince Edward Island (PEI) mussels are your next best bet. We just don't ever go for those green-lipped New Zealand guys—they're pallid and flabby. If you can't find mussels you're excited about, you could substitute large littleneck or butter clams.

⅓ cup denjang (Korean fermented bean paste) or, failing that, shiro (white) miso

2 tablespoons sherry vinegar

2 tablespoons minced peeled fresh ginger

2 tablespoons sliced scallions (greens and whites), plus ½ cup scallions cut into 1½-inch-long julienne

6 garlic cloves, thinly sliced

4 to 5 pounds mussels

¼ cup grapeseed or other neutral oil

1 cup dry sake

Freshly ground black pepper

1. Smash together the denjang, sherry vinegar, ginger, sliced scallions, and garlic cloves in a small bowl. Set aside.

2. Clean the mussels: Put them in a large bowl of cold water and let them sit for a few minutes to purge any grit, then scrub their shells clean of any debris, and rip off the "beards"—the little fuzzy strands sticking out of the side of the shells.

3. Pour the oil into a deep wide pot with a lid that will later comfortably accommodate all the mussels, and set over high heat. After a minute or so, when the oil is hot but not smoking, add the mussels. Cook, stirring, for 1 minute, then add the sake. Cover the pot and steam the mussels until they've all opened, about 4 minutes.

4. Remove the lid from the pot, scoot all the mussels to one side, and add the denjang mixture to the liquid in the bottom of the pot. Stir to incorporate it, which should happen rather quickly, then toss the mussels to coat them with the sauce and pan juices.

5. Using a slotted spoon, transfer the mussels to four deep bowls. Discard any mussels that did not open. Pour the broth-sauce from the pot over the mussels, and garnish each portion with a heavy dose of black pepper and some of the julienned scallions. Serve at once.

bacon dashi with potatoes & clams SERVES 4

Simplicity rules in Japanese cuisine. One of my favorite dishes—and one of the simplest—from the repertory is clams cooked in dashi. That's it. The whole dish, the recipe: clams cooked in dashi. The clams steam open, releasing their essence; the smokiness of the dashi perfectly and politely complements the sweetness of the clams. So simple, so good. That was the first dish I ever made with our bacon dashi; this is a lightly souped-up version.

Bacon Dashi (page 45)

1 pound small fingerling potatoes, scrubbed

2 dozen littleneck or butter clams

¼ pound (3 or 4 slices) smoky bacon, preferably Benton's (see page 147), cut crosswise into 1- to 1½-inch-long batons (½ cup)

Usukuchi (light soy sauce) if needed

Mirin if needed

Greens from 6 scallions, cut into 1½-inch lengths and finely julienned, or ¼ cup Scallion Oil (opposite)

1. Heat the bacon dashi in a large soup pot over high heat. Once it boils, turn the heat down so the dashi simmers and add the potatoes. Cook for 10 to 15 minutes, until tender. (Check by tasting one.) When the potatoes are cooked, remove them from the pot with a slotted spoon and reserve; leave the bacon dashi on the stove over low heat.

2. While the potatoes are simmering, put the clams in a large bowl of cold water and let them sit for a few minutes to purge any grit, then scrub their shells clean of any sand.

3. Heat a 10- to 12-inch cast-iron skillet over medium heat for a minute or so, until very warm. Add the bacon and cook, stirring occasionally, until it shrinks to about half its original size and browns but does not become overly crisp, about 4 minutes. Remove the bacon with a slotted spoon and drain it on paper towels (reserve the bacon fat for another use if you like).

4. Meanwhile, when the bacon's getting close to done, raise the heat under the dashi and bring it to a boil. Add the clams, cover the pot, and boil the clams until they're all open, 8 to 10 minutes. Remove the pot from the heat, add the potatoes to warm them up in the broth, and taste it for seasoning. Although bacon dashi is salty and the liquid the clams added to the broth is also salty, the broth might need a splash of soy sauce; or if it needs sweetness or acid, add a splash of mirin.

5. Ladle the soup out into bowls, avoiding the liquid at the very bottom of the pot if the clams threw off sand while they were cooking; discard any clams that didn't open. Garnish each bowl with some of the crisped bacon and a scattering of julienned scallions or a ring of scallion oil.

scallion oil

MAKES ABOUT 1 CUP

1. Roughly chop the scallions. Put them in the jar of a blender, along with the salt and oil, flip the switch to puree, and let the blender do its thing until the scallions and the oil are almost one—stop it before they're totally emulsified.

2. Set a fine-mesh strainer lined with a piece of cheesecloth over some sort of receptacle to collect your scallion oil. Pour the scallion sludge into the strainer. Use a wooden spoon to press the oil out of the scallion mush, but don't force the issue: you want just a limpid green oil, so leaving some behind in the strainer is fine. Use the oil immediately or keep it for a day or two in the refrigerator.

1 bunch scallions, whiskers trimmed and any limp greens excised

1 teaspoon kosher salt

1¼ cups grapeseed or other neutral oil

sichuan crawfish SERVES 2

One of the best times I ever had was in 2003, after I'd finished up cooking in Japan and was in Beijing visiting an old friend who knew the back alleys and underbelly of that city like nobody else. After a night doing something we probably shouldn't have in a place where we could, my friend took me to this dump of a restaurant in one of the *hutongs*—the ghettos—of the city (many of which were bulldozed to make way for the 2008 Olympics, as this place was). My friend, Tully, and the waiter exchanged little more than a glance and a grunt before we sat down and had the most ridiculous pile of crawfish I've ever seen dumped on the table in front of us.

They were unbelievable: wok-fried with dried chiles, Sichuan peppercorns, and soy. While we were crushing these crawfish, chucking the shells all over the place and drinking a river of beer and bai xiu, I remember thinking to myself, "*This* is eating." And it cost all of five bucks. I knew I would never forget that dish or that meal.

The first time Bobby, my fish guy, mentioned he had live crawfish, I ordered them and knew we'd do 'em straight Sichuan-style: throw them live into a ripping-hot pan, then add peppers, peppercorns, and soy, and serve them whole in a bowl. That was it. Simple. And probably the most "authentic" dish we've ever served.

At home, you'll have to cook them in batches: Do them in two or more pans at the same time if you can manage it, dividing the ingredients appropriately. Watch out for runners—crawfish are the jailbreak kings of crustaceans—and watch out for those pinchers: crawfish should be alive when you buy them, and feisty.

4 to 6 pounds live crawfish, depending upon how hungry you are

¼ cup grapeseed or other neutral oil

20 to 30 dried red chile peppers, to taste

2 tablespoons Sichuan peppercorns

¼ cup usukuchi (light soy sauce)

½ cup sliced scallions (greens and whites)

NOTE: If you or any of your eaters are crawfish virgins, the basics of eating them are as follows: Rip off the head. Suck the juices from the head, or crush it between your fingers and let the juices soak any rice or bread you're serving alongside. Peel away the largest pieces of the carapace, then pinch and wiggle the tail to squeeze out the meat from it. Eat that, possibly dipped in some of the spicy pan juices accumulated in the bottom of the serving bowl. Repeat until full.

1. Put the crawfish in a large bowl of cold salted water and let stand for 15 to 30 minutes before you intend to cook them so they have a chance to purge any dirt in their systems. (They don't call them mudbugs for nothing.)

2. Heat the oil in a couple of wide skillets or sauté pans over high heat. After a minute, add the dried chile peppers, crushing them in your hand as you add them, along with the Sichuan peppercorns. Once the oil is good and aromatic, maybe 30 seconds to a minute, add the crawfish and begin tossing and stirring them in the oil. Keep tossing and stirring for 4 to 5 minutes, until the crawfish are bright red, then add the soy, stir a few more times, and turn the crawfish out into a large serving bowl. Sprinkle with the scallions and serve hot. Repeat for the remaining crawfish.

grilled octopus salad konbu, bamboo shoots & pickled chiles SERVES 4 TO 6

This dish, one of the most popular things on the Noodle Bar menu, was devised largely by Kevin Pemoulie to use up all the leftover konbu we were generating by making our ramen broth. Could we have come up with something simpler? I'm sure. Something tastier? Probably not.

Note that almost all the work in this recipe can happen a long time before you're gonna serve it. It's not weeknight cooking, but it's not hard—it just takes some planning. Or a bunch of leftover konbu to motivate you.

1. If frozen, thaw the octopus in its bag in a bowl of cold water in the sink. Remove the octopus from the bag, rinse it, and check to see if the little bit of cartilage in the heads needs to be removed. If it's there, just squeeze the top of the head, and it should slide right out.

2. Heat the oven to 275°F.

3. Make a court bouillon of sorts: Stir together the water, soy, mirin, sake, and vinegar in a large oven-safe saucepan or pot—a vessel roomy enough to accommodate the octopus and the liquid. Bring the liquid to a boil, then reduce the heat so it bubbles at a steady strong simmer.

4. Add the octopus to the pot one at a time: Hold each by its head and dip its tentacles into the simmering liquid, the way you'd dip your toe into a swimming pool to check the temperature of the water. After just a second, the legs will curl up, and at that point you can drop the octopus into the braising liquid. Cover the pan, put it in the oven, and braise the octopus for 2 hours. When the octopus are ready, drain them and discard the liquid. Use at once or, if you are preparing the octopus in advance, cool, cover, and refrigerate for up to a couple days.

5. While the octopus cooks, rinse the bamboo shoots (discard the liquid they were packed in) and put them in a small saucepan over low heat. Cook, stirring occasionally, until tender, about 15 minutes. Set aside to cool.

6. Ideally you've got some cooked sheets of konbu in the fridge, maybe from making Ramen Broth (page 40) or Traditional or Bacon Dashi (pages 44 or 45). If not, rinse the konbu under running water, put it in a saucepan, and add water to cover by an inch. Bring to a simmer and then turn off the heat. Let steep for 10 minutes; drain. Separate the konbu sheets. Working with one at a time, roll each into a tight cylinder, then finely slice crosswise into ribbons.

octopus

2 pounds baby octopus, fresh or frozen

2 cups water

1¼ cups usukuchi (light soy sauce)

1 cup mirin

1 cup sake

¼ cup plus 3 tablespoons rice wine vinegar

1 tablespoon grapeseed or other neutral oil

konbu and bamboo shoot salad

One 12-ounce can bamboo shoots

Four 2-by-6-inch sheets konbu (see step 6)

¼ cup sliced scallions (greens and whites)

Freshly ground black pepper

Octo Vinaigrette (page 107)

1 cup julienned carrots

1 teaspoon sesame seeds

RECIPE CONTINUES

7. Combine the konbu, bamboo shoots, and scallions in a large mixing bowl, season with a few twists of black pepper, and douse with the octo vinaigrette. Toss the salad well, making sure the konbu is particularly well coated, then lift the salad from the bowl and transfer it to your serving bowls. Reserve the leftover octo vinaigrette in the mixing bowl to finish the octopus.

8. Time to char the octopus: Heat a large cast-iron skillet over medium-high heat for a minute or two, or fire up the grill. You want a hot direct fire, so either crank your burners or pile your lighted charcoal so the area directly above it is hard-to-hold-your-hand-over-it-for-more-than-a-second-or-two hot. Put the octopus in a large mixing bowl, add the oil, and use your hands to toss and film them lightly with the oil. Stand the little soldiers up on their tentacles on the grill or in the pan: The legs should crisp and char, but not burn, and they will cook quickly—1 to 3 minutes, depending on your heat source.

9. Transfer the cooked octopus to the mixing bowl you tossed the salad in—the one that's holding the excess vinaigrette—and toss the grilled octopus in it. Divide the octopus among the serving bowls and garnish each portion with a large pinch of carrot and a small pinch of sesame seeds.

octo vinaigrette
MAKES ABOUT 1 CUP

From Kevin Pemoulie, creator of this vinaigrette, one of the world's finest condiments and food-improvers—a sauce so good it makes anything taste better:

So, the "octo vin" is how she's formally known. I think of it as an interesting flip-flop of a traditional vinaigrette in that the ratio of vinegar to oil is reversed. It's designed to hold up to the char of the octopus and to dress the seaweed, which, unlike lettuces, requires a very forceful, pungent sauce. I wish my prom date had worn a pungent dress.

If we used this to dress a salad, it would probably be too strong. However, it is really fucking delish with meats: grilled or fried. We served it once with whole fried sole. We've served it with grilled hamachi collar. And, obviously, the Fried Chicken (page 89).

Combine the garlic, ginger, chile, vinegar, soy, grapeseed oil, sesame oil, sugar, and a few turns of black pepper in a lidded container and shake well to mix. This will keep in the fridge for 4 to 5 days, and is good on everything except ostrich eggs, which is really more the ostrich's fault than the vinaigrette's.

NOTE: When preparing the garlic and ginger for this recipe, make sure to take your time and work your knife skills: small, even pieces of garlic and ginger (not the mush that a garlic press or a ginger grater creates) really make a difference. Big bits of raw garlic can have an acrid sting; chunks of ginger will deliver a too-spicy blast and can be unpleasantly fibrous.

2 tablespoons finely chopped garlic

2 tablespoons chopped peeled fresh ginger

¼ teaspoon finely chopped Pickled Chiles (page 68), or 1 fresh bird's eye-chile, seeded and chopped

¼ cup rice wine vinegar

¼ cup usukuchi (light soy sauce)

2 tablespoons grapeseed or other neutral oil

¼ teaspoon Asian sesame oil

1½ tablespoons sugar

Freshly ground black pepper

shrimp & grits SERVES 4

Noodle Bar's first fall and winter: bleak, bad business, maybe not such great cooking. Its first spring and summer: expanded menu, better cooking, crazy amounts of customers. Heading into the second fall, Scott and Kevin and Quino and I were trying out new dishes and ingredients all the time to see what would stick, what would make it onto the menu and stay there. We were starting to find our voice, to push the boundaries of what we felt comfortable serving.

One afternoon, Quino made mention of missing breakfasts of hominy and fried eggs. The next morning, I went up to Hearth, a restaurant up the avenue from us that my old chef, Marco Canora, owns, and stole a couple pounds of polenta. We cooked it off to feed ourselves, using our ramen broth, and then cracked slow-poached eggs over each bowl. And it was so good we decided we'd start developing it into something better and put polenta on the menu.

Then there was that lightbulb moment: grits, not polenta. Waffle House, not Cibrèo. Grits and shrimp is a classic. Anson Mills, a supplier I knew of from my time at Craft, makes the killerest grits ever. Everything started tumbling into place.

And when we finally got the dish right, it was an important moment for me with Momofuku, because other than the ramen broth (which you couldn't see), there was no Asian foundation, relation, or appearance to the dish. No other "noodle bar" was serving shrimp and grits.

But the flavor . . . I imagined what it would be like if my ancestors had ended up in Charleston, South Carolina, a few generations before I was born. They would have eaten corn, they would have eaten grits, they would have cooked with bacon. Or, if Southerners were magically transplanted to Korea, they'd eat jook instead of grits at breakfast. And you know a people who can handle the salty power of a country ham certainly could have gotten down with kimchi. I imagined a Japanese cook making grits—you know he'd boil it in dashi and season it with soy.

I guess these were all conversations I was having with myself. I didn't want to be cooking shitty fusion food. I consoled myself by thinking about how Vietnamese cuisine and Cajun cooking adapted French techniques into something that might have looked French but tasted totally different. But it was with this dish that I decided—or accepted—that if we reached past "tradition" to create the truest and best version of a dish for our own palates, then what we were doing wasn't bullshit. Momofuku was going pretty strong at this point, but this is the dish that allowed us—or me, certainly—to really look outward and onward.

2 cups water

2 cups white or yellow quick-cooking grits from Anson Mills

2 cups Ramen Broth (page 40) or Bacon Dashi (page 45)

2 tablespoons usukuchi (light soy sauce)

Kosher salt and freshly ground black pepper

8 tablespoons (1 stick) unsalted butter, cut into pieces

½ pound smoky bacon, preferably Benton's (see page 147), cut crosswise into 1- to 1½-inch-long batons

1 pound medium shrimp (16 to 20 shrimp per pound), shelled and deveined

2 tablespoons grapeseed or other neutral oil

4 Slow-Poached Eggs (page 52) or regular poached eggs

½ cup chopped scallions (greens and whites)

1. Assuming you have the foresight to do so, combine the water and grits and let the grits soak overnight (or for at least 8 hours) in the pot you'll cook them in.

2. If you soaked the grits, drain them, then add the broth to the grits and bring to a simmer over medium-high heat, whisking all the while. If you didn't soak the grits, bring the water and broth to a simmer in a pot over medium-high heat and add the grits in a thin stream, whisking neurotically. Continue to whisk for 5 minutes after the liquid simmers, then turn

the heat down to low. Per Anson Mills, this first 5-minute cooking period is called "cooking to first starch." Here's the deal on that: "First starch," they say, "refers to the early stage of grits and polenta cookery in which fine corn particles thicken the liquid enough to hold the larger particles in suspension. It is crucial to stir constantly until the first starch takes hold and to reduce the heat immediately after it does so." So there: it's "crucial." Keep stirring.

3. Add the soy sauce, a large pinch of salt, and a few turns of black pepper. Keep the heat low and whisk regularly if not constantly; the grits should be thickening, undulating, and letting occasional gasps of steam bubble up and out. Soaked grits will be cooked after about 10 minutes over low heat; unsoaked grits will take 20 to 25 minutes. They're ready when they're no longer grainy, when they're thick and unctuous.

4. Add the butter, stirring until it has melted and been absorbed into the grits. Taste them and add additional salt or pepper as needed. Set aside, covered to keep warm, while you get the rest of the dish together (or serve at once if you're eating them on their own).

5. Cook the bacon: Heat a 10- to 12-inch cast-iron skillet over medium heat for a minute or so, until very warm. Add the bacon and cook, stirring occasionally, until it shrinks to about half its original size and is crisp and browned, 5 to 6 minutes. Remove the bacon with a slotted spoon and drain it on paper towels. Drain the bacon fat from the pan (reserve it for another use if you like) and return the pan to the stove.

6. Put the shrimp in a mixing bowl, pour the grapeseed oil over them, and add a couple of large pinches of salt. Toss them in the oil and salt until they're coated. Wipe the pan cleanish with a paper towel and turn the heat up to high. Cook the shrimp, in batches if the shrimp will crowd your pan, which is probably the case. As soon as the shrimp hit the pan, press down on them, using a bacon press or the back of a spatula, or a smaller pan or whatever works, and sear them for 1 to 2 minutes on the first side. Watch as the gray-pink flesh of the raw shrimp gradually turns white in the side pressed against the hot metal, and when that white line creeps about 40 percent of the way up the shrimp, flip them and press down on the second side. Sear that side only long enough to get a decent but not necessarily superdeep brown on them, about a minute. They should be just slightly shy of cooked when you pull them from the pan— they'll continue to cook after they come out of the pan. (And nobody likes overcooked shrimp.)

7. Make up plates for everybody: start with a big helping of grits, nestle an egg in the middle of the dish, and arrange some of the bacon and shrimp in separate piles and then some sliced scallions in another. Serve at once.

ssam bar

ssäm bar

I was Ahab, and the burrito was my white whale.

Let me explain: Noodle Bar, after flirting with death in its early days, had taken off by the end of the first year it was open. We finally had good cooks. Every stool was taken all day long, thanks to more media attention than really made any sense—so much press that friends and colleagues started to resent it.

With only a 600-square-foot space and twenty-seven very cramped seats, we needed to open a second place, so we could attract, pay, and keep more and better cooks, and so the business could grow.

There are a lot of ways that expansion could have gone.

The natural progression in the restaurant business, especially when you get the kind of attention we were getting at Noodle Bar, is to parlay your success and profile into more success and a higher profile: a Noodle Bar II, for example, or maybe a fancier operation. But I wanted a place that made money simply, that didn't need constant tweaking and babysitting. I figured if we could get a system down and a few talented guys to oversee it, the second restaurant wouldn't have to be the constant worry that Noodle Bar was.

That's when I came up with my genius idea: to take the ssäm—an unpopular lunch-only item at Noodle Bar with a name nobody could pronounce—and use it as the basis for a second restaurant. In Korean, a *ssäm* is a wrapped food. Lettuce is the traditional wrapper. At summertime backyard barbecues when I was growing up, there'd always be a basket of lettuce leaves on the table, always the opportunity to make a ssäm out of something. There's really no limit on what you can eat ssäm-style.

Ours was something like a marriage of a *bo ssäm* and a northern California–style burrito. It was a large flour tortilla painted with hoisin sauce and wrapped around rice, shelled edamame, shredded pork shoulder, roasted onions, kimchi, and soy-pickled shiitakes. The restaurant would be called Ssäm Bar, and it would serve these burrito-ssäms, like a Korean-ish version of Chipotle. It would become a fast food hit, allow us to build Ssäm Bars across the country, make us wealthy beyond our wildest dreams. Then, if we wanted to, we could chase other goals.

Everybody, all my cooks—even those who were then or would soon be given a partnership interest in the business—thought I was nuts. But I can be very, very hard to deter when I've got my mind set on something. If we build it, I thought, they will come.

. . .

We found a space at 13th Street and 2nd Avenue, a few blocks from Noodle Bar. It had
been vacant for twelve years; the last place
that had legally done business there was Spring
Joy Village Restaurant, which I assume was a
crappy Chinese take-out place. (I'm saying
that affectionately; I love crappy Chinese
takeout.) I had to take the place out of receiv-
ership, and during that process, I learned that
the previous owners were named Chang too.
At the time, I did not take that to be a portent
of doom.

The first floor, where Ssäm Bar is now,
looked like London after the Blitz: there was a
crater in the rusted tin ceiling, extensive water
damage to the façade, the floors, and the ceiling. A steam pipe had broken sometime dur-
ing the nineties, and nobody did anything about it. The place was a disaster,
a wasteland.

Downstairs, where the prep kitchen is now, was even freakier: there was
an Amex credit card sign right by the exit to the building's staircase and a
table shower in a secluded alcove under the stairs. The entire sprawling, low-
ceilinged, subterranean brick-walled space was filled with cubicles, every one
of them with a dirty mattress in it, and every mattress rotting from the years
of water trickling from the first floor. Apparently the space had a double life
as a whorehouse sometime during or after the reign of Spring Joy Village.

Among the decay, there was some magically well-preserved detritus:
unopened soda cans, a *Time* magazine from the first Gulf War, and unmen-
tionables related to the downstairs business. When we got around to demoli-
tion, we found a bar behind a fake wall that had bottles of half-full booze
from a time when fruit cordials were more popular ingredients in cocktails
than they are now and that hinted at an even longer, more sordid history
than we had first imagined.

It was just a couple blocks from Noodle Bar, it was a corner location, and
even if it wasn't cheap, it wasn't as overpriced as everything else we'd seen at
the time. So it was going to be the home of the ssäm.

. . .

While we were building the restaurant—for which I'd taken out a million-dollar loan using Noodle Bar and my apartment as collateral—things started to get surreal.

In March 2006, the James Beard Foundation nominated me for Rising Star Chef of the Year, alongside four other contenders. That's a big deal in the restaurant world. But the gulf between the competition and me was hilariously vast; my inclusion on the list seemed more like a prank than anything else. It's easiest to illustrate if you look at the bio of Corey Lee (another nominee, and the eventual winner of the award): he was, like me, a Korean cook in his late twenties. But, very unlike me, he was running the kitchen at the French Laundry, Thomas Keller's restaurant in Napa Valley, a place that's synonymous with perfection and elegance and ambitiousness in cooking. I ran a fucking ramen joint. So I knew I'd be losing that, which was a relief, but it was awkward and stressful to have my name thrown around with his and other guys of that caliber.

I was prepared for it on some level, though, because I'd been told that *Food & Wine* magazine was naming me one of their Best New Chefs of 2006. I was so embarrassed: I was *that* guy, the undeserving winner of some big award. When Dana Cowin, the editor in chief, called to congratulate me, I asked if she would give the honor to someone else. I told her I didn't know if I was ready for it, that those weren't shoes I felt ready to fill, that I was petrified by the pressure. She told me to be excited—and that no one had ever tried to ditch the award in all her years of giving it.

The *Food & Wine* announcement came out in April, which was when I found out that Jonathan Benno, the chef at Per Se, Keller's East Coast analogue to the French Laundry, was also a Best New Chef. That made it all the more harrowing an experience. Benno was a superior cook to me in every single way and he'd played a massive part in teaching me what good cooking was—about the importance of the details and minutiae—when we worked together at Craft. It made my head hurt to think about it: he was the mentor, I was his charge, and there we were together.

The awards convinced me that I wanted to do something different, something to deflect expectations. The burrito bar was going to be the perfect thing for it. I didn't want to make my bones as a mainstream badass cook like my heroes. I liked the periphery of the culinary world: fast food, ramen, subs, pizza. Simple and delicious food people could afford. I wanted to succeed, but I wasn't eager to play the game I'd come up in. I wanted to succeed on my own terms.

I mean, after all, Noodle Bar, in the early days, should've joined the ranks of thousands of other restaurants that filed for bankruptcy. Actually, the place probably should have never opened. I was twenty-seven years old at the time and I had a decent-enough résumé; I should have been jockeying for a position at Per Se or wd~50, trying to gain experience, to move up, with the goal of opening a real restaurant when I knew enough to do so. But somehow it didn't work out like that.

Before all the press and everything, we'd been an underdog. We'd had nothing to prove. We could "undersell and overdeliver" and have fun and put out good food. But then there began to be so much bullshit swirling around Momofuku. People hated us and hated me. Former friends—folks I had worked with and worked for—talked shit about me and didn't mind if it got back to me. I remember I went online a few times early on to try and defend the restaurants or myself when people were taking the piss out of us on the Web, but I pretty quickly gave up on that—it only fired them up. I felt as if I hadn't signed up for any of this shit. So I just focused on trying to become a burrito baron.

· · ·

Construction was a clusterfuck; construction in New York almost always is. The particularly stress-inducing twist at Ssäm Bar was that the building was so old there was no Certificate of Occupancy on file with the city. Without that document, you can't get a beer and wine license, or get your gas turned on, or open for business. We only found out about it when we already had a half-million dollars sunk into the renovation, so we had to either stop construction and wait to work it out with the city or throw the rest of our money into the pit and hope everything worked out in the end. That is, of course, what we did, but there were plenty of nights I couldn't sleep thinking about what would happen if it didn't work.

We got the C of O, we got the restaurant built, and we had an opening-night party for friends and fellow chefs and people who write about restaurants on August 20, 2006. The front of Ssäm Bar is a glass garage door that we rolled open to let in the warm summer night air and the throngs of people we'd invited to the party. The place was packed.

But when we opened for regular business the next night—and for the weeks that followed—things were different. We were busy a couple hours a night, and there'd be a tiny bit of business during the day. That was it. Most of the time it was scary slow, going-out-of-business-in-a-hurry slow.

The general take on the Ssäm Bar in its first incarnation was, "This place sucks, the food is stupid, this guy was a total one-hit wonder. Let's move on to somebody else." We were almost instantly irrelevant, a footnote on the blip that had been the excitement of Noodle Bar. We had some loyal customers who were down with the burritos, but they were few and far between.

Spending time in the restaurant, watching a bunch of unhappy cooks with nothing better to do than wipe down the stainless steel that surrounded them, was like passing a kidney stone every service. Nobody wanted to work there, because standing around in an empty and soon-to-fail uppity fast food restaurant is a total fucking bummer.

I was the source of a lot of the problems: I altered the pork buns, the most popular Momofuku menu item ever (at Ssäm Bar we originally used shredded shoulder and cole slaw instead of belly and hoisin); I didn't even put our original burrito-style ssäm on the menu the way we'd served it at Noodle Bar (I subbed black beans for edamame). Friends and customers asked why we weren't serving noodles, and I had no good answer for them. (Then they'd rub salt in the wound by asking if Nike was paying us to house such an ugly old John McEnroe poster—my idea of decor— in the front of our restaurant.) My naive vision of hordes of people clamoring for ssäm was just that: naive. It was high time to deal with a dilemma we should've addressed much ear-

lier, of how we could replicate the success of Noodle Bar without simply cloning it.

The problem was that Noodle Bar's success was an anomaly, a happy pileup of accidents that somehow morphed into something that people really seemed to like. That kind of organic conversion is hard to replicate.

Fortunately, my obstinate and deep-seated self-doubt was working in our favor. I had told Hiro, our architect, and Swee, our contractor, to make the restaurant nice enough that if the fast food experiment didn't work, we could switch it up into a more conventional restaurant. We had always planned on doing a late-night, anything-goes menu to have some fun and extend our hours of operation, so we had some real fire power back in the kitchen in terms of equipment. We had planned on rolling out the late-night menu after the burrito empire was well established. But it quickly became obvious that the burrito empire wasn't happening and that we needed to do something *now*.

I had always known Ssäm Bar was probably a bad idea. Now I was spending my nights in this near-empty restaurant listening to Neil Young and wondering if I was trying to sink the ship. Whatever. When you're bleeding money like we were, introspection is not the thing that helps the bottom line. So we pushed up the schedule on the late-night thing and started it

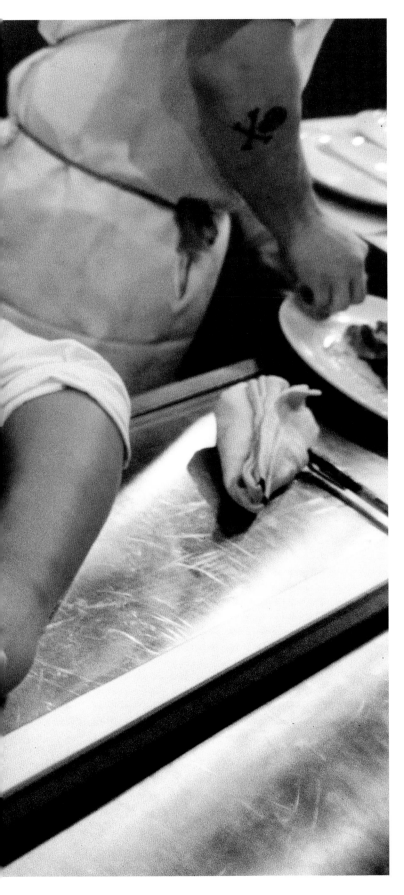

almost immediately. No menu development, no planning, no plan, really—just to try and get people in the restaurant eating and drinking and spending money so we didn't lose everything.

We had all these talented guys around—like Tien Ho, whom I'd worked with at Café Boulud, a total badass in the kitchen and a master of terrines and pâtés—and my ego-driven burrito failure was keeping them from really cooking. Somehow they had been lured by the success at Noodle Bar, and I guess by the idea of eventually having a no-holds-barred late-night menu. Thank God.

Starting around the end of September, Cory Lane, our general manager, Quino, and Tien spearheaded the late-night operations. From 10:30 until about 2 a.m., we cooked anything we wanted to. We had a good time. Cory made sure anybody who stumbled in had a good time too, and Quino and Tien came up with a late-night menu—with corn dogs, veal head terrines, and Vietnamese spring rolls—that I've been given too much credit for.

Late-night quickly became a hit. People came and ate oysters and country hams and corn dogs at one in the morning and didn't quibble with the setting. They stopped asking why we didn't serve noodles and started asking why we didn't serve the late-night menu all day.

As with Noodle Bar, it turned out the early faceplant that Ssäm Bar had to go through was a blessing in disguise. There's no way it could have gotten to where it is today without the faceplant, without the liberating

ssäm (Korean for wrap)

Step 1: Choose ssäm or bowl

1. **Flour Pancake Ssäm**	$9
2. **Bibb Lettuce Ssäm** (with rice bowl)	$12
3. **Toasted Nori Ssäm** (with rice bowl)	$11
4. **Rice Bowl**	$9
5. **Chap Chae Bowl**	$9

Step 2: Choose protein

- Berkshire Pork
- Organic Chicken
- Angus Beef Brisket
- Braised Tofu

Step 3: Choose extras

- bacon black beans
- red azuki beans
- kewpie slaw
- red kimchi puree
- white kimchi puree
- roasted onions
- pickled shiitake
- edamame
- bean sprouts
- whipped tofu

6. **The Original Momofuku Ssäm** $9
flour pancake, rice, berkshire pork, onions, edamame, pickled shiitake, red kimchi puree

7. **Steamed Buns (2 per order)** $8
Berkshire Pork or Organic Chicken
hoisin, pickled cucumber, kewpie slaw

8. **Beverages**

Dr. Pepper, Diet Dr. Pepper	$1.5
San Pellegrino Limonata, Aranciata	$1.5
Smart Water	$2
OB Beer	$5

Dietary Information:
Red Kimchi Puree contains salted shrimp & fish sauce
Kewpie Slaw contains MSG & Mayo / Buns contain Dairy

Vegetarian Friendly:
Chap Chae, Azuki Beans, White Kimchi Puree, Tofu & Edamame

Pork is from Eden Family Farms / Chicken is from Bell & Evans

momofuku ssäm bar

207 Second Avenue at 13th Street   212-254-3500
www.momofuku.com
Momofuku means "Lucky Peach"

effect that imminent failure can have: the house was on fire, and we were just trying to keep it from burning down.

We were going to serve good food regardless of the environment, regardless of the paper napkins, the shitty silverware, the fast food–style condiment island in the middle of the dining room. We were going to outwork everybody around and serve smart food, even if it didn't make the most sense when you wrote all the names of the dishes down on the same piece of paper. Texture was paramount at Ssäm Bar—if Noodle Bar was about bombast and fat and kind of aggressive and rustic food, Ssäm was about balancing sweet and sour and bitter, about paying attention to temperature, about making sure there was some kind of crunch in every dish.

So by Thanksgiving, with late-night booming and the burritos-by-day concept still not, we knew we had to start serving the late-night menu—the non-burrito cuisine—at 6 p.m. We planned to make the switch on the first day of spring—three or so months out, during which time we'd bulk up the staff, work on some dishes, alert people to the change.

But in a typical Momofuku move (in my mind, "Momofuku" could also be a synonym for "ill-advised"), around Christmastime, while I was standing in the near-empty dining room for what felt like the millionth time, I decided that we'd make the switch *that night*. I remember storming down into the kitchen and yelling at everybody and then getting on my Black-Berry to e-mail the cooks who would need to be there. Were we prepared? No. But it was better than just watching the ship go down.

And, almost overnight, things with the restaurant changed: it seems as if our customers were just waiting for the change. Suddenly the place was packed. Suddenly it looked like I wasn't going to default on my loans and lose everything. For a moment, financial ruin and public embarrassment were back at arm's length.

We organized the menu into categories that were untraditional but worked for us and worked for our customers: raw bar; country hams; small dishes (which might be a *bánh mì* or an order of pork buns); local (for anything from the market); and seafood, offal, or meat if we had enough of any one category to group together, or "large format" if we didn't. Ssäm was a menu category for a long time, though by the first anniversary of Ssäm Bar, the burritos were headed for the shitter. It was "late night" food all the time.

Once Ssäm Bar late night was rolling, we were able to pick up some more great cooks: Josh Kleinman, Sam Gelman, and Peter Serpico all joined Momofuku around that time; Tim Maslow graduated from a cook at Noodle to a sous-chef at Ssäm. When we hired Christina Tosi, who had worked stints at wd~50 and Bouley, to help us create a HACCP plan for sous vide cookery (in other words, to help us navigate city bureaucracy), we had no idea that she'd put desserts on the menus—which we had almost entirely avoided up to that point—and become our pastry chef.

But then one night we saw Frank Bruni, the restaurant critic of the *New York Times,* in the dining room, and then again, and I was bugging out because I knew we were getting reviewed. He had never even been to Noodle Bar. I was confident about what we were doing—the food tasted good—but I had no confidence that he was going to see past the paper napkins and the hand dryer that went off the second you opened the bathroom door and the blasting AC/DC as anything but drawbacks.

By February, Ssäm Bar had two stars from the *Times.* It was an almost-unprecedented turnaround. We had received a mediocre "$25 & Under" review from the *Times* in October, the gist of which was, "Your daytime menu sucks but would probably be okay at a soulless midtown restaurant." *The New Yorker* had given us a "meh."

When the *Times* review came out, we were still a month away from when we'd thought we'd have enough cooks and testing time to debut a new menu. It was awesome to get two stars, and we drank heavily to celebrate. But a few months later, I wished he had waited to review us. Ssäm Bar was far better come springtime.

(And, in fact, Bruni came back in December 2008 and awarded three stars to the restaurant, a testament to Tien's growth as a chef, to Cory Lane and the front-of-house stepping it up on all fronts, to the young guys who'd been with us since the beginning turning into killer cooks. It also coincided with a kitchen renovation that killed off the last vestiges of the burrito bar that Ssäm was originally meant to be.)

After the first Frank Bruni review, things kept getting weirder. I was nominated for Rising Star Chef by the Beard Foundation again, which there was at least precedent for, and Ssäm Bar was nominated for a Beard award too, as one of five contenders for Best New Restaurant in the entire country, alongside restaurants run by Wolfgang Puck and Joël Robuchon. Real restaurants. Measured against them, we looked like a bunch of fucking clowns. That year we bought tickets to the Beard awards gala for every cook we could give the night off to, rented a huge party bus outfitted with smoke machines and laser lights and flat-screen TVs, and threw down, because it was so funny to us we couldn't do anything but toast our ridiculous luck.

Then I won the Rising Star Chef award that night, which was crazy. I guess it was around that time that I really started having to deal with who I was as a cook.

The cooking was amateurish at Noodle Bar at the outset, but it had evolved to something very simple and solid. Though my chosen path—opening a restaurant before I'd really done enough cooking for other chefs—may have stunted my growth, I decided that was not going to be an excuse. No one was going to spoon-feed me knowledge about food; I would have to teach myself and learn from anyone I could. Privately, deep down somewhere, I wanted to prove to everyone that I could do it.

My top priority was the food. Every day, I'd walk through the kitchens and look for the tiny mistakes that are the enemy of good cooking. We had a crack support team of cooks and sous-chefs to rely on and try to grow with, and we were all trying to get better every day. Whenever someone came up with a new dish at one of the restaurants, we all asked, "How can we make this better?"

We started something we call the roundtable, which required hooking up all our top guys with BlackBerrys. For the roundtable e-mail, each night, the chef or sous-chef in charge of the kitchen for the evening e-mails all the other chefs and managers with the postmort after service (which VIPs were in, who's a shitty tipper, etc.) and, more important, notes on food: new dishes, new ingredients, who had good stuff or bad stuff or overpriced stuff at the market, how an ingredient was prepared that night and how the dish went over with diners. With these e-mails, we were able to share what was going on in both kitchens all the time, and to edit and comment on each other's cooking even when we weren't all in the same room. We use it to document successes and failures—and to take those failures and learn from them, to find the weak link and fix it.

With all the recognition that Ssäm Bar had gotten, it was time for me—for us—to put up or shut up.

. . .

Fortunately—well, not really—Noodle Bar was physically falling to pieces around that time. We had the greatest and most expensive kitchen staff of any noodle restaurant in history, but every time somebody flushed something weird down the toilet (seriously, the signs in restaurant bathrooms are there for a reason), the downstairs office would get soaked. We didn't have room to store enough food to serve everybody who was coming to eat, even after outsourcing the restaurant's pickle production to Ssäm Bar. We were doing three hundred covers a day in a space with twenty-seven seats. It was too much.

So we decided we'd move Noodle Bar up the block—there was a big space with an unpopular Filipino restaurant in it that I knew we could get our hands on—and do something different with the Noodle Bar space, our baby, the spiritual home of our now-growing empire. We kicked around a few concepts, like a taquería that Quino or Pedro might run, but ultimately concluded that we needed to do a lot fewer covers to make that space manageable.

That's when I came up with the idea of doing Ko (the name means "son of" in Japanese). It was going to be a cook-centric restaurant with just a few stools, a collaborative kitchen, and a constantly changing menu. And we'd put more money in the pockets of the cooks who worked there (cooks don't typically get any part of the tip pool at a restaurant—in fact, it's illegal to give them a cut in New York unless they actually serve the food too—so this was a way of addressing the fact that servers can make a ridiculous amount more than the cooks who prepare the food). We wanted it to be the anti-restaurant. That's all we knew at the beginning.

The move was motivated both by ambition and by the simmering animosity I felt directed at us at the time. We had won all these awards, and there were a lot of doubters. I was among them. This restaurant was going to attempt to answer all those doubts.

By the height of the summer, I was running myself ragged, working a couple shifts at Ssäm, supervising construction on the new Noodle (which had to be completed before we could start work on Ko, though, against logic, I was trying to open them at the same time), and trying to manage the business and do events and press stuff so people would keep coming through the door. I was insufferable to work with, I'm sure, always yelling about the small things in the kitchen. I started feeling more tired and worse than I ever had before.

Then one week, the shit hit the fan more than usual. I caught a guy who I'd hired as a favor—to give him work while he was waiting for his boss's new restaurant to open—trying to steal our cooks. An old friend with a great résumé wasn't working out in the kitchen. Quino and I didn't see eye to eye on where the restaurants were going, which added more strain to our already strained relationship. The Filipino mobsters who owned the new Noodle Bar space were squeezing us for more money.

I felt terrible. I was wracked with stress. So I did the only thing restaurant cooks know how to do: worked harder and harder. I interviewed EunJean Song for an office job and realized after a couple minutes that I couldn't hear anything she was saying—that my left ear was completely out. My back went out one day, but I got pain meds and kept working. When my left leg would barely support me one morning, I went to the emergency room. Nothing they could detect. Bed rest was prescribed, but I went back to work. My jaw eventually went out—I couldn't talk or chew very well—and after another inconclusive emergency room visit, I went back to work.

All of this was happening on my left side. It was like a stroke. No doctor could figure it out. I went to the emergency room seven times in two weeks. Finally, when my skin started to break out into sores, I went to a dermatologist. He diagnosed me with shingles. If you get chicken pox as a kid, the virus never really leaves your body, though for most people it's no problem. But if you're stressed out and in poor health—a diet of take-out Chinese,

fried chicken, Pappy Van Winkle, OB beer, and loads of pork apparently can lead to that—the virus comes back with a virulent vengeance. I split town on doctor's orders and hopped a plane to Montreal for a week to hide out and recuperate and just get away from it all.

I was sick for the next few months while we were building out Ko and Noodle Bar, but I kept a hand in what was going on in the kitchen at Ssäm, and I started to develop dishes for Ko.

And so we started down the path that any successful business does: growing from a mom-and-pop operation to a fledgling company. Drew Salmon joined the company behind the scenes and brought the hammer down: we couldn't run the company like we had been—no more spending the restaurant's money at strip clubs, for example. He and EunJean and Alex Magnan-Wheelock became Team Papercut and started running the business like a business.

I would have loved to keep the burritos. I would have loved it more if the burrito-bar business model had worked out. When I go back and make one for old time's sake, I still think they're delicious. I think it was a failure on my part, a failure in execution that did them in. If we had opened in midtown, I believe the original Ssäm Bar would have worked.

A single bad oyster taught me a lot about what it means to cook with integrity, why it's important to do things the right way. Well, a single bad oyster and Marco Canora.

Back when I was working for Marco at Craft, a customer complained that the kitchen had sent out a bad oyster. Oysters were coming off my station that night, which meant that the bad oyster was my fault. Marco destroyed me: he told me that I had ruined someone's dinner (which means I had ruined all the effort the rest of the kitchen had put into the meal), that he couldn't trust me. He had been riding me for weeks about serving only oysters that were pristine and unblemished. I fucked up bad enough that he heard about it from a customer, and he let me have it.

I couldn't sleep that night. I didn't want to go into work the next day. I wanted to blame Marco for being an asshole, anything to avoid accepting that I sucked as bad as he had told me (and everyone within earshot). But as I was sitting in my apartment the next morning, stomach in knots, I understood: I did suck. I wasn't cooking with integrity. In essence, I didn't care enough—obviously I tried to send food out the right way and tried to make sure the oysters were perfect, but I didn't really care about the outcome in terms of life and death. That was the difference—the Grand Canyon—that separated aspirant poseurs like me from guys like Marco. That was why he, and any great cook or chef, goes totally nuclear when food gets fucked up. They care too much.

I manned up and went back to Craft the next morning, and I tried to care about every single thing I did. Not to waste a step or a scrap or an unnecessary paper towel. Not to cook on autopilot. To respect what I was cutting or cooking or plating. Maybe I haven't always lived up to all of that, but I have never served another bad oyster.

You don't need to become an obsessive or a rage-oholic to do oysters right, you just need to acknowledge and accept that oysters should be perfect. They are a perfect food from Mother Earth and a gritty oyster, a popped belly, a dead oyster in the progression of a meal—is as bad as serving a rib eye well-done when it was ordered rare, as bad as anything that can happen to a diner at a restaurant (or a guest at your house).

If you don't know oysters, take a minute to orient yourself with one. The meat is sandwiched between two shells: one is flat or almost flat, one is convex, or cupped. You can think of the cupped shell as the "bottom" shell, since you always hold oysters flat side up when shucking them. Some oysters are more symmetrical than others and sometimes it takes a couple of seconds to differentiate the two with particularly gnarled and twisted shells, but there's always a cupped side and a flat side.

One end of the oyster—the end you slurp it from—is rounded and is called the bill. The other end is pointed (sometimes bluntly, sometimes sharply), and it's the hinge. That's where you'll be prying the oyster open. Inside, there's the oyster itself, which holds the shell closed with adductor muscles that are attached to the top and bottom shells.

The big teardrop of juicy meat of the oyster is called the "belly." You do not want to puncture or pop the belly. (Whenever I see someone do that, I cringe; when I see someone at one of the restaurants serve a popped belly, I am powerless against the anger that overtakes me. An oyster with a popped belly should never be served.) The oyster shell will have some seawater inside it, and if you can preserve that and serve a clean oyster, free of mud or shell fragments, great. But even if that all gets rinsed out in the cleaning of the oyster, the really sweet oyster liquor is still inside the beast, and it's by not popping the belly that you preserve it.

Veteran shuckers can open oysters with anything—bottle openers, screwdrivers, whatever. If

oysters

you are not one of them (and if you've read this far, you probably aren't), get an oyster knife, which looks like a dull round-tipped metal shank with a handle. Using a kitchen knife to open oysters is poor form—you can easily puncture and sully the oyster, you can chip the blade of the knife, and you can—and probably will—stab yourself.

Speaking of stabbing yourself: use protection. Hold the oyster in your non–knife hand in a kitchen towel that's been folded over on itself a few times. Doing so will give you a firm grasp on the oyster and protect you from cutting yourself on a sharp shell edge or jagged lip. You should never use so much force when opening an oyster that you'd actually stab through it and jab your hand, but the towel gives you a little bit of insurance against that.

Before you get to actually opening the oysters, ready whatever you're going to serve the oysters on (see opposite), as well as any garnish (see pages 134–136).

Wash the oysters under cold water, scrubbing them clean with a soft brush. Handle them gently, work quickly, and keep them cold. If you're working with a large number of oysters or are slow, keep most of them in the refrigerator and work in batches, both when cleaning and when opening them.

now, on to the shucking

1. Fold a kitchen towel over itself and use it to hold an oyster in your non–knife hand. Hold the oyster flat side up, cupped side down, with the hinge facing you. Alternatively, instead of holding it in your hand, hold it in place with the kitchen towel on a cutting board.

2. Think about it like popping the lock on a car with a coat hanger: you're not roto-rooting the interior of the door, you just want to get it in and out and get the door open. Use the tip of the oyster knife to scrape away any mud still lodged in the hinge (at this and all points forward, remember that any time the oyster knife gets dirty, it must be wiped clean). Gently but firmly wriggle the oyster knife into the hinge. Use the tiniest bit of pressure to jimmy the knife in, and gently rock the knife back and forth until you feel the ligament pop and the oyster give up on staying closed.

3. Slide the knife into the oyster, keeping it absolutely flush with the flat inside of the top shell so you don't puncture the oyster, and slide it along the right-hand edge of the shell to separate the oyster from the top shell. Some oysters are more firmly attached to life than others, and you may need to go around the left side or whatever, but stay flush against the top shell, and know that the adductor muscle you're looking to sever is near the bill and right-hand side of the oyster. Twist off and discard the top shell, keeping the oyster level all the while so as not to spill out its liquor.

4. Wipe or rinse the oyster knife clean. Then, keeping the knife as flush as possible against the bottom shell, slide it underneath the oyster to loosen the adductor muscle holding it to the shell.

The oyster is now shucked, but your work is not done. Smell the oyster: it should smell clean and fresh and sweet; it should smell like the sea in an appetizing, elemental way. If it smells off or fishy or weird in any way, discard it. Every batch of oysters has some clunkers in it, no matter how fresh or expensive they are, and some have more than others. Better safe than sorry: bad oysters are bad news, and your nose knows which are what.

If the oyster passes the smell test, clean it. Some oysters shuck superclean and require little more than a cursory swabbing of their rim with a clean thumb. Sometimes the shucking leaves a few shell fragments floating in the liquor. If that's the case, use your clean thumb or the tip of the clean oyster knife to fish them out. Occasionally, despite your best efforts, the oysters will have a lot of shell fragments or maybe even some mud in them. In those cases, use your (clean) thumb to rub out the dirt and shell, doing this under cold tap water, which will help with the process.

Once you've got the oyster shucked and cleaned, it's ready to be garnished, if you're garnishing, and served.

what to serve oysters on

Because oysters come in cupped shells that won't sit well on a flat plate, you need some kind of serving setup you can nestle the shells in and keep the oysters upright, or their juices will spill everywhere. There are three common methods for this.

ice: Restaurants that serve a lot of oysters usually have an ice machine that makes the crushed pebbles of ice you're used to seeing oysters served on. You probably don't. To make crushed ice at home, fill a clean sturdy sack with ice cubes and bludgeon them with a mallet or hammer. Repeat as needed.

seaweed: Seaweed is another classic. When we started serving oysters at Noodle Bar, we used konbu salvaged from making our ramen broth, cut into a fine julienne. It's less of a pain in the ass than sitting around pounding bags of ice.

salt: Probably the easiest way to go is to cover a platter or plate with a thick layer of rock or kosher salt, then create little divots in it into which you can nestle the oysters.

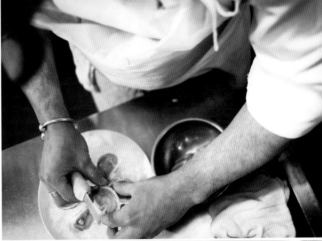

oyster garnishes

When we started serving oysters, back in the primordial days of Noodle Bar, we garnished them with a fine dice—a brunoise—of radish kimchi, because in Korean cuisine, kimchi and oysters go together like milk and cookies. Around that time, we signed on to do a dinner at the James Beard Foundation in New York, the sort of thing you do as a young restaurant to get people to pay attention to you. (Which doesn't necessarily work, but you do it anyway.)

As Quino and I were prepping, we realized it would be absolute madness for one of us to brunoise enough radish kimchi to top oysters for 150 people along with everything else we had to tackle. So we decided we'd puree the kimchi. It needed a little vinegar to help get it going in the blender, and I added a little bit of sugar, because I was worried that it was too hot and pungent. We funneled the pureed kimchi into squeeze bottles and used it to garnish the oysters.

It was a breakthrough moment for me: because of the vinegar and sugar, the puree was skewed to taste more like prepared horseradish or mignonette than regular kimchi, but it still had its roots in Korean cooking (oysters are frequently used in the fermentation process of making kimchi), so the flavors made sense to us. The preparation was a breeze. Service was easy. And the puree was delicious on the Fishers Island oysters we served that night.

Lemon wedges, a bottle of hot sauce, freshly ground black pepper. You can be as uncreative as you like when it comes to garnishing oysters, because oysters are pretty perfect the way they come out of the water. But at Momofuku, we are interested in the act of cooking, in working with and manipulating flavors in a creative way. So the kimchi puree was the beginning of our experiments in garnishing oysters. Use these garnishes sparingly, ¼ teaspoon or so per oyster. These comprise just a partial inventory of some of the dozens of things we've dabbed onto oysters.

kimchi puree: Puree Napa Cabbage Kimchi (page 74) in a blender.

pickled fennel & yuzu kosho: Stir ⅛ teaspoon green yuzu kosho (yuzu chile paste) into 1 cup chopped Pickled Fennel (page 69).

pickled asian pear & black pepper: Finely chop Pickled Asian Pear (page 66) and add a little of the pickling liquid to approximate the liquid-to-solid ratio of a mignonette (i.e., the pears should be bathed in liquid but not swimming in it). Season with a lot of freshly ground black pepper, tasting as you go, until you can taste the heat of the pepper.

melon gelée MAKES ABOUT ⅔ CUP

One summer we were making a watermelon consommé for oysters, and somebody put the gelatin-and-juice concoction in the refrigerator, not the freezer. Hence, that night we had jellied watermelon juice, or watermelon gelée if you will, to put on our oysters. Luckily, it tasted good and looked cool on top of the oysters. Melon gelées are now a regular part of the Ssäm Bar oyster arsenal. To make melon juice, puree the flesh of a melon in a food processor or blender and strain it through a fine sieve.

1. Bloom (soak) the gelatin in hot tap water for 5 minutes, then wring it out and combine it with the melon juice and vinegar in a small bowl.

2. Put the bowl in the refrigerator to chill for 6 to 8 hours, until set, using a long-tined fork to stir and break up the gelée thoroughly once an hour to give it the look of shattered glass. This gelée keeps for up to a week, covered, in the refrigerator.

1 sheet gelatin

⅔ cup strained melon juice

1 tablespoon rice wine vinegar

kimchi consommé for oysters MAKES ABOUT 1 CUP

So, the oyster garnish that was radish kimchi brunoise morphed into kimchi puree. When Ssäm Bar opened, we took that idea to the next level and started making kimchi consommé to top oysters. It works because kimchi + oysters is such a good combination—and also because sometimes serving clean oysters means rinsing out some or all of the seawater in their shells, and having a cold, flavorful, salty liquid to replace it is perfect.

We adapted a technique called "gelatin clarification," which we learned about from Wylie Dufresne, to make the consommé—a perfectly limpid, flavorful broth or liquid. It's a radically easier and less work-intensive way to make consommé than the old-school method (which involves a raft of egg white and meat and a lot of ladling; see page 248 for one of those). And, unlike the old-school method, you can use it to turn any liquid into a consommé.

The process is simple: season the liquid you want to clarify, add gelatin, and freeze. (When working with a solid like kimchi, add the solid to water in such a ratio that the water takes on the flavor of the solid.) You can also clarify a traditional meat stock with this freezing method, without the addition of gelatin, since the meat and bones will have added enough to the liquid on their own. Then you defrost the frozen mixture in a fine-mesh strainer (lined with cheesecloth if it's not truly all that fine-mesh) in the refrigerator and collect the liquid.

Kimchi was a starting point for us; see the variation opposite for other ideas. Add these consommés to oysters by the teaspoonful until the shell is brimming with liquid.

2 sheets gelatin

1½ cups hot water

½ cup Napa Cabbage Kimchi (page 74), preferably pureed, though that's not necessary, or more to taste

1 tablespoon rice wine vinegar

1 teaspoon sugar

Freshly ground black pepper

1. Combine the gelatin and water in a container you can later seal and put in the freezer. After a minute, stir to dissolve the gelatin.

2. Add the kimchi, vinegar, sugar, and 5 turns of black pepper to the gelatin mixture and taste. The kimchi should be present, if not strong. If the liquid tastes too dilute, add more kimchi and taste; repeat as necessary until you're satisfied. Cover the container and freeze the mixture. You can freeze it for months at this point.

3. Line a strainer with cheesecloth and set it over a clean container (bowl, pan, dish; it doesn't matter). Run hot water over the outside of the container you've frozen the kimchi mixture in so you can slide it out into the cheesecloth-lined strainer, then put the whole setup in the refrigerator and allow the kimchi ice cube to melt in its cheesecloth hammock.

4. After 12 to 24 hours, you'll have a container of clear (or maybe very light red) kimchi consommé, and a puck of thick nasty stuff in the cheesecloth, which you should discard. The consommé will keep, covered, in the refrigerator for at least a week.

xo consommé

We started making Xo Sauce (page 154) to use up the scraps and skin of the country ham we serve (see page 144). Xo is so strong flavored that we don't go through that much of it, so we eventually ended up with a huge quantity of unused xo sauce in the fridge. And you know what they say: when life gives you a refrigerator full of xo, make some xo consommé. Follow the recipe opposite, substituting xo for the kimchi and adding another ¼ cup water.

bay scallops dashi, chive oil & pineapple

MAKES 4 CANAPÉS

Here's the challenge: a dish with bright, clean, appetite-whetting flavors. It has to be made with impressive haute cuisine precision, but it is not an occasion for involved, multistep à-la-minute cooking: it's called an amuse-bouche, and it's the first bite that's given to a customer at a fancy restaurant. Amuse-bouches were one of my responsibilities when I was working the canapé station for Andrew Carmellini at Café Boulud.

When I worked there, amuses were typically little bites of something served in Chinese soupspoons; canapés (also my responsibility) ranged further and could include raw fish, arancine, special pâtés, bite-sized pieces of foie gras torchon—anything luxe, impressive, and delicious.

One afternoon, I was tapped out of ideas and struggling to keep up with my regular workload. Carmellini stopped by my station at around 4 p.m. every day to taste—and approve or alter—the night's first bite. So, when I didn't have one ready that day, he disappeared for a second and then came and dropped a 150-count bag of Taylor Bay scallops on my cutting board. He told me to get them shucked. I was to devise a first bite featuring them for that night's service, which started an hour and a half later, as well as finish the prep for the rest of the dishes coming off my station.

I got to shucking, with the help of Grande, the head butcher at Café, who saved my ass on occasions too numerous to count. I figured we would serve them in the shells with a pinch of Maldon sea salt and tiny splashes of dashi (which I had to make) and chive oil (which I would be stealing from the grill station).

Once I had my mise-en-place finished, moments before service was about to start, I put one together: it was good—but something was missing. The gears in my brain were turning but weren't getting any traction, and I was cooking against the clock. Hmmm. Something to go with those dots of green chive oil would be nice, I thought. Something to complement and echo the sweetness of the raw scallop, something to bring it together. I thought mirin, which would nicely round out the flavors of the dish, but I knew we didn't have any in the house, and it wouldn't do anything for the color.

That's when Andrew came by to check on my progress. He tasted one of the scallops with dashi. After a second of flipping through the Rolodex of flavors in his brain, he told me to brunoise some pineapple and it would be perfect. That was it: scatter some pineapple cut into minuscule cubes over the scallop.

I thought he was nuts. I thought it would taste like some kind of Roy Yamaguchi flight of fantasy. But he seemed pleased with the solution, and the pineapple solved my problem of the moment, so I got to brunoise-ing. And when I tasted another dressed scallop, this time with the addition of pineapple, I was blown away: the fruit more than made up for the sweetness deficit. Even more illuminating and encouraging to me was that the acidity, sweetness, and flavor of the pineapple were not that far removed from the same qualities in mirin, and I've used one for the other on many occasions since. It was a genius touch. Plus, the fruit added the right textural accent without getting in the way of the central pleasure of the dish: those Taylor Bay scallops.

I always use that dish, and that encounter with Carmellini, as a benchmark. In a few seconds, I learned so much about him as a cook—his knowledge, his speed, his creativity—and gained a reference point by which to judge other cooks (and a standard to aspire to myself). And I knew that I would use that dish again in some form or fashion in the future. It was so simple, but it was so smart, and the flavors were so clean and bright. A great fucking dish.

1. Combine the grapeseed oil and chives in a blender and puree. Pass the mixture through a fine-mesh strainer (twice if necessary to strain out all the solids), to yield a bright green, chive-flavored oil.

2. Divide the scallops among four scallop shells or soupspoons. Top each with a tablespoon of dashi, a scant tablespoon of pineapple, a few dots of chive oil, and a pinch of salt. Serve at once.

½ cup grapeseed or other neutral oil

1 bunch chives

8 bay scallops (see note)

¼ cup Traditional Dashi (page 44), at room temperature or chilled

¼ cup ripe pineapple brunoise (1/16-inch dice)

Maldon sea salt

NOTE: Finding bay scallops in the shell can be tough even for a restaurant with a reliable fishmonger on speed dial, so don't skip this dish if all you can land are already-shucked bay scallops. Make sure that they're sparkling fresh, and serve them in soupspoons. Otherwise, substitute pristine diver scallops, thinly and neatly sliced.

Also, if you want to multiply this to feed a crowd (or to make more than just one for each guest), you won't need more chive oil than is called for here until you start getting into banquet-size affairs, but multiply the other ingredients normally.

maine jonah crab claws
with yuzu mayonnaise SERVES 4

I'm embarrassed at how Sandra Lee–simple this dish is.

But you need crab claws from Jonah crabs—like Florida's stone crabs, but from the cold waters off Maine—which you probably won't find at your local fish market. No problem. You can do what we do, and what most every restaurant that serves them does: have them shipped to you frozen (and parcooked and cracked open) from Maine, ready to be defrosted and eaten.

Then you need a few shelf-stable pantry items—Kewpie mayonnaise and two condiments made from yuzu, a crazily aromatic Asian cousin of the lemon—that can be picked up at any Japanese grocery or ordered online. And the yuzu mayo is just the tip of the iceberg. When Fran Derby—formerly of wd~50 and Tailor here in New York City—joined the kitchen at Ssäm, he swapped out the yuzu stuff for harissa, a spicy Moroccan condiment you can buy in a tube, and it worked perfectly, even if the flavor of the whole dish was totally different. The moral of this story: crab + flavored mayonnaise = lots of possibilities.

And that's it. A little defrosting, a little stirring: a seafood snack that you can have anytime. Embarrassingly simple.

1. Defrost the crab claws according to the shipper's directions.

2. Combine the mayonnaise, yuzu kosho, and yuzu juice in a dipping bowl and mix well. Serve alongside the crab claws.

4 pounds frozen Jonah crab claws

1 cup Kewpie mayonnaise

¼ teaspoon green yuzu kosho (yuzu chile paste)

1½ teaspoons bottled salted yuzu juice

cured hamachi horseradish-edamame puree
& furikake SERVES 4

We started messing around with this combination at Noodle Bar, but it only coalesced at Ssäm. The inspiration was sushi, the kind of everyday sushi we eat in America: raw fish with a horseradish and soybean puree that's passed off as wasabi. (The horseradish adds pungency; the soybeans make it green like real wasabi.) We thought we'd amp up the horseradish and edamame, bring them out front. We garnish this with *furikake,* a crunchy, salty, delicious packaged Japanese "rice seasoning" that contains seaweed and tiny puffed rice balls. You can buy it at Japanese markets.

hamachi

1 heaping teaspoon Sichuan peppercorns

1 heaping teaspoon coriander seeds

3 tablespoons kosher salt

2½ tablespoons sugar

One 9-ounce piece skinless hamachi fillet

edamame puree

½ cup plus 2 tablespoons shelled edamame (frozen soybeans are fine)

½ teaspoon kosher salt

½ teaspoon sugar

1 teaspoon usukuchi (light soy sauce)

½ cup finely chopped peeled horseradish (trim away any darkened areas before chopping)

About ½ cup water

4 teaspoons wakame chazuke furikake (Japanese "rice seasoning")

A few pinches of pea shoots or micro–pea greens

1. Combine the Sichuan peppercorns and coriander seeds in a spice grinder and process until coarsely ground. Pour into a small mixing bowl and stir in the salt and sugar.

2. Dredge the hamachi fillet in the ground seasonings, coating it well, then wrap it in plastic wrap and put it in the fridge to cure for 2 to 3 hours, until it is slightly firmer. (If you want to prepare the hamachi more than 2 to 3 hours before serving, wipe it clean of cure at this point, so it doesn't overcure and turn into hamachi gravlax, and rewrap in plastic.)

3. Make the edamame puree: Bring a large pot of salted water to a rolling boil. Prepare an ice bath in a large mixing bowl. Drop the edamame into the boiling water and blanch them for 30 seconds, then scoop them out and shock them in the ice bath. Drain, set aside a couple of tablespoons of beans for garnish, and transfer the rest of the beans to a blender jar.

4. Add the salt, sugar, soy, horseradish, and ¼ cup of the water and puree, adding more water as necessary. Don't add too much water right up front—it might take a minute or two for the whole mixture to "catch" and the blender to get going. Hold tight and ride it out, then process the mixture on high speed for a minute after it's pureed: it should be as smooth as possible. Pass it through a fine-mesh strainer, tamis, or chinois after pureeing it to be sure. The puree will keep for up to a day, covered, in the fridge. After that, the horseradish's spiciness will be diminished.

5. To finish the dish, sharpen your knife. Twice. Wipe the excess cure off the fish. Cut the fish into 16 slices, each about ¼ inch thick (if the slices are too thin, the textural benefit of the curing process is lost; if they're too thick, the saltiness will be exaggerated), cutting either straight down or with your knife at a slight angle, no more than 15 degrees.

6. Plop a dollop of edamame puree down slightly off the center of each of four plates. (Chill your plates in advance for extra points.) Use the back of the spoon to smoosh the puree across the plates. Shingle 4 hamachi slices across each of the smooshes of edamame puree. Scatter 1 teaspoon of the furikake over the fish on each plate, then scatter some of the reserved edamame and a few pea shoots around them, as suits your taste.

country ham

When Ssäm Bar started serving late at night, we cooked some things—corn dogs and braised chicken miso clay-pots—and served a bunch of ready-to-eat foods, like purchased frozen mochi for dessert, whole wheels of Époisses cheese for whenever, and, what has turned out to be the most enduring one, American country ham.

Dave Arnold—who is, in title, the "Director of Technology at The French Culinary Institute"—is the reason we serve ham. (Things to know about Dave: He is the smartest person I have ever met. He carries a spelunker's headlight and a length of rope made out of some indestructible material with him *at all times.* There are some aspects of cooking and eating that he probably knows more about than anyone who's ever lived. He's also an impossibly good guy to get drunk with on a train.)

Dave wrote an article about country ham for an industry magazine called *Food Arts,* but it was hanging around with him and tasting and hearing all about the hams and what went into their production that got me convinced we had to serve country ham, had to put money in the pockets of people who are preserving an old American tradition, and had to do it in New York before anyone else. We serve it uncooked and sliced thin (the way the best cured hams of Europe are served) with warm bread and some kind of condiment: first, apple butter, later—and still—red-eye mayonnaise (see opposite). Here's a little bit from Dave Arnold on country hams. Plus a transcript of a visit with Allan Benton and a step-by-step look at Mr. Benton's ham-making process.

Just in case you didn't get it: eat more country ham. It is delicious, easy, and inexpensive. Isn't that American enough for you?

dave arnold on country ham

People ask "What's American cuisine?" and all we have to point to is "new American cuisine," which is really just using semiregional ingredients in a European and often Mediterranean style. But American cuisine does have a few touchstones, and country ham is one of them. It's our product, our unique product—it's not a rip-off of somebody else's thing. It's world class and it's ours. Why is bourbon important, other than because it's delicious? Because it's only made here, in a traditional way that yields a unique result. We have, as Americans, precious few things that we can treasure like that.

American hams are robust; they have a characteristic twang to them that I think comes from the higher temperatures at which they're aged. It's hard to taste European hams after eating American ones—part of that is the higher salt content of American hams, which I enjoy. Plus they're way cheaper than prosciutto, which is crazy, given how good they are.

If you don't believe me, go and read Escoffier's *Guide Culinaire,* written more than one hundred years ago, and check out his lists of world-class hams: Virginia ham is on that list. Those were Smithfield hams made from peanut-fed pigs (and maybe we've lost a little bit of that luster because few if any pigs are raised or finished on peanuts anymore in this country), but American country hams are still world-class products, even if we, as a culture, seem to have forgotten about them.

We can do something about this: eat them constantly. One caveat: learn how to serve them right, which is thinly sliced with few if any accompaniments (and none salty). There's a perception that country ham is too salty—and it *is* salty, but it's not *too* salty. Do not cook it (even if the package gives directions for doing so); cooking it amplifies the saltiness as does slicing it too thick. Use it anytime you would prosciutto but are looking for something more delicious and robust. And remember: God made the egg to go with country ham.

how we serve country ham

Country ham is good just about any which way. Traditionally, it's thinly sliced and browned in a skillet. You can substitute it for bacon in a lot of cases, like in the Shrimp and Grits recipe on page 110.

But at Ssäm, we were inspired by Dave Arnold to treat it like what it is: America's indigenous answer to prosciutto. And thinly sliced and served uncooked, it's great—it doesn't need anything to elevate it. We serve it with warm chunks of good-quality baguette and "red eye" mayonnaise to dip it in—because what becomes fat more than more fat?

red-eye mayonnaise
MAKES ABOUT 1 CUP

Red-eye gravy, for the great mass of Northerners who may not know better, is made by using coffee, often instant coffee, to deglaze a skillet in which country ham has been fried. It is traditionally poured over grits. This is our riff on red-eye gravy, which is a way of not calling it coffee-flavored mayonnaise. We serve it alongside our country ham platters, but it's excellent in a sandwich with country—or any—ham, too.

Combine the egg, instant coffee, water, vinegar, salt, and sriracha in a food processor or blender (or, if making the mayonnaise by hand, in a mixing bowl). Start the machine (or start whisking) and add the grapeseed oil in a slow, steady stream. Process (or whisk) until the mixture is thick and creamy. Check it for seasoning (it may, but probably won't, need more salt) and use immediately, or store in the refrigerator for up to a week.

1 large egg (use a Slow-Poached Egg, page 52, if you have one on hand)

1 tablespoon instant coffee crystals

2 tablespoons cold water

1½ teaspoons sherry vinegar

½ teaspoon kosher salt, or more to taste

½ teaspoon sriracha (Asian chile sauce)

1 cup grapeseed or other neutral oil

allan benton

on how allan benton became allan benton

The first time I called Allan Benton to order his bacon for Momofuku, I asked him to send me some written information about his products. I figured I'd get a press release. Instead, I got a scroll of butcher's paper, filled with Allan's handwritten account of his story—how he started doing what he does, and a description of how he makes his hams and bacon. It will pain me until death that I lost that scroll during the early crazy Noodle Bar days, but in its spirit, here's Allan's story in his own words. Knowing it and getting to know him—which isn't that hard, since he's usually the guy taking the phone orders—has deepened our already profound love of and profane reverence for his smoked meats.

The fella who started this business was not me. He was a dairy farmer here in Madisonville named Albert Hicks. Back in 1946, a gentleman came to visit the dairy farm—a gentleman from New York City, if you'd believe it; he was a relative of Albert's wife—and when he was getting ready to leave after a couple weeks, he inquired about the kind of ham and bacon he'd been having. Albert explained it was just meat from a smokehouse, which doesn't seem too unusual if you've grown up around it.

But the guy kept on asking questions and asking questions and eventually expressed an interest in buying some of these products. Albert told him he had some ham from his own smokehouse that he'd let him have. Then he told Albert he wanted one hundred hams to take back to the city.

Albert didn't know what to do: he'd never so much as thought of butchering fifty hogs. They talked for a while, and Albert told him if he'd come back and visit the following year, he'd go around and buy fresh hams from the local farmers and cure them so they'd be ready. And that's what they agreed on.

True to his word, Mr. Hicks cured the hams in a little shack right in his backyard and the gentleman from New York did come back and did get them. By that time, word had gotten out about what Mr. Hicks was up to, and that's when people from around here—some of them the farmers he bought those fresh hams from—started knocking on his door. Some were asking if they could buy one of his hams, others wanted him to cure the hams from their own pigs. (That is a business we're still in today—folks bring us fresh hams from hogs they've slaughtered and we cure and smoke those hams just like we do for our own products.) Albert thought there may be something to this ham-making business.

So he went to a local packinghouse and bought two or three hundred fresh hams and started curing them in that little shack. And he ran that business from the late 1940s until 1973.

Before we get to 1973, let me tell you that I grew up in Virginia and only moved to Tennessee to go to college. My parents and their parents, where we lived was about as isolated as could be in the 1950s and '60s. Both sides of my family homesteaded adjoining sections a mile apart there in Scott County, about twenty-two miles from Gates City, the nearest town and the seat of the county—which really wasn't much more than a wide spot in the road.

And I didn't know it growing up, but my grandparents lived in the absolute depths of Appalachian poverty. We were poor, we had nothing, and all the neighbors were just like us. There was nothing to think of it. My family's house is 175 years old today, and it's still never seen a coat of paint.

Neither side of my family owned so much as a car or a tractor. They farmed with horses and mules. They raised everything they ate. We had cows for milk and chickens for eggs. It was a very mountainous part of Virginia, with just a little flat land on which they raised corn and grain and other crops. To fatten our hogs, my family turned them loose to forage in the mountains. As a kid, I had no idea they were raising fantastic pork, I just knew it tasted good.

And we butchered hogs on Thanksgiving Day every year. We'd spend that Thursday, Friday, and usually Saturday working up all the meat from the hogs we'd butchered. Each side of the family would kill two to four hogs. And they were heavy hogs, six- to seven-hundred-pound hogs back in those days, because they really wanted the lard, and they didn't waste a single part of those animals—curing and smoking those hams was the way to keep that meat good for as long as possible.

That was my background. I never had a turkey on Thanksgiving Day until I was grown and moved to Tennessee. We always ate fresh pork.

I graduated from the University of Tennessee in 1969—never stepped a foot off the Ag campus in all my time there—and afterward I took a job as a high school guidance counselor in Florida near Cape Canaveral, which had a very progressive school system at that time. I came home from Florida one spring break (while everybody from up here was down there vacationing), and I ran into the local superintendent of schools. I told him what I was up to and he immediately told me he had a job for me and that I needed to come back to Tennessee and take it. I told him I was happy down there, that I was living the good life, that I was being paid well.

He said, no, no, no, I needed a master's degree or more if I was going to work in education and that the University of Tennessee was just up the road and that I needed to move back here and take this here job and go back for more school. I'm twenty-two and so flattered the guy wants to hire me that I decide to take it. So I come back and I get that certification at Middle Tennessee University and take that job as a guidance counselor in the schools here. And when I finally take a hard look at the pay scale that goes with that degree and that job . . . I realize I've made a horrible career choice. That there's no way I can live on it.

I quit my job right there in 1973. I had to. I'd pump gas—do anything to make a living. I couldn't make any less than I was.

That was the year Mr. Hicks quit the ham business. He was sixty-eight years old and had just hauled off about $25,000 worth of fresh hams 'cause they had spoiled and he had no idea why. I knew about Mr. Hicks and his ham situation because my family had begun to purchase hams from him after I had graduated from high school, when my grand-parents were too old to be curing hams.

I was naive and desperate and willing to try anything, so I drove out to Mr. Hicks's place, which was so far out in the hills you couldn't find it with a road map, and I convinced him to lease me the building. I'd made hams growing up, I could try making hams now, I thought.

I wrote to every university in the South—Virginia, Tennessee, Kentucky, Alabama, North Carolina—to anybody that I thought might shed light on what I was going to be doing and what Mr.

Hicks had done wrong. And I listened to what Mr. Hicks, as an older gentleman, had to say, but he really resented me calling those universities. He told me, "Boy, you go listenin' to those educated fools, you're soon gonna be outta business." But I went ahead and worked with the food tech people from Tennessee and tried to blend it with my own background and make it work. (Of course, Mr. Hicks never did believe in what I was doing. He just told people I was the luckiest boy he ever saw.)

Now that I'd solved his spoilage problem, I knew what I wanted to do: I wanted to make a better ham and a better bacon than a lot of people were doing at the time. Mr. Hicks was curing his hams as quick as he could—get 'em in and get 'em out. If he could sell 'em at three or four months, he wanted to sell 'em at three or four months.

That's not unusual: most of the country hams that are made in this country today are made in a hundred days, max. I told my father I didn't know how I could compete, especially because the big operations sell them so cheap. He said, "Son, if you play the other man's game, you'll get beat every time." He said, "Stick with quality. There's always going to be a market for quality. If you make something that's truly outstanding, there will always be people there to buy it."

And that's what I decided to do: I lengthened the curing process and tried to improve it over the years. There's nothing fancy about the way we cure our hams—rubbing them with salt and sugar and spices—but I've found that it takes me about a year to get somebody to the point where they really know what they're doing, where they really have the feel, where they're really focused on the quality. I guess we're particular about what we do.

It hasn't been easygoing all these years: the business only started turning a profit five or six years ago, and there was a good long stretch where I'd spend a lot of sleepless nights tossing and turning and wondering what I was gonna do. I am lucky and thankful that chefs like John Fleer and Damon Wise took an interest in our products and helped introduce people like David Chang to them. Their business has helped me stay in business, and it's always a thrill when someone as far away as New York City takes an interest in what we do.

And what I can say for what we're doing is that I want to make something people want. Something better than what you get at the local supermarket. Because if we do that, there will always be a market. I won't tell you that we do that. But I will tell you that we honestly strive to do so.

CURING

Hams—we bring 'em in, cure 'em, stack them in the racks, and after a week or seven or eight or nine days, we take them out and we rework the cure into them and then stack 'em again. And then they stay in this cool room for almost two months.

MORE CURING

This is the second stage of cure, where we start the hams by hanging 'em shank down in netting. It shakes the ham up and gives it a prettier shape. We're always working on the flavor, but anything we can do to improve the aesthetics of the ham, I'm gonna do too, because I want to make a superior product. We leave 'em hanging in that stocking for anywhere from thirty to sixty days. Then we'll take 'em out and hang 'em shank up for another thirty to forty-five days, 'cause they'll dry out better without that netting, and by that time they've got the right shape.

AGING

Next we wheel the racks of hams out of the refrigeration and age them at about 75°F for at least thirty-five days but usually much, much longer than that.

SMOKING

Then we wheel the hams out to the smokehouse, where they spend three days in a haze of hickory and applewood smoke. The smokehouse is powered by a little woodstove I bought from a cousin for $50 thirty years ago, and knowing my relatives and how poor they all are, it couldn't have been a very expensive stove—they probably got it second-hand before I bought it.

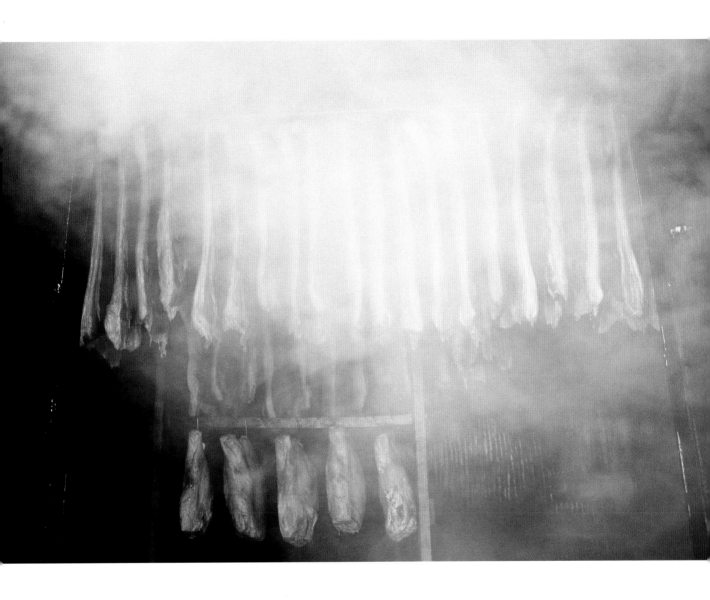

xo sauce MAKES 2 CUPS

We started making xo sauce to use up the scraps from the country ham platters we serve. And since we make a lot of ham scraps, we make a lot of xo.

For the uninitiated, xo is a Chinese sauce—"sauce" is a loose term here, because the finished product is actually dry and flaky, not at all loose and saucelike—invented in the 1980s. It takes its name from the "XO" designation given to Cognacs, obviously intended to confer a luxurious aura to the sauce. (Peter Serpico, the source of xo knowledge at Momofuku, notes that a touch of cinnamon added at the end is "a VIP move.")

Xo is good on almost everything—vegetables, eggs, a bowl of rice and whatever pickles you've got lying around after a hellish night of dinner service—and it keeps forever. Its pungency and funk pair well with seafood with a high sugar content, like scallops, shellfish, and squid. Because you only need a few tablespoons for any dish you add it to, the return on the investment of cooking time it takes to make it is so worth it. And once you've had a tub of xo sauce at the ready in the fridge, you'll never want to be without it again.

2 ounces (about ½ cup) dried scallops

2 ounces (about ¾ cup) dried shrimp

½ cup peeled garlic cloves

½ cup sliced peeled fresh ginger

1 cup chopped country ham, ham scraps, or, failing that, chopped Chinese sausage

½ cup grapeseed or other neutral oil

1 tablespoon crushed dried red chile

1. Combine the dried scallops and shrimp in a bowl and cover them by ½ inch or so with room-temperature water. Cover the bowl and let them sit out overnight to rehydrate.

2. Put the garlic and ginger in the work bowl of a food processor and pulse on and off until finely chopped. Scrape out into a small bowl and reserve. Drain the scallops and shrimp and follow the same protocol to finely chop; then add to the bowl with the garlic and ginger. Finish by finely mincing the ham or sausage in the food processor; keep it separate from the rest of the ingredients.

3. Heat the oil in a 10- to 12-inch sauté pan over medium-high heat. After 1 minute, add the minced ham and cook, stirring occasionally, for 3 to 4 minutes, until it has started to brown and crisp. Add the chile and cook, stirring, another 2 to 3 minutes.

4. Turn the heat down to very low and add the dried seafood mixture. Stir to mix the contents of the pan, and stew the sauce over low, low heat for about 45 minutes, stirring every once in a while to make sure nothing's sticking to the pan, until the mixture appears dry and the garlic and ginger are a dirty, dirty blonde. You can use the xo sauce immediately, or cool it and store in a covered container in the refrigerator for months if not years: you'll use it before it will ever go bad.

xo with baby bok choy

For 4 people, split 4 or 5 heads of baby bok choy in half if they're any bigger than truly "baby." Heat a tablespoon or two of grapeseed or other neutral oil in a wide sauté pan over medium-high heat. After a minute, when it's hot, add the bok choy and a splash—maybe 2 to 3 tablespoons—of water (or broth, if you've got it kicking around). Cook, stirring and shaking the pan, for 1 minute, then add 2 to 3 tablespoons xo sauce. Cook, stirring, for a minute more, then add a splash of soy sauce and a knob of butter. Once the butter melts, toss the bok choy in the pan sauce to coat, and turn out into a serving dish. Taste a leaf, and add another scoop of xo if the dish needs it. Serve at once.

xo with sugar snap peas

For 4 people, blanch 1 pound peas in a pot of boiling salted water for 1 minute. Plunge the peas into an ice water bath, then drain, pull the string that runs down their edges off them, and split each pea into two halves. (Split this way, they'll really scoop up and carry the sauce nicely.) Heat a tablespoon or two of grapeseed or other neutral oil in a wide sauté pan over medium-high heat. When it's hot, add the peas. Then immediately add 2 to 3 tablespoons xo sauce, a splash of soy sauce, and a knob of butter. Cook, stirring, for a minute or so, just until the peas are coated, and turn them out into a serving dish. Taste a pea, add more xo if needed, and serve.

xo with long beans (or green, wax, or purple beans)

For 4 people, blanch 1 pound beans in a pot of boiling salted water for 1 minute. Plunge the beans into an ice water bath; drain. Cut long beans into a manageable length—say, 3- or 4-inch sections; split green or other similar beans in half along their seams. Cook long beans, which tend to be sturdier, as you would baby bok choy, above; cook green beans (etc.) in the same manner as snap peas. Either of these preparations is made that much more soigné with a finishing garnish of grated hard-boiled egg.

roasted mushroom salad braised pistachios, pickled sunchokes & radishes SERVES 8

Quino used to call it fat-kid-in-a-candy-store syndrome. I admit: I do have a hard time controlling myself anywhere I can shop for food. (I buy my weight in beef jerky and ice cream bars at highway rest stops even when I'm not hungry.) For a few weeks, until there was an intervention staged, I'd go over to Murray's Cheese in the West Village and load up on really expensive artisanal butters that we'd then have to sell at cheese-like prices or else eat our shirts for serving for free. (That was the genesis of the $8 plate of bread and butter at Ssäm Bar.)

This recipe was the result of a shopping problem I had at SOS Chefs, a specialty food shop in the East Village. SOS deals mainly with the trade and their specialty is mushrooms: they have a whole refrigerated room loaded with baskets of yellow chanterelles, pale porcelain porcini, angry-red lobster mushrooms, anything you could want.

I was there one afternoon, covetously eyeing the black truffles. But as fiscally freewheeling as I am, I knew they were too expensive for us to use at Ssäm Bar. So I rewarded myself for my thriftiness by taking all the money I could have spent on truffles on a basket's worth of other stuff: beautiful Turkish pistachios, perfect hon shimiji and king oyster mushrooms, fleur de sel, and pistachio oil. Like a fat kid in a candy store. Then I had to figure out how to turn it into a dish.

The result is a hodgepodge of ideas cribbed from dishes I've eaten over the years: The composition—a number of seasonal ingredients, each prepared separately in a way that highlights its intrinsic qualities—is loosely pinched from Michel Bras's famous composed salad "gargouillou," one of my top five dishes of all time. The idea for braised pistachios comes from a dish I had at Grant Achatz's restaurant, Alinea, in Chicago. And the idea of marrying cooked nuts and fish sauce from Tien Ho, who was roasting peanuts with fish sauce and chiles for an early version of the apple and bacon salad on page 162.

1. Toss the radish wedges with the sugar and 1 teaspoon salt in a small bowl. Reserve until ready to use.

2. Bring the dashi and mirin to a boil in a medium saucepan and add the pistachios. Boil for a minute, then turn down the heat so that the liquid simmers and cook the pistachios until very tender, about 1 hour.

3. Drain the braised nuts, discarding the dashi. Segregate ⅓ cup of the pistachios to use whole in the finished dish and transfer the rest to a blender. Add the water and process to a smooth, thick, creamy, peanut butter–like texture. Scoop out and reserve.

4. Heat 1 tablespoon grapeseed oil in a wide (12- to 14-inch) skillet over medium-high heat. When the oil is hot, add a batch of the oyster mushrooms one at a time, making sure not to crowd the pan. Season with pinches of salt and pepper and sear the mushrooms, undisturbed, for 2 minutes, then turn and sear the second side for 2 to 3 minutes more.

8 red radishes, trimmed and cut into wedges

1 tablespoon sugar

Kosher salt

4 cups Traditional Dashi (page 44) or instant dashi

¼ cup mirin

1 cup shelled roasted pistachios

½ cup water

Grapeseed or other neutral oil as needed (about ¼ cup)

½ pound oyster mushrooms, cleaned and cut lengthwise into ¼-inch-thick slices

Freshly ground black pepper

2 garlic cloves, smashed

2 tablespoons unsalted butter

3 tablespoons sherry vinegar

1 cup Pickled Sunchokes (page 69), cut into ¼-inch-thick batons, or Pickled Crosnes (page 68), halved (1 cup)

One 3½-ounce package enoki mushrooms, root ends trimmed

A couple handfuls of microgreens, like mizuna

Maldon or other high-quality coarse sea salt

RECIPE CONTINUES

Remove the seared mushrooms and repeat with the remaining mushrooms, adding additional oil to the pan as needed.

5. When all the mushrooms have been cooked, return them to the pan and add the garlic and butter. When the butter melts, add the vinegar, turn the heat to high, and cook, stirring, until most of the liquid has boiled away. Remove from the heat and discard the garlic.

6. To serve the salad, smear a heaping tablespoon of the pistachio puree across the center of each plate and top with a portion of the sautéed mushrooms. Scatter the radishes, pickled sunchokes, reserved braised pistachios, and enoki mushrooms on top, and finish each salad with a few pinches of microgreens and a large pinch of Maldon salt. Serve at once.

fried (or roasted) cauliflower
with fish sauce vinaigrette SERVES 4

This is one of the best Ssäm Bar dishes—a staple there since the late-night days and a fine way to dispatch either cauliflower or Brussels sprouts in season (see the variation).

There's not too much of a story to it: we had a deep fryer, we had vegetables in season that we needed to cook, we had Tien's fish sauce vinaigrette on hand, and we were looking for a way to use *boondi,* a fried chickpea snack used in Indian cooking that Tien brought with him from his days working for Gray Kunz. They all found each other, and the results were awesome. Sometimes it's just that easy.

Later we swapped out the *boondi* for puffed rice—which is what Rice Krispies are—seasoned with shichimi togarashi.

1. Combine the vinaigrette, cilantro stems, and mint in a bowl, and set aside.

2. To fry the cauliflower: Heat 1½ inches of oil in a wide skillet over medium-high heat until a deep-fry or instant-read thermometer registers 375°F. Line a plate with paper towels. Fry the cauliflower in batches that don't crowd the pan for 4 to 5 minutes each, until the florets are golden and dotted with spots of brown. Drain on the paper towels.

To roast the cauliflower: Heat the oven to 400°F. Put the florets in a large mixing bowl, add a splash of oil—enough to coat them, start with a couple tablespoons—and toss. Spread the cauliflower out on a rimmed baking sheet (or two—you want space around the cauliflower so it roasts, not steams) and pop into the oven. After 20 to 25 minutes, the cauliflower should be browned in spots and tender. Proceed.

3. Fry the cilantro leaves. If you fried the cauliflower, you're all set up. Make sure the leaves are dry and fry them by the handful, dropping them into the 375°F oil and agitating them with a slotted spoon or spider so they don't clump together. Give them 5 to 10 seconds to crisp, then drain on paper towels. If you roasted the cauliflower, heat about 1 cup of oil in a small sauté pan or skillet—the oil should be ½ inch or so deep—over medium-high heat until a deep-fry or instant-read thermometer registers 375°F. Fry, stir, and drain the leaves as directed.

4. Toast the puffed rice: Heat a small skillet over medium-high heat for 1 minute or so, until it's hot, then add the puffed rice. Toast, stirring occasionally, until it's aromatic and perhaps a shade darker than it was when you added it to the pan, just a couple of minutes. Remove the pan from the heat.

5. Divide the cauliflower among four bowls (or serve it all out of one big bowl), top with the dressing, and toss once or twice to coat. Sprinkle the fried cilantro and puffed rice over all, and serve.

RECIPE CONTINUES

Fish Sauce Vinaigrette (page 177)

2 tablespoons very thinly sliced cilantro stems, plus ½ cup cilantro leaves

3 tablespoons chopped mint

Grapeseed or other neutral oil, as needed (lots for frying, little for roasting)

4 cups cauliflower florets (about 1 head)

½ cup puffed rice tossed with ½ teaspoon grapeseed oil and ½ teaspoon shichimi togarashi (Japanese 7-spice powder)

fried (or roasted) brussels sprouts
with fish sauce vinaigrette

This recipe works equally well with Brussels sprouts. The method is almost exactly the same. You want about 2 pounds Brussels sprouts for 4 servings, and smaller Brussels sprouts are better than bigger ones for this dish, so if you're shopping at a market where you can pick out which you want, angle for the smaller guys. Peel away any loose or discolored outer leaves and cut the sprouts in half. If frying them, follow the instructions for frying cauliflower. Brussels sprouts will take about 5 minutes: when the outer leaves begin to hint at going black around the edges—i.e., after the sprouts have sizzled, shrunk, popped, and browned but before they burn—remove them to a paper towel–lined plate or tray. To roast them, heat 2 tablespoons grapeseed oil in an oven-safe wide skillet (12 to 14 inches) or 3-quart sauté pan over medium heat. When the oil slides easily from side to side of the pan, add the Brussels sprouts cut side down. When the cut faces of the sprouts begin to brown, transfer the pan to the oven to finish cooking, about 15 minutes. The sprouts are ready when they are tender but not soft. Proceed as above.

fuji apple salad
kimchi, smoked jowl & maple labne SERVES 4

In the winter, there's practically nothing in the Greenmarkets around New York other than apples, cabbage, potatoes, and more apples. So we don't really have much choice about whether or not we're going to cook with them, and since we tend to take a minimal approach to our dessert offerings, we have always tried to incorporate them into our savory menus.

We're really into the Fuji apple: it's tart and sweet and crisp. We messed around with making apple kimchi, but even the crispest apple gets too soft for my taste after a day or so in a salty kimchi marinade. Still, the flavors work together perfectly, so we started tossing apples in kimchi puree so they could take on some of the flavor but not lose their texture. The combination might sound counterintuitive, but the heat and funk of the kimchi really bring out the sweetness of the fruit.

We needed pork with it, and we knew exactly what we wanted to use: smoked country jowls from Burgers' Smokehouse in California, Missouri. Dan Phillips, who runs the online bacon emporium that is the Grateful Palate, had sent us a box of just about every bacon on the planet (I think the final count was forty-three different bacons) for a bacon tasting. Benton's bacon shone bright and proud, but Burgers' smoked jowls—sweet and smoky and with a crisp texture just a little bit different from belly bacon—was the star of the new crop. (Okay, the fact that it was face bacon was also a major point in its favor.)

We needed an element to bring it all together, and the maple syrup–labne mixture bubbled up to fill the gap: the labne (a Middle Eastern yogurt) serves as a counterpoint to the heat of the kimchi (much in the way Indian cooks use yogurt); the maple syrup rounds out the dish and complements the smoked jowls. Because what's better than bacon and maple syrup?

4 Fuji apples, peeled

½ cup Napa Cabbage Kimchi (page 74), pureed

½ cup labne, or more to taste

¼ cup maple syrup, or more to taste

1 pound sliced country jowl from Burgers' Smokehouse (see Sources, page 294) or thick-cut smoky bacon

1 loosely packed cup arugula (I know, I know, there are like 3 leaves on the salad in the photo, but that was just to make it look pretty)

2 tablespoons olive oil

Kosher salt and freshly ground black pepper

1. Cut the apples into wedges or very large cubes: The size of the apples will dictate what works best—what you want are pieces that are one big bite or two small bites. If they're too thin or small, they'll be limp and won't assert their appleness; if they're too big, they won't take on enough kimchi flavor and the salad will be hard to eat. Toss the apples in the kimchi puree. You can do this just before making the salad or up to 6 hours in advance—any longer, though, and the apples will be sublimated by the kimchi.

2. Combine the labne and maple syrup in a small bowl and whisk together until they're married in a smooth and homogeneous mixture. It should be assertively sweet from the syrup and perceptibly tart from the labne. Adjust if necessary, but don't play down the sweetness too much. You can do this days in advance and keep the labne-syrup mixture in the fridge—it's good with granola or spread thickly on a piece of toast.

3. Heat the oven to 350°F.

4. Arrange the bacon on a rimmed baking sheet and pop it into the oven. Bake for 18 minutes, or until it is browned and crisped. Transfer the meat to a plate lined with paper towels to drain. It needn't be any more than lukewarm when you serve the salad, but it shouldn't be cold or greasy. (If you're preparing all the elements in advance, slightly undercook the bacon up to a couple hours ahead of time and then reheat and recrisp it in a 200° to 300°F oven.)

5. Just before serving, toss the arugula with the olive oil, a large pinch of salt, and a few turns of black pepper.

6. To serve, plop a dollop—1 to 2 tablespoons—of the sweetened labne in the middle of each plate and top with one-quarter of the kimchi apples. Stack 3 or 4 pieces of bacon over the apples and drop a handful of the dressed arugula over the bacon. Hit each plate with a couple turns of black pepper, and serve at once.

bo ssäm SERVES 6 TO 8

Our bo ssäm was a long time in the making before it showed up on the menu. I'd had an inkling for years it would be a good idea—bo ssäm is a supercommon dish in Korean restaurants, though the ingredients and cooking that go into it are frequently an afterthought. The oysters are usually Gulf oysters from a bucket, the kind that are really only suited to frying; the pork is belly that's been boiled into submission. Almost every time I ate it at a restaurant, I'd think about how much better it would be if all the ingredients were awesome.

The first time we made one was for family meal back when we'd just started serving kimchi puree on our oysters at Noodle Bar. One of the new cooks was fucking up oysters left and right, so I made him shuck a few dozen perfectly, and then we ate them ssäm-style: wrapped up in lettuce with rice, kimchi, and some shredded pork shoulder that was otherwise destined for the ramen bowl. (The shoulder in our bo ssäm is, essentially, the same shoulder we put in the soup at Noodle Bar, except that we add more sugar in the last step to make the crust even more delicious—it's like a shoulder encrusted in pig candy.) So there, in the cramped, dark subterranean kitchen of Noodle Bar, I ate the best bo ssäm of my life.

I think that experience and our take on the bo ssäm are typical of the way we approach "traditional" dishes: with one foot rooted in tradition and the other foot kicking it forward. There is a great line from Emerson that sums up my perspective perfectly: "Meek young men grow up in libraries, believing it their duty to accept the views which Cicero, which Locke, which Bacon have given, forgetful that Cicero, Locke, and Bacon were only young men in libraries when they wrote these books."

pork butt

1 whole 8- to 10-pound bone-in Boston pork butt

1 cup granulated sugar

1 cup plus 1 tablespoon kosher salt

7 tablespoons light brown sugar

accompaniments

1 dozen oysters, shucked (see page 132 for instructions)

1 cup Napa Cabbage Kimchi (page 74), plus 1 cup pureed

1 cup Ginger Scallion Sauce (page 57)

Ssäm Sauce (opposite)

2 cups Short-Grain Rice (page 279)

3 to 4 heads Bibb lettuce, leaves separated, well washed, and spun dry

Maldon or other high-quality coarse sea salt

1. Put the pork shoulder in a roasting pan, ideally one that holds it snugly. Mix together the granulated sugar and 1 cup of the salt in a bowl, then rub the mixture into the meat; discard any excess salt-and-sugar mixture. Cover the pan with plastic wrap and put it into the fridge for at least 6 hours, or overnight.

2. Heat the oven to 300°F. Remove the pork from the refrigerator and discard any juices that have accumulated. Put the pork in the oven and cook for 6 hours, basting with the rendered fat and pan juices every hour. The pork should be tender and yielding at this point—it should offer almost no resistance to the blade of a knife and you should be able to easily pull meat off the shoulder with a fork. Depending on your schedule, you can serve the pork right away or let it rest and mellow out at room temperature for up to an hour.

3. When ready to serve—sauces are made, oysters are ready to be shucked, lettuce is washed, etc.—turn the oven to 500°F.

4. Stir together the remaining 1 tablespoon salt and the brown sugar and rub the mixture all over the pork. Put it in the oven for 10 to 15 minutes, until the sugar has melted into a crisp, sweet crust.

5. Serve the bo ssäm whole and hot, surrounded with the accompaniments.

ssäm sauce

MAKES 1 CUP

Ssämjang—a spicy fermented bean paste sold in Korean markets—is a traditional accompaniment to grilled meats. Ssämjang is like the love child of two Korean sauces: a mix of *denjang* (Korea's funkier answer to Japanese miso) and *kochujang,* a spicy chile paste.

Anyway, rather than just thinning out the ssämjang with oil or water as is most commonly done, we've allied ssämjang with extra kochujang and added vinegar in the mix to bring up the acidity of the sauce.

Combine all the ingredients and stir until evenly mixed. Ssäm sauce will keep in the fridge for weeks.

1 tablespoon ssämjang (fermented bean and chile paste)

½ tablespoon kochujang (chile paste)

¼ cup sherry vinegar

¼ cup grapeseed or other neutral oil

marinated hanger steak ssäm
red kimchi puree & ginger scallion SERVES 4 TO 6

When it comes to cheap steak—not shit that the supermarket puts on sale because it's been sitting around, but steaks that aren't from the expensive and cherished rib and loin of the cow—hanger steak is the steak to get. When we were thinking about putting a beef ssäm on our menu, we knew the cut would be hanger.

The trick: there's only one hanger steak on each cow, and it's not widely available in butcher shops or supermarkets in the States. But you can order it from Niman Ranch very easily (see Sources). Or substitute New York strips if you're feeling fancy and/or are afraid of the Internet and/or are not into economy. The marinade on this steak is almost exactly what my mom uses when she makes *kalbi* (marinated short ribs), so, like her, we use Mott's apple juice.

1. Make the marinade: Combine the apple juice, soy, onion, garlic, sesame oil, and pepper in a large freezer bag (or another container that will snugly accommodate the steaks and marinade) and seal and shake (or stir or whisk) to combine. Add the steaks, seal or cover tightly, and marinate in the refrigerator for 24 hours.

2. Light a good hot fire in your grill.

3. Remove the steaks from the marinade (discard the marinade). Grill for 6 to 10 minutes total for medium-rare, taking care to first char the two flattest sides of the steaks, which should take about 2 minutes per side. Monitor the doneness closely after that—depending on how hot your fire is, they could be cooked in 6 to 8 minutes. When they're ready, remove the steaks to a platter and let them rest for at least 5 minutes. More resting time won't hurt: you can't overrest steak.

4. When ready to serve—sauces are made, lettuce is washed, etc.—cut the steaks into ¼-inch-thick slices, cutting on a slight bias (i.e., your knife at a 15- to 30-angle to the cutting board). Serve the steaks flanked by the accompaniments.

RECIPE CONTINUES

hanger steak

2 cups apple juice

½ cup usukuchi (light soy sauce)

½ yellow onion, thinly sliced

5 to 6 garlic cloves, thinly sliced

1 teaspoon Asian sesame oil

1 teaspoon freshly ground black pepper

Four 8-ounce hanger steaks

accompaniments

1 cup Napa Cabbage Kimchi, pureed (page 74)

1 cup Ginger Scallion Sauce (page 57)

2 cups Short-Grain Rice (page 279)

2 to 3 heads Bibb lettuce, leaves separated, well washed, and spun dry

Maldon or other high-quality coarse sea salt

"ghetto sous vide"
marinated hanger steak ssäm

We got into sous vide cooking through the back door (we now do it on the up and up and are certified to do so), and through this dish. The hanger steak was one of the few popular items we had at Ssäm Bar during the burrito phase, but the ten or so minutes it took to cook was way too long for anyone waiting in a burrito bar.

We didn't have all the gear to do real sous vide cooking at the time (there's more information on sous vide cooking on page 273), but we knew that low-temperature cooking—the category sous vide falls into—could save us a bunch of time.

How? The idea behind low-temperature cooking is that it is possible to cook a steak—or anything—to an exact temperature. If you know what temperature you want the thing to be, just cook it at that temperature for long enough to bring the whole thing up to that temperature and presto! It's like magic; you're not sitting there poking or prodding the meat or worrying that it's rare or raw or overcooked. It's a very rational, logical approach to cooking food, which is probably why so many cooks seem to think it's bullshit.

Back to low temperatures: hanger steak is best rare, and hanger steak is rare when the meat is cooked to 120° to 125°F, when it's no longer squishy and raw but is far from tough, overcooked, and chewy. Using low-temperature cooking allows us to cook the *entire* steak to exactly that temperature. There's no guessing involved. Get the whole steak to 120°F, and the whole steak will be perfectly rare. That takes care of the texture. But the char on the outside is what gives the steak so much of its flavor, so we finish it quickly on the grill: a thin layer of char (the sweetness in the marinade helps the steak char up extra quick) around a ruby center of perfectly cooked steak, and the pickup—kitchenspeak for what you have to do between the time the order is barked out and when you hand it over to go out to the dining room—is minimal.

Low-temperature cooking requires more preparation time, but unless somebody really fucks up, the food will be perfectly cooked every time. That was a boon to us in the kitchen, and if you've ever stressed over whether a steak was going to come out right or how much longer your friends are going to have to wait until dinner is ready, it can be a boon to you at home.

There are some concerns related to what we call "ghetto sous vide" cooking at home—like the possible but unlikely leaching of chemicals out of plastic bags—we never had a problem with it when we did it at the restaurant, and in the course of testing it for this book, no one had any adverse reactions to it. If you are going to be lazy, sloppy, unhygienic, or careless, it's not worth trying. If you're the kind of person who wears a football helmet every time you take a city bus, or you litigate recreationally, or you're with child, ghetto sous vide is not for you.

For the curious rest:

Marinate the steaks individually, each with a portion of the marinade in its own high-quality Ziploc (or comparable brand) freezer bag. (Cheap plastic bags are made with cheap plastic; avoid them.) Force as much air out of the bags as possible when you seal the steaks and marinade inside. (Tien used to suck the air out of bags with a straw, though he's found that submerging the bag in water while sealing it—using the water to squeeze the air out of the bag—works best.) Marinate in the refrigerator for 24 hours.

The next day, put the largest pot you own into a sink that you don't need to use for an hour. Overfill the pot with hot water from the tap and, using a digital instant-read thermometer, take the temperature of the water—both what's coming out of the tap and what's in the pot—making sure to measure it in a few different places and at a few depths. Adjust the tapwater until you've got the water in the pot at a reliable temperature somewhere between 120° and 125°F.

Take the steaks in their bags from the fridge and put them directly in the warm-water bath. Use the thermometer to monitor and adjust the temperature of the bath and keep it at a steady temperature in the desired range for 45 minutes, adding water as necessary. You may need to keep a steady trickle of water running into the pot to do so, or you might be able to pull it off by refreshing and replenishing the bath every 5 or 10 minutes. That's between you and your faucet.

After 45 minutes, prepare an ice bath in a big pot or mixing bowl. Snag your steaks from the warm water and plunge them into the ice bath. Chill them down for 20 or so minutes, then transfer them to the refrigerator. You can hold the cooked steaks in the fridge until dinner is almost ready—up to 3 or 4 hours (the marinade is still working).

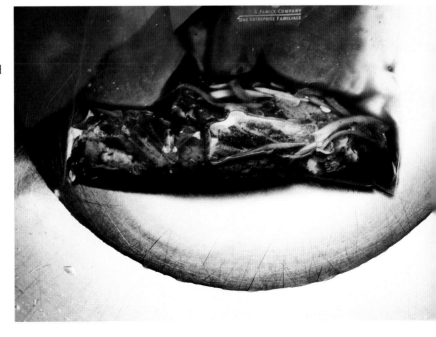

To cook, remove the steaks from their bags, discard the marinade, and pat the steaks dry with paper towels. Char the outsides evenly and fully over a blazing-hot fire in a grill or in a ripping-hot cast-iron pan on the stove, 1½ to 2 minutes a side. Rest, slice, and serve as directed in the recipe.

pork belly ssäm
(aka sam gyup sal ssäm) with mustard seed sauce SERVES 4 TO 6

Sam gyup sal is "three-layer fat"; it was a no-brainer addition to our ssäm list because: (a) we love pork belly, and (b) see (a). It's a very traditional ssäm, though in Korean restaurants the belly is often simmered or braised, and rarely as tasty as it is when it's cooked this way.

We first served *sam gyup sal ssäm* with a sauce that was a ceviche of razor clams (echoing raw oysters), but the wavering availability of the clams, plus the cost they added to the dish (for us and our customers), eventually led the team to develop this mustard seed sauce. It's good on the pork belly and anything that needs a sharp, pungent, pickle-dotted sauce to brighten it up.

pork belly

One 3-pound slab skinless pork belly

⅓ cup kosher salt

⅓ cup sugar

accompaniments

Mustard Seed Sauce (opposite)

2 cups Short-Grain Rice (page 279)

2 to 3 heads Bibb lettuce, leaves separated, well washed, and spun dry

Maldon or other high-quality coarse sea salt

1. Nestle the belly into a roasting pan or other oven-safe vessel that holds it snugly. Mix together the salt and sugar in a small bowl, and rub the mix into the meat; discard any excess salt-and-sugar mixture. Cover the pan with plastic wrap and put it into the fridge for at least 6 hours, and as long as 24.

2. Heat the oven to 450°F.

3. Discard any liquid that has accumulated, put the belly in the oven, and cook for 1 hour, basting it with the rendered fat at the halfway point, until it's an appetizing golden brown.

4. Reduce the oven temperature to 250°F and cook for another 30 minutes or so. The belly should be a little resistant, a little firm, shy of jiggly tenderness. Remove the pan from the oven, decant the fat and the meat juices from the pan, and reserve (see page 50). Allow the belly to cool somewhat.

5. When the belly is cool enough to handle, wrap it in plastic wrap or aluminum foil and put it in the fridge until it's thoroughly chilled and firm. (You can shortchange this step if you're pressed for time, but the only way to get neat, nice-looking slices is to chill the belly thoroughly before slicing it.)

6. Light a good hot fire in your grill.

7. Cut the pork belly into ½-inch-thick slices that are about 2 inches long. Grill the pieces of belly until well browned on one side, about 2 minutes. (We typically turn them 45 degrees at the midway point to get a cross-hatch of grill marks on the meat. Do so if your grill grate gets hot enough; if not—and most home grill grates, like those that come with kettle grills, don't—just get a good, even char.)

8. Serve the grilled belly warm with the accompaniments.

mustard seed sauce

MAKES ABOUT 1 CUP

Combine the mustard seeds, Dijon and Chinese mustards, mayonnaise, scallions, and cucumber in a small bowl and stir until evenly mixed. Season to taste with salt and pepper. Store in the fridge, and use within a day or two.

6 tablespoons Pickled Mustard Seeds (page 72)

3 tablespoons Dijon mustard

1 tablespoon Chinese hot mustard

3 tablespoons mayonnaise, preferably Kewpie

3 tablespoons thinly sliced scallions (greens and whites)

3 tablespoons diced Quick-Pickled Cucumbers (page 65)

Kosher salt and freshly ground black pepper

grilled lemongrass pork sausage ssäm
daikon, carrot, herbs & fish sauce vinaigrette SERVES 4 TO 6

When we started serving the night menu at Ssäm Bar, this sausage was stuffed into a made-to-order summer roll with herbs and rice noodles. When late-night started to get busier and busier, we learned why so few places make rolled-to-order summer rolls: it's a pain in the ass.

So we simplified things and added the sausage to our growing roster of ssäms. As Tien Ho will tell you, *coung* (meats or fishes served with lettuce to wrap them in) are the ssäm of Vietnam, so it's not like this recipe is that much of a stretch.

A couple of notes about the recipe: The flour in the sausage helps keep it firm and saves it from going crumbly or loose. In Vietnam, they would add toasted rice ground to a powder, which adds an amazing level of depth to the dish, and which you're welcome to substitute.

And then there's the lemongrass, which people always seem to cut the wrong way. The right way: Peel away the outer leaves—anything green or woody. Cut off the woody and tough bottom 1 to 1½ inches of the stalk—the 4 to 5 inches of the somewhat tender core above that is what you want—and trim off the tapering top. Cut the 4- to 5-inch piece lengthwise in half, finely slice it, and, finally, go over the pile a few times with your knife until it's finely minced. Save all the trimmings for soup; they freeze just fine if you don't have plans to use them immediately.

1. Heat the oven to 300°F.

2. Combine the lemongrass and shallots with the salt, sugar, fish sauce, and sriracha in a food processor and process until finely chopped. (Or do it by hand.) Put the mixture in a large mixing bowl. Add the ground pork and flour to the bowl and toss together with your hands, working the seasonings into the meat.

3. Pat the meat into an even 1-inch-deep layer in an 8-by-11-inch baking pan or similar vessel. Put the pan in the oven and bake the meat for 20 minutes. (This step cooks the sausage meat most of the way through and helps render out some of the fat that would otherwise create crazy flare-ups on the grill.) Pour any rendered fat off the pan and let the sausage cool to room temperature. The sausage can be cooked through this step, covered, and refrigerated for up to a day.

4. Light a good hot fire in your grill.

5. Cut 1-inch-wide by 3-inch-long "sausages" out of the cooked meat the same way you'd cut brownies out of a pan. Brown the sausages on the grill, no more than 1 or 2 minutes per side. Serve with the suggested accompaniments.

Scant ½ cup loosely packed minced lemongrass (from 3 reedy or 2 meaty stalks)

½ cup roughly chopped shallots

1 tablespoon kosher salt

2 teaspoons sugar

2 tablespoons plus 2 teaspoons fish sauce

2 tablespoons sriracha (Asian chile sauce)

3 pounds ground pork

½ cup all-purpose flour

accompaniments

1 cup Pickled Daikon Julienne (opposite)

1 cup Pickled Carrot Julienne (opposite)

1 cup Fish Sauce Vinaigrette (opposite)

1 cup loosely packed mint and cilantro leaves (one or the other is fine, a combination of both is better)

2 cups Short-Grain Rice (see page 279)

2 to 3 heads Bibb lettuce, leaves separated, well washed, and spun dry

Maldon or other high-quality coarse sea salt

pickled carrot & daikon julienne

First peel your carrots and daikon, then cut them into 3-inch lengths and julienne them. The right thickness of julienne for this ssäm (and for the bánh mì sandwich, page 205) is 3/16 of an inch. Most Asian mandolines come with a set of three blades for cross-cutting vegetables. The widest is too thick to be useful, the thinnest just shreds things, but the middle blade, like warm porridge, is just right—especially for these pickles.

Once you have the vegetables cut, pickle them in separate containers, using 1 batch of the brine for vinegar pickles (see page 66), split equally between the carrots and the daikon. After 1 day, they'll be good; after 2 days, they'll be perfect; and they'll keep for weeks after that.

If you haven't planned that far in advance, use the salt-and-sugar method: Put the julienned vegetables in separate small bowls and sprinkle each with a tablespoon of sugar and a teaspoon of salt per cup of cut-up vegetable. Toss well and let sit for as long as possible before using.

fish sauce vinaigrette

MAKES ABOUT 1 CUP

This stuff is totally Tien Ho, who says, "Fish sauce vinaigrette is like the ketchup and mustard and mayonnaise of Vietnam all in one. If you go into a Vietnamese family's house and there's not a jar of it in the fridge or out on the table, there's something wrong. There is nothing it doesn't go with, there is no possibility of overusing it, and there's no chance anyone ever gets tired of it. Growing up, when we were dirt-poor, I'd get a bowl of rice and a tiny little piece of meat for dinner and then just add enough fish sauce vinaigrette on it to make every last grain of rice taste good."

Our fish sauce vinaigrette is lighter and sweeter than whatever Tien's ma would have made (just as our kimchi is sweeter and less fermented than my mom's), so feel free to adjust it to your taste.

Combine the fish sauce, water, vinegar, lime juice, sugar, garlic, and chiles in a jar. This vinaigrette will keep for up to a week in the refrigerator.

½ cup fish sauce

¼ cup water

2 tablespoons rice wine vinegar

Juice of 1 lime

¼ cup sugar

1 garlic clove, minced

1 to 3 red bird's-eye chiles, thinly sliced, seeds intact

spicy pork sausage & rice cakes
chinese broccoli & crispy shallots SERVES 4 TO 6

½ cup grapeseed or other neutral oil

3 large yellow onions, cut in half and thinly sliced

2½ teaspoons kosher salt

1 pound ground pork

2 very loosely packed cups (1½ ounces) dried red chiles

2 garlic cloves, thinly sliced

2 tablespoons toban djan (jarred Chinese fermented bean and chile sauce) or ssämjang (the Korean analogue to toban djan)

1 tablespoon Sichuan peppercorns

1 tablespoon kochukaru (Korean chile powder)

6 tablespoons water

1 tablespoon usukuchi (light soy sauce)

1 tablespoon sugar

2 cups sliced or coarsely chopped Chinese vegetables, such as Chinese broccoli or bok choy

8 long cylindrical rice sticks, cut into 1-inch lengths

8 ounces silken tofu, drained

1 cup sliced scallions, greens and whites

½ cup packaged Chinese fried shallots

There's a branch of the Grand Sichuan on St. Mark's Place in the East Village, just a few blocks from our restaurants. I eat there a lot. A lot. Fish with noodle hot pot, braised chile beef, house special pork, dan dan noodles—there's lots of good stuff on that menu.

After one of many meals there with the crew from Ssäm Bar, I goaded them into doing something like the oily, spicy food we were eating so much of. I think I had about this much input on the dish: "Use some Sichuan peppercorns, lots of red peppers, and make it really oily. It'll be banging." Tien and Tim Maslow did their thing with it. *Ma po tofu* was their point of departure. They melded it with a dish from the first late-night menu—rice cakes with a kinda-sorta-but-not-really Asian pork Bolognese sauce. The result isn't Sichuan or Korean or Bolognese or anything, but it is very Momofuku. And banging.

1. Heat 2 tablespoons of the oil in a wide skillet over medium-high heat. After a minute or two, when the oil is hot, add the onions and ½ teaspoon of the salt. Cook, stirring occasionally, until the onions start to take on color and begin to shrink in the pan, about 10 minutes. Turn the heat down to medium and cook, turning the onions over on themselves every 5 or so minutes, until golden and soft and sweet, about 20 minutes longer.

2. Meanwhile, heat another tablespoon of the oil in a wide skillet over medium-high heat. After a minute or two, when the oil is hot, add the ground pork and cook, jabbing at the meat with the edge of the spoon to break it up, for about 10 minutes, just until it has lost its raw pinkness but not so long that it browns or threatens to dry out. Transfer the pork to a bowl and reserve it. Return the pan to the stove.

3. Add the remaining 5 tablespoons oil to the pan, turn the heat down to medium, and let the oil heat up for a minute. Add the dried chiles and warm them through in the oil for about 1 minute, until they're fragrant. Add the sliced garlic and cook, stirring, for a minute to infuse its flavor into the oil—it doesn't need to color, but when the aroma of garlic is rising from the pan, it's ready. Remove the pan from the heat and stir in the Chinese chile bean sauce, Sichuan peppercorns, and kochukaru. Reserve until the onions are cooked.

4. Add the water, cooked onions, and pork to the pan with the chile sauce and stir to combine. Stir in the soy, sugar, and remaining 2 teaspoons salt. At this point, you can cool the sauce and refrigerate it (for a few days) or freeze (for a few weeks), if desired.

5. Meanwhile, put a large pot of water on to boil and salt it well.

6. Bring the sauce to a simmer over medium heat and stir in the chopped greens. Cook them for 3 to 5 minutes, stirring occasionally, until the stems are just tender.

7. Drop the rice cakes into the boiling water and cook them for 2 to 3 minutes, until warmed through. Drain and add them to the pan with the pork sauce. Whisk the tofu until creamy and fluid and then stir it into the rice cake mixture.

8. Divide the rice cakes and ragu among serving bowls, garnish each with some scallions and packaged fried shallots, and serve hot.

bev eggleston's pork shoulder steak

SERVES 6

Bev Eggleston came into Ssäm Bar one night and asked to speak with the chef. (Restaurants have that advantage over home cooks: people will just ambush you out of the blue with great products sometimes.) We didn't know Bev or his meat at that point, but the waiter he spoke to, Rhasaan Manning, happened to be reading Michael Pollan's *Omnivore's Dilemma* at the time and had the presence of mind to recognize Bev's name from the book. He told Tien that Bev was in the restaurant and about his mention in Pollan's book—that this guy raises very happy pigs and sells meat from a collective of farms called EcoFriendly foods in the Shenandoah Valley of Virginia. Tien and Bev chatted, and it turns out that Bev is one of the coolest and nicest guys ever. He agreed to bring some meat by on his next weekly delivery run.

When we got some of his pig in and cooked it, we couldn't believe what we were tasting. There was general and collective disbelief at the tenderness and flavor of the flesh and the succulence of the fat: it was the best pork we'd ever tasted. Hands down, Bev's pork is magic. It makes the cruelly raised pink cardboard they sell at supermarkets seem even more ridiculous. Bev raises what he calls "crossabaws," pigs that are a crossbreed of Ossabaw pigs and more common heritage breeds like Tamworths.

Bev's meat is very expensive compared even to other high-quality producers like Niman Ranch (from whom we buy literally tons of meat every year), so we looked for an affordable way to showcase it. Talking through possibilities with Tien, Bev suggested blade steaks—pork shoulders, one of the cheapest cuts, cut into thin steaks. Tien, in his many years of kitchen cooking, had never eaten or cooked one, and after trying one of Bev's over at my old mentor Marco Canora's wine bar (Terroir, just around the corner from the Momofuku restaurants), he was sold: it's like a pork chop with character. It's been on the menu every night since, an affordably priced introduction to Bev's excellent pig meat for anyone who comes to Ssäm Bar.

If you live in the D.C. area, you can buy EcoFriendly's meat at some local markets; if you don't, they will ship it to you, but the shipping costs a bunch. Regardless, if you've got access to a butcher with a band saw and some good pig, you can get your hands on steaks cut like these: ask him for ⅝-inch-thick steaks cut from the shoulder. All you need after that is salt, pepper, and a blazing-hot grill.

We always serve the steaks with Tien's ramp ranch dressing, though the vegetables we add change with the season: ribbons of raw zucchini and sliced red onion during the summer, batons of raw celery root and spaghetti squash during the winter. They're less important to the dish than the meat and the sauce, so improvise as you see fit.

1. Light a hot fire in your grill. (Yes, you can grill-pan these, but you're going to want that pan scorching, hellfire hot.)

2. Season the steaks very generously on both sides with salt and pepper—enough so plenty will shake off when the steaks hit the grill. Lay the steaks on the grill, leaving a little space between them. Don't leave the grill: these are steaks that need tending. Have a grilling spatula at hand to flatten the steaks against the grill grate when they start to buckle: a bunch of different muscles collide in the shoulder, and some that are cooking and contracting more quickly may act up—with a firm hand and a spatula, you can keep the steaks flat. Grill for 4 minutes on the first side, or until well charred, then flip and grill the steaks for 3 to 4 minutes, until the second sides are charred but the meat is still a little bit giving and tender. Remove the steaks from the grill and allow them to rest for at least 5 minutes.

3. Serve the steaks whole, with sharp steak knives, and drizzled in ramp ranch. Or slice the steak into ¼-inch-thick strips, transfer them neatly to plates, and dress them. Serve hot.

Six ⅝-inch-thick pork shoulder steaks (about 1 pound)

Kosher salt and freshly ground black pepper

Ramp Ranch Dressing (recipe follows)

ramp ranch dressing
MAKES ABOUT 1½ CUPS

Stir together the mayonnaise, buttermilk, and pickled ramps in a mixing bowl. Season with the lemon juice, a pinch of salt, and a few turns of black pepper and stir to combine. Taste and correct the seasoning, paying particular attention to the lemon and pepper. This will keep in the fridge for about a week; use whatever leftovers as you would any ranch dressing.

1 cup Kewpie mayonnaise

¼ cup buttermilk

½ cup Pickled Ramps (page 69) or substitute half store-bought pickled pearl onions and half raw scallion greens, both finely chopped

Juice of ½ lemon, or more to taste

Kosher salt and freshly ground black pepper

gauging doneness

The times, temperatures, and cooking methods for meat presented here were all well tested, but recipes can tell you only so much. You need to know how to gauge doneness by feel to be able to guarantee you're going to cook your meat right. Softer meat is rarer meat. Firm, resistant meat is overcooked. You can use your hand to help you gauge what every level of doneness feels like, but there's no better teacher than the piece of meat in front of you. Prod it when it hits the heat (that's raw), then regularly after that, paying attention to how much more resistance it offers.

raw to rare: Hold your hand out and let it dangle lifeless and limp. Poke the flesh between your thumb and index finger. The slack, soft tenderness that yields to pressure easily is similar to the feeling of prodding a raw or rare piece of meat.

medium-rare hedging toward medium: Flex the muscles and stretch the fingers on your extended hand. Notice that the flesh between your finger and thumb is more taut, more resistant to pressure, firmer. That's the texture of steak cooked to medium or medium-rare. Unless you like overcooked beef, you want to pull the steak from the heat right before or right at this stage. Remember that meat will continue cooking after you remove it from the heat, while it rests, so you want it on the softer side of this texture if you want it medium-rare. Which you do.

well-done/way overcooked: Ball your hand into an angry fist. Poke it. Rigid. Dense. Unyielding. That's what well-done meat is like: like eating a fist. And it's worse when you order it in a restaurant, because everybody who works in the kitchen will make fun of your order.

Of course, poking meat is just one way to check on its progress. At Momofuku, we are far more likely to check doneness with a cake tester. Cake testers are long, needle-thin metal sticks designed for—surprise, surprise—making sure cakes are cooked through and no longer gooey in the center. But they're a fixture on the savory sides of better kitchens around the world, too.

To use a cake tester (or, really, any long, super-thin metal rod) to gauge the doneness of your meat, do this:

Remove the meat from the heat.

Insert the cake tester in the meat—go in from the side, not from the top. Slide it in far enough so that the tip of the tester is in the middle of the piece of meat. Let it sit there for 5 seconds or so.

Now pull out the tester and immediately press it just below your lower lip. As soon as you feel the heat of the metal, you know where the meat is: If it's cold, it's not ready. If it's just barely, barely warmer than body temperature, you're right where you want to be. If it's hot, that thing is cooked—and probably overcooked.

pan-roasted dry-aged rib eye

SERVES 2 TO 4

We ran an $80 rib-eye special around the holidays the first winter Ssäm Bar was open, and it flew out the door. This was when we were still serving burritos, and before anyone thought Ssäm Bar was a good restaurant. Tien and I were both goofily surprised people would drop coin on an expensive steak at Ssäm. It was great for our bottom line, but it was also great for us. We liked strutting out the old-school cooking we both revered. Cooks who are worth anything love cooking a piece of meat like this, love slicing it, love just being in a kitchen where it's happening. At least that's how we felt.

Soon we took our pet project and made the steak program *professional.* We went from using a high-quality prime rib from a good purveyor to using a dry-aged one from an even more exclusive purveyor to buying pasture-raised dry-aged steaks from Sylvia and Steve Pryzant, who run the Four Story Hill Farm cooperative in Wayne County, Pennsylvania. The price of the steak climbed every step of the way, but we were obsessed at that point: there's something thrilling about cooking a big slab of best-quality meat. It starts when you get your hands on the primo beef, stuff that's been dry-aged for a few weeks, and smell it raw: it has a minerally aroma, like a cured salami. Incredibly appetizing. Browning it is a pleasure; the smoke and steam it sends off smell about as good as cooking meat can. And then there's the basting, the real money shot of the whole operation. As far as cooking tasks go, cooking the steak this way is not very difficult. You could sum it up in a text message:

Season it.

Sear it.

Roast it.

Baste it.

Rest it.

Slice it.

Eat it.

But it's not easy, because cooking a piece of meat that costs maybe $40 or $50 takes balls. If you fuck up, you fucked up a piece of meat that cost a lot of money. That somebody took care to raise and slaughter and dry-age and butcher. That makes you an asshole, especially at Momofuku. Of course, we should extend the same care and fear of God to cooking beets or greens or eggs or anything. But I find there's nothing like the threat of a medium-well dry-aged rib eye to drive the point home.

And when you get it right, it's magic. Magic to cook. Magic to eat. This is a pricey dish, yes, but it's a special one.

1. Heat the oven to 400°F.

2. Heat a 10- to 12-inch cast-iron pan over high heat. While the pan is heating, season the steak liberally with salt—like you'd salt a sidewalk in New York in the winter—and then with pepper.

3. When the pan is good and hot—the steak should sizzle aggressively when it touches the pan—brown the steak. Put the steak in the pan and

One 2- to 2½-pound bone-in rib-eye steak, very preferably dry-aged

Kosher salt and freshly ground black pepper

4 tablespoons unsalted butter

A few sprigs of thyme

3 garlic cloves

1 medium or 2 small shallots

Maldon salt

Confit Fingerling Potatoes (optional; page 189)

RECIPE CONTINUES

don't touch it or press it or do anything stupid like that after you add it. After 2 minutes, take a peek: the steak should release easily from the pan and the seared side should be on the golden side of browned. Flip it. Sear the second side for another 2 minutes, following the same program. Stand the steak up with the wide fatty side opposite the bone against the pan for 30 seconds, then turn the steak back over so the side that was seared first is against the pan.

4. Put the steak in the oven and leave it untouched for 8 minutes.

5. Return the pan to the stovetop over low heat. Add the butter, thyme, garlic, and shallots to the pan. As soon as the butter melts, start basting: Use one hand to tilt the pan up at a 45-degree angle and, with the other hand, use a very large spoon to scoop up butter from the pool in the pan and spoon it over the steak. Repeat this motion constantly, cloaking the steak in an eddy of aromatic melted butter. After about 2 minutes of basting, give your pan-holding hand a break and give the steak a poke—it should be squishy-soft, or somewhere close to that. If it's there, and if you like your steak the kind of ultrarare the French call *bleu,* pull the steak from the pan and put it on a plate to rest. If you're going more medium-rare, which is what I prefer, baste it for another minute or two more, then remove it to a plate. Do not cook a steak like this beyond medium-rare. Please. (And do not think about dumping the fat from the pan either. After the steak has had time to rest and it's time to eat, reheat the pan sauce until it's hot to the touch, pour it into a small bowl, or a couple of small bowls, and bring it to the table. It goes on everything.)

6. Let the steak rest. Just leave it the hell alone. No touching for at least 10 minutes. Get the rest of your meal together. Get out a cutting board and a good knife to slice the meat.

7. Slice it: Cut the steak off the bone, then slice it against the grain (cutting in the direction that was perpendicular to the bone) into ½-inch-thick slabs. Put on plates and pour any juices from where it rested and the cutting board into the pan drippings. Scatter the steak with Maldon salt and serve with the potatoes and drippings on the side.

confit fingerling potatoes

SERVES 4

At Ssäm Bar, we usually serve our rib eye with a side of potatoes that have been stewed in pork fat and then deep-fried. In the summer, we might augment the offering with a big, ripe heirloom tomato cut into thick slices and sprinkled with Maldon salt. The sides don't matter as much as the steak, as long as you've got something on hand to sop up the pan sauce with.

1. Melt the pork fat in a medium pot over low heat. Once it's warm, add the potatoes. Simmer them over low heat until they are just tender—not tender-mushy-mashed-potato-time tender, but just-past-firm tender—about 10 minutes. Use a slotted spoon to remove them from the oil, then turn the heat under the oil up to medium-high. Line a plate with paper towels and have it near at hand to drain the potatoes on.

2. When a deep-fry or instant-read thermometer inserted into the oil registers 375°F, begin frying the potatoes in batches that don't crowd the pan for 2 to 3 minutes each, until the edges of the potatoes are crisp and browned. Drain the potatoes on the paper towels and salt them generously while they're still hot. Let the oil return to temperature between batches.

3. Toss the still-warm potatoes with the crumbled bacon and chopped greens, and serve.

4 cups rendered pork or duck fat or grapeseed or other neutral oil

2 pounds fingerling potatoes, scrubbed and sliced lengthwise in half or quartered, if large

Kosher salt

4 slices smoky bacon, preferably Benton's (see page 147), cooked and crumbled

1 cup baby mustard greens or other similar bitter lettuce, roughly chopped

roasted fingerling potatoes: If you can't be bothered to slow-cook and then deep-fry the potatoes, you can opt to roast them: Toss the sliced potatoes with a few tablespoons of rendered pork or duck fat or grapeseed or other neutral oil to coat, season them liberally with salt, and arrange them cut side down on a baking sheet. Bake for 20 minutes in a 400°F oven, until crisp outside and tender within. Toss them with the bacon and greens if you like, or just dunk them in the pan sauce from the steak and call it a day.

fun with meat glue

Once Ssäm Bar was up and running, and the burritos were behind us, and the kitchen was pounding away on all cylinders, I wanted very much to elevate our cooking. I wanted to be, and I thought we needed to be, educated about all techniques and cooking methods—not just how to grill a steak (though without that, you've got no starting point), but what creative, progressive cooks were doing with the new powders and technologies that are expanding the realm of "cooking" past hot fire and sharp knives.

I used the example of a heart surgeon when I talked about it with the crew: a surgeon who's been practicing for thirty years and knows every trick in the book still has to stay on top of the advances being made in his or her field. What are the newest ways to save a heart, what's the least invasive way of opening up a chest? Some medical methods might be more effective on one patient or another, so that comprehensive knowledge the surgeon acquires means he or she has, at his or her immediate disposal, medical methods from the very old to the very new. Maybe the doctor rejects the new methods in favor of the old ones in most cases, but those decisions do not release the surgeon from the need to stay up on advances made by science. The example doesn't need to be so highfalutin: if a plumber swears by copper only, rejects PVC pipe, and has no idea what kind of tape or insulation to use with it, that plumber is of limited usefulness and skill.

There was a stretch where I ate dinner at wd~50, Wylie Dufresne's restaurant on the Lower East Side, every Sunday night, not just because I like Wylie and I like the restaurant, but also because Wylie typifies that approach to cooking—he is at the vanguard of almost everything in the kitchen. His chicken ball with mole paper and egg carpaccio is one of the greatest dishes of all time (and the follow-ups, like the chicken ball with sake soubise and the quail ball with banana tartare and nasturtium leaves, were all awesome). The chicken ball was a boneless piece of chicken meat, the dark meat around the white, the skin still attached, that was fried until crisp—it was the platonic ideal of chicken eating. I was nuts for it, and it was made with something called "meat glue," which Wylie taught me about and gave me my first bag of. I'm going to turn it over to Wylie, who's really the master of meat glue, to explain what it is and why you should cook with it.

wylie on meat glue

I found out about meat glue from Heston Blumenthal—and it was Heston, or someone at his restaurant, the Fat Duck [in Bray, in the UK], who coined the term "meat glue." Chris Young, who was working as Heston's research scientist at around the time we opened wd~50, brought me some and told me I might find it interesting. I did. In fact, we went bananas with it. I don't think there's anyone who uses as much meat glue as we do.

The basics, quickly: Meat glue is an enzyme called transglutaminase. When it comes into contact with certain amino acids—specifically lysine and glutamine—it forms covalent bonds that act like a glue. Virtually all fish, meat, and poultry contain enough lysine and glutamine for that reaction to take place.

The first dish we ever made with transglutaminase at wd~50 was a rabbit sausage. It was a variation of a dish I'd learned to make when I cooked at Jean Georges, an old dish of his for which there is a recipe in his book *Simple Cuisine*. He'd take rabbit meat, a little bit of chicken breast, pistachios, herbs, and some of the rabbit's liver, and he'd mix them with egg yolks, wrap the mixture in foil, and poach it. It was cool to me because it was a sausage without a casing. As soon as I got my hands on some meat glue, I thought, "I'm gonna try that. I'm going to make a sausage without a casing and without the egg to bind it." It worked. We had our take on that sausage on our menu in the first year we were open.

So it started with the rabbit. And then we realized there were no more end cuts. Two tails of

something—like a fish fillet, where the tail ends are thinner than the middle of the fillet, and harder to use in a dish—can be put together into a good-sized piece of meat. We were saving money by eliminating scraps, having a little bit of fun, being creative with it. Then it dawned on me: if you can glue A to B, you can glue A to A. Rather than taking two shrimp and gluing them to each other, why couldn't I make a puree of shrimp and extrude it, to make noodles out of shrimp? It turned out we could.

We had some successful but painfully slow attempts that, among other things, involved making a kind of mousse out of the shrimp, pushing the mixture through a pastry bag, and refrigerating the noodles to set them. Then one day I was talking to somebody at Ajinimoto, the company that makes transglutaminase, and he told me that it is really happiest between 125° and 140°F—that's the temperature range the enzyme is most active in, where the reaction will happen at an accelerated rate. So Shea Gallante from Cru lent me this Japanese extruder, I set the bath temperature in a water circulator to the right range, and I extruded out these gigantic ten-foot-long noodles into it. After 15 minutes at the right temperature, we snipped them to the right lengths with scissors, portioned them, and had them ready to be reheated when a diner ordered the dish. Worked perfectly.

The finished dish was warm shrimp noodles with smoky paprika yogurt and prawn crackers. In some ways, that was the dish that really put us on the map, one of the first things that got us some ink. And from there we just opened our brains up to meat glue.

The dish that I think Dave really got into was the chicken ball. My sous-chef at the time, Mike Sheerin (now the chef de cuisine at Blackbird in Chicago), is a master butcher. He noticed he could bone out half a chicken and if he did it right, he could fold it so the breast meat would be completely wrapped in dark meat. We'd do that, put the meat glue inside, and wrap it in plastic to shape it into a ball, then let it sit in the refrigerator overnight so the glue could set. We'd cook it at a specific temperature in a water circulator and when an order came in, we'd baste the chicken ball in a pan with butter for a bit and then right before we sent it out, we'd drop it in the deep fryer to really crisp up the skin. We'd slice off the end of the ball to show the cross section of dark meat and light meat inside and plate it with a slab of egg yolk that looked like American cheese, some carrot confit, and mole paper. A very simple dish that we churched up a bit and wd~50-afied or whatever.

We're always looking for new things to do with meat glue—always scouring patents to see what people are doing with these ingredients. Back in 2004, I had a link to fifty patents that Ajinimoto had for uses of transglutaminase that ranged from field dressings for the military to keeping chocolate from blooming during temperature changes in shipping to nonacidified gels—gels that are thermo-irreversible, which means they will not melt.

That last one was very interesting to me, and has led us into meat glue 2.0 or 3.0—taking it further than just gluing two things together. Right now we're making a take on yuba—a flat noodle made from dried soybeans—but ours is a noodle made from fresh beans, so it has their fresh green flavor. It's a noodle made from a pureed vegetable and has very similar characteristics and mouthfeel to pasta. Now the amino acids you need for meat glue to work—the lysine and glutamine—aren't present in fresh vegetables, but they are in gelatin, and because of that, meat glue and gelatin have a near-perfect relationship. So I add a little gelatin to a soybean puree, introduce meat glue to it, and roll it out in sheets. Voilà: a vegetable turned into a pasta that's actually a thermo-irreversible gel. I can heat it, and it won't melt. I know it's a thermo-irreversible gel, but it just registers as a vegetable pasta on the plate.

If you can get past the fact that you're playing God on some level—that I can actually make a turducken that is one solid piece of meat—then why not? If we can agree that it's okay to peel a carrot or boil a potato and mash it, then why not re-form a chicken? What's the cut-off point? I don't see a good argument against meat glue. Once we get to the point where we know it's perfectly healthy—and it is, it has been studied and approved by the Food and Drug Administration (and your body makes the stuff—it's what repairs muscles when they tear)— then what's the issue? Can we exist without it? Sure. You could also rub two sticks together every time you wanted to make a fire.

In the end, meat glue, like so many hydrocolloids, is a neat product. It's fun. It expands what you can do in the kitchen. When people ask me why— why glue a chicken together or deep-fry mayonnaise or try to do something that hasn't been done before—it brings out the philosophy major in me. Why? Do we really need to get existential about it? I've read Camus; I know we're all going to die. So, why? There is no point. It's a dead-end question. I don't understand asking what the point of playing with your food is when I think playing with your food is fun and an inherent part of cooking. If you can get past the why and the hang-ups and have some fun in the process, apply some creativity to what you're cooking, then that's the goal, the end point, and the answer for me.

When I got my first bag of the stuff from Wylie, I popped my meat glue cherry by re-creating the chicken ball—not for serving at the restaurant, just to do it and to see that it could be done. Then we got crazy with it—sticking all kinds of pork together in a way God never intended—before realizing that it was the ultimate tool for making ballottines. A ballottine is a boned-out chicken (or other animal) wrapped around a savory stuffing, and the old method requires that you handle it gently and tie it neatly. With meat glue, I'd make one, sprinkle it with the glue, and torque it into a tube with plastic wrap (much the same way as we'd done for the pig's head torchon on page 201), and the next day we'd have a ballottine.

We had some failures along the way, but Tien, who fell hard for the stuff, came up with a couple of awesome dishes: the Frankensteak and brick chicken. The Frankensteak was created as a way to use up leftovers: when we got an aged rib eye in, there was usually an inch-thick cap of aged beef fat on it that we'd have to trim off. We'd been saving that fat, because it was incredibly delicious, but we didn't have a use for it. That's when Tien came up with the Frankensteak. He took the fat, pounded it out into a thin sheet, then meat-glued a blanket of the fat around a hanger or other cheaper, unaged steak. The

genius of it was that as the steaks cooked, they were basted in and infused with the flavor of well-aged beef, even though they were the sort of cuts of meat that don't lend themselves to long aging.

The brick chicken is essentially a lazy rip of Wylie's chicken ball and a send-up of chicken cooked under a brick. People have been cooking chicken under stones and bricks for millennia. This was a "brick chicken" only in as much as the chicken is re-formed into a brick-like shape.

"brick" chicken SERVES 4

Your goal is to completely bone out a whole chicken and end up with two boneless halves, each a breast and a leg connected by skin. Hey, if you're going to go to the trouble to find transglutaminase (see Sources) to make this recipe, I'm thinking that deboning a chicken is something that's right up your fun alley.

1. Trim off the wing tips from the chicken, easing your knife into the chicken's elbows to do so. Reserve the wing tips for another use, like making Taré (page 42) or adding to stock or broth.

2. Cut out the wishbone: Use your fingers to locate the wishbone, which runs from the chicken's shoulders to the high point of the breastbone. Using the bone to guide your knife, make an incision along the inside of the breastbone—the inside being the part closest to where the neck would have been. Then, again running the knife along the bone and using it as a guide, cut the breastbone away from the breast meat on the outsides of the wishbone. Grab the wishbone and pull it away from the carcass. It may break into two pieces, it may not. As long as it's out, no problem.

3. Make an incision through the skin down the breastbone, from the neck end all the way down. Cut the breast meat away from the rib cage, letting the bones of the rib cage guide the blade of the knife.

4. Cut off the wing bones: pull the skin back to reveal the shoulder joint on one side of the chicken. When you find that joint, cut through the joint—you may need to use some pressure to make the cut.

5. Pop—hyperextend—the legs to detach them from the backbone, then, with the backbone guiding the blade of the knife, cut the boned breast and bone-in leg away from the backbone. Be careful to follow the shape of the meat, and to keep the oyster—the nugget of meat that rests above the ball socket of the back legs and is nestled against the backbone— intact. When you get all the way around to the back of the chicken, make an incision through the skin and meat along where the backbone used to run to release the first boned half. Repeat on the other side. Reserve the backbone and rib cage scraps for another purpose, such as stock.

6. Cut the bones out of the legs. Make an L cut: Use the tip of your knife to cut along the thighbone to make an incision that reveals the whole bone. When you've gotten to the knee joint, make a cut (through the skin and flesh) that runs from the knee to the end of the drumstick, flaying open the drumstick. Run your knife around the end of the drumstick to sever the tendons that are attached to it. Pull the thighbone away from the flesh, using the tip of your knife to scrape or cut away the meat holding the bone in place, then repeat for the drumstick, and pull the bone away from the meat. Repeat for the other leg.

One 3- to 4-pound chicken

Kosher salt and freshly ground black pepper

1 teaspoon Activa-brand transglutaminase (aka meat glue)

if deep-frying

About 8 cups grapeseed or other neutral oil

if pan-roasting

2 tablespoons grapeseed or other neutral oil

8 tablespoons (1 stick) unsalted butter

6 garlic cloves

A few branches of thyme

RECIPE CONTINUES

7. Pull the tenderloins off the breasts, and cut the tendons out of the tenderloins. Comb your meat looking for any silverskin, veins, or bone fragments to trim out or off.

8. Spread a couple of pieces of plastic wrap out on the counter in front of you so that you've got a roughly 2-foot-square work space of plastic wrap. Lay one of the half chickens skin side down on the plastic wrap. Arrange the tenderloin on the thigh. Season the chicken generously with salt and pepper. Sprinkle the chicken with ½ teaspoon of the meat glue—it should be a fine dusting, like a really restrained dusting of confectioners' sugar on a coffee cake. Use your hands to spread it around and make sure it's applied in an even, gentle coat.

9. Fold the breast over onto the leg, then gather the loose skin around the bird and start forming it in a "brick" shape, tucking it in on itself. Once you've got it most of the way there, use the plastic to help, and then wrap the plastic wrap around the bird. Repeat the process for the second half chicken.

10. When the brick chickens are shaped and wrapped, put them in the refrigerator with something on top of them to weight them down evenly and gently. Let them sit in the refrigerator overnight, or for at least 12 hours, so the meat glue has a chance to work its magic.

11. Unwrap the chickens the next day, and—presto!—they're firm, solid pieces of meat that won't unfold or unfurl.

12. To fry the chicken bricks: Have a cooling rack (like you'd use to cool cakes or cookies) ready to drain the bird on. Heat 3 inches of oil in a deep pot over medium-high heat until a deep-fry or instant-read thermometer registers 375°F. Fry the bricks one at a time for 8 to 10 minutes each, until the chicken skin is a deep, gorgeous brown, at which point the chicken will be cooked inside too. Remove the fried chicken to the cooling rack to drain (draining it on paper towels would make the skin on one side soggy).

To pan-roast the chicken: Heat the oven to 400°F. Put a 10- to 12-inch cast-iron pan over high heat on the stovetop. Blot the chicken dry with paper towels. When the pan is good and hot, add the oil, wait half a minute, and then add the chicken bricks. After 4 to 5 minutes, use a spatula to take a peek at the skin on the bottom of the chicken, which should be a deep brown. Sneak the spatula under the chicken, gently loosening it from the pan if it hasn't loosened its grip already, and flip it over.

Put the pan in the oven and roast for 30 minutes, or until an instant-read thermometer reads 160°F when you plunge it into the center of the chicken. (Do so from the side of the brick, not the top, as to not have a hole in the middle of that pretty skin you worked so hard to brown.)

13. Return the pan to the stovetop over low heat. Add the butter, garlic, and thyme. As soon as the butter melts, start basting: Use one hand to tilt the pan up at a 45-degree angle and, with the other hand, use a large spoon—like a serving spoon—to scoop up butter from the pool in the pan and spoon it over the chicken. Repeat this motion constantly, cloaking the chicken in an eddy of aromatic melted butter. After about 2 minutes of basting, remove the chicken to a cutting board.

14. To serve, slice each of the bricks into 4 or so thick slices and fan them out on serving plates. If you roasted the chicken, pour the butter sauce in the pan over the bird.

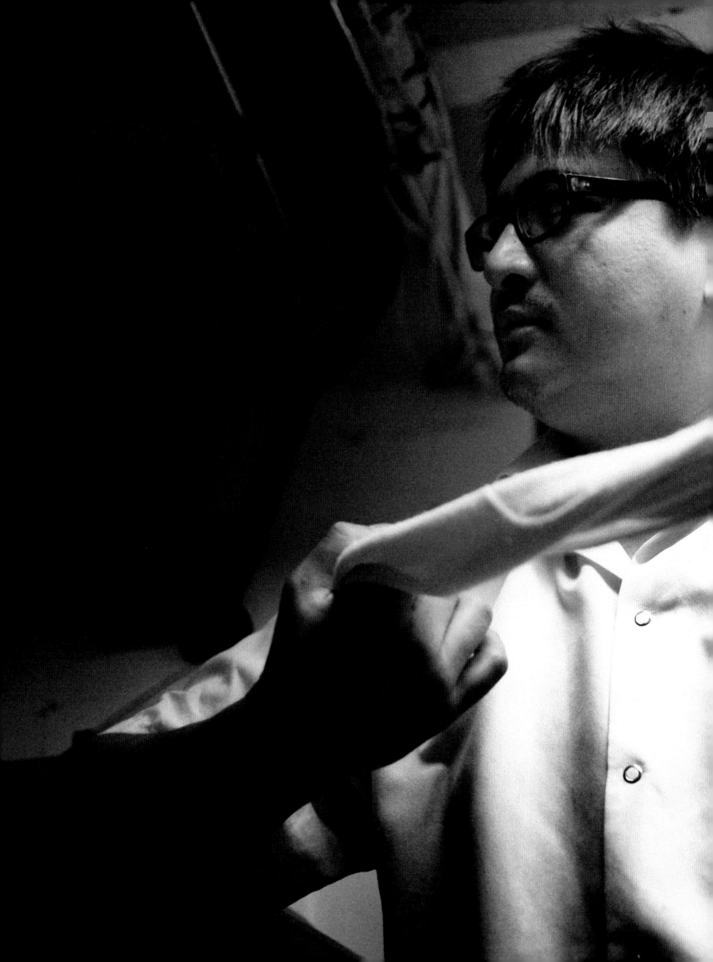

pig's head torchon SERVES 6

Pigs have heads. Every one of them does. Farmers do not raise walking pork chops. If you're serious about your meat, you've got to grasp that concept. And if you're serious about sustainability and about honestly raised good meat—which is something that we're dead serious about at Momofuku and we try to get more in touch with every day—you've got to embrace the whole pig.

A farm turns out a head on each beautiful, well-raised pig, but nobody's rushing to eat it. That's where the cook steps in: you take it, cook it, make it delicious. That's the most badass way you can connect with what you cook: elevate it, honor it, lavish it with care and attention—whether you're slicing scallions or spooning out caviar or boiling up half a pig's head. Turning ingredients into food, and sometimes almost literally turning a pig's ear into a silk purse, is what cooks do in the kitchen.

And this is, no shit, an easy way to cook a pig's head. Boil it, pull it into pieces, roll it up, slice it, and fry the elegant little pucks that couldn't be any further from the carnage that is the whole head. I strongly, strongly recommend a pair of rubber gloves—they'll make the job much more pleasant.

1. Inspect the head for hair. A 1 o'clock shadow isn't much to worry about, but if there are any hairy patches, dispense with them: a blowtorch works, as will a disposable razor.

2. Put the head in a large enough stockpot. Add the scallions, carrots, onion, and water to cover. Salt the water aggressively (it's better if it's on the too-salty side) and bring to a boil. As soon as it boils, reduce the heat so it simmers gently—bubbles here and there. Simmer the head for 3½ hours, until it's tender but not falling to pieces. Remove from the heat.

3. Before dissecting the head, cook the garlic: Heat the 2 tablespoons oil in a small skillet over medium heat. After a minute or so, when the oil is hot, add the garlic and cook, stirring, for 5 to 6 minutes, until it's deep golden in color and decisively aromatic. Remove it from the heat and reserve.

4. Prepare your kitchen counter for the task at hand: Have three bowls ready—a large one for waste and two smaller bowls, one each for meat and fat. Cover the counter with a few sheets of overlapping plastic wrap, creating a work surface about 4 feet wide and 2 feet deep. Have paper towels, a sharp small knife, and, if you have them, rubber or disposable plastic gloves on hand.

5. Remove the head from the pot and put it in your large waste bowl to drain. Discard the broth the head simmered in. (You could go super-hard-core and salvage it for a simple soup or something, but we find that it's typically too porky for us—which is saying something.) Give the head a few minutes to cool—it will be easier to prevail over it. Put on your gloves. When the head is cool enough to handle, transfer it to the plastic

torchon

Half a pig's head (8 to 10 pounds)

1 bunch scallions

2 carrots

1 onion, split in half

Kosher salt

2 tablespoons grapeseed or other neutral oil

¼ cup finely chopped garlic

Freshly ground black pepper

About 1 cup all-purpose flour, or as needed

3 large eggs

At least 2 cups panko, or as needed

About 8 cups grapeseed oil or other neutral oil for deep-frying

garnish

One 1.52-ounce tube spicy Japanese mustard (we use S&B brand)

1½ tablespoons Kewpie mayonnaise

2 tablespoons rice wine vinegar

Butter lettuce leaves

Pickled Cherries (page 68) or fresh cherries, pitted and halved

RECIPE CONTINUES

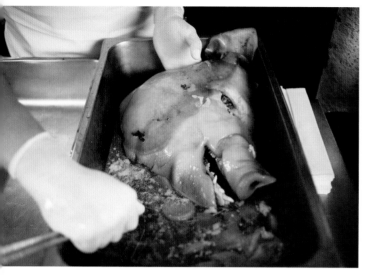

wrap, cheek down, cut side up. Pull out the top of the skull, and put it in the discard bowl. Discard the eye. Look for a nice little nugget of meat around the eye. Pull out the jaw; discard it. Twist off the snout (if it's not coming off easily, use a knife to help you) and discard it.

6. Without resorting to a bunch of veterinary terminology here, let me put this step as simply as possible: meat goes in one bowl, good fat in another, and everything else joins the skull in the discard pile. Let your fingers tell you what's what: meat is stringy and soft and pulled pork–like. Most of it is in the cheek, but there's a good store of it near where the head used to be attached to the neck, and little pockets of it all over. Fat is fat. If things worked out right, the skin should come off in a few big pieces—and the skin is, for this purpose at least, the same thing as fat, so put it in the fat bowl. Avoid or discard veins, and when your fingers are burrowing for meat and they find tough little clumps of . . . pig stuff . . . attached to it, especially around the mouth, discard those, because they're probably glands, which can be bitter. (If it makes you feel any better, know that none of what you don't really want is inedible; it's just less than delicious.) Turn the tongue inside out when you come to it; put the meat from inside the membrane in the meat bowl and the membrane/tongue skin in the discard pile. We don't

use the ear in this recipe, but if you were so inclined, you could deep-fry it right now, slice it, and eat it with mustard, and it would be an excellent snack. Otherwise, into the discard pile it goes.

7. When you've dispatched the charge of separating the head into its constituent bits, it's time to lay the meat out to make the torchon. Season the meat with salt, if needed, and pepper. Start by laying a carpet of the reserved fat down on the plastic: whole pieces of skin should form the largest proportion of it; intersperse them with globules of fat. The carpet should be about rectangular and 3 to 4 inches shy of the edges of the plastic on all sides. Once the carpet's laid, taste a bite from the meat bowl. Does it need salt? Probably. Hit the meat bowl with a large pinch of salt and the reserved golden garlic, and toss it well. Arrange the meat like a blanket over the carpet, covering it almost completely but leaving a barren inch of fat trim around the edges. Remove your gloves.

8. Now roll up the torchon: Start by lifting up the near edge of the plastic wrap and bringing it toward you, using it to guide the pork; you're rolling this thing up jelly roll–style into a log. Once it's loosely shaped into a log, push from the ends of the log to tighten up the pile of meat, then twist the ends in the plastic wrap to force it into a tidy cylindrical shape. Once it is neat and tight, tie the ends of the plastic wrap closed and put the torchon in the refrigerator to chill for at least 2 hours, so the gelatin and fat have time to firm up and the log shape will hold. You can complete the recipe through this step up to 2 days in advance or, once the torchon is chilled and solidified, put it in the freezer for a couple of months; defrost it in the refrigerator for 24 hours before proceeding.

RECIPE CONTINUES

9. When you're ready to cook the torchon, prepare three bowls: put the flour in one, the eggs in a second one (beat them lightly), and the panko in the third.

10. Remove the torchon from the refrigerator and remove the plastic. Cut the torchon into 1-inch-thick pucks. Dredge the pucks one at a time in flour, mounding it over the puck and then shaking the excess off, then in egg, thoroughly coating it, and then in the panko, mounding the bread crumbs over the puck to make sure it is amply coated.

11. Have a plate lined with paper towels at hand. Heat 3 inches of oil in a deep pot over medium-high heat until a deep-fry or instant-read thermometer inserted in the oil registers 375°F. Fry the pucks 2 at a time for 3 minutes each, until the panko coating is a medium dark brown. Drain the fried pig on paper towels.

12. To serve, stir together the mustard, mayonnaise, and rice vinegar until well combined, then plop down a generous tablespoon of the vinaigrette just off the center of each plate. Use the back of the spoon to smear it across the plates. Place 2 pucks of torchon atop each smear and flank them with butter lettuce leaves and pickled (or fresh) cherries. Serve hot.

bánh mì MAKES ABOUT 12 SANDWICHES

The Ssäm Bar bánh mì is 100 percent Tien Ho. I just eat it. Here's Tien:

Though there are two terrines involved, and it's got a Vietnamese name, and you might have never had one, let me assure you: bánh mì are one of the world's most delicious meat sandwiches, standing shoulder to shoulder with burgers and tortas and whatever else you want to put in that category.

Bread baking—crucial to the creation of the bánh mì sandwich—was introduced to Vietnam when the French colonized the country in the mid-nineteenth century. The arrival of the French continues to have a profound influence in the Vietnamese diet: baguettes aren't foreign to any Vietnamese table; terrines and forcemeats are commonplace; even pho, the elemental soup of Vietnamese cuisine, owes a debt to French cooking.

In Vietnamese, *bánh mì* means "bread," and in Vietnam, there are a host of dishes, like *bánh mì bo koh* or *bánh mì carri,* that are stews—often made with beef braised in coconut water or coconut milk—served with crusty bread on the side, just like a stew would be served in any self-respecting French home. But when you say "bánh mì," especially in America, it's often understood to mean a Vietnamese sandwich: a crusty baguette filled with meat and lightly pickled vegetables, almost always with mayonnaise (another thing the Vietnamese adopted lovingly from the French), cilantro, and something like sliced jalapeños to add some heat. The meat component in a bánh mì is, most classically, a mix of terrines, which are sometimes boiled or fried before they are put in the sandwich. And the list of things that couldn't be stuffed into a bánh mì is shorter than the list of things that can.

I'd never attempted to make bánh mì before Ssäm Bar, but I grew up eating them, like other kids did hamburgers. When we started out, we made it with three terrines—the two here, plus a veal head terrine. It was common back in Houston where I grew up that if you ordered a "special" bánh mì, it would have all those elements—liver, headcheese, and some kind of ham product. Over time, we settled on this simpler, two-terrine formula.

A couple of things to note: It doesn't really work to scale it down more than we have here, so you'll have leftover terrine for sure, which I consider a good thing. You can freeze the terrines in parts or whole, as indicated in the recipe, or use them up as you'd use any terrine—smear them on bread, put them on Triscuits, eat them by the spoonful while standing in front of the fridge wondering what you're going to cook for dinner. The chicken liver one is easier than making meat loaf; the ham terrine is like a ghetto-simplified and lightly Vietnamesed *jambon persillé.*

Kewpie mayonnaise

Good, airy baguettes, cut into 6-inch lengths and sliced almost all the way open

Chicken Liver Terrine (opposite)

Ham Terrine (page 208)

Pickled Carrot and Daikon Julienne (page 177)

Cilantro sprigs, thicker stems discarded

Sriracha (Asian chile sauce)

1. Heat the oven to 300°F, or work in batches out of a toaster oven like they do at bánh mì shops in New York. Your call. You can make more sandwiches at once using the oven.

2. Squirt a line of Kewpie mayonnaise down each face of a split-open 6-inch length of baguette. Schmear about ¼ cup of chicken liver terrine on top of it and put a few thin slices (or a healthy scoop, smeared) of ham terrine on top of that. Leave the sandwich open-faced and pop it in the oven until the bread is good and hot and crusty, 3 to 4 minutes. (It doesn't need to toast or brown, however.)

3. Scatter one side of each sandwich with pickled carrots, the other with pickled daikon. Lay some cilantro down on one side and give the other a good squirt of sriracha. Fold each sandwich closed. Cut it in half. Serve it hot.

chicken liver terrine MAKES ONE 3-POUND TERRINE, ENOUGH FOR AT LEAST 12 SERVINGS OR SANDWICHES

This is a loose, sometimes crumbly, terrine, not some neat-slicing piece of fancy French footwork. It gets smushed into and onto the bread for the bánh mì, so keeping it in the brick-like loaf shape it comes out of the refrigerator in is not necessary if it is inconvenient. For speed and ease at Ssäm Bar, we typically break it up and pack it into quart containers, then scoop out spoonfuls of the meat when we're making bánh mì.

1. Heat the oven to 275°F.

2. Rinse and pick over your chicken livers, removing any large veins or little green blobs of bile. Don't worry about keeping the livers intact and pretty; they're going into the food processor.

3. Put the garlic and shallots in the work bowl of the food processor and pulse on and off until finely chopped. Scrape them out into a medium mixing bowl. Return the work bowl to the processor (no need to clean it) and add the chicken livers. Pulse the machine on and off until the livers are chopped coarsely but evenly. Add them to the mixing bowl with the garlic and shallot, then add the pork, 5-spice, fish sauce, sugar, and salt. Mix gently but thoroughly. (A rubber-gloved hand is the best tool for this.)

4. Pack the mixture into a baking pan with a 6-cup capacity—like a terrine mold or an 8½-by-4½-inch loaf pan. Set the terrine in a deep roasting pan and add hot tap water to come up nearly to the lip of the terrine pan. Put the terrine in its water bath in the oven and bake for 1 hour and 15 minutes, or until an instant-read thermometer stuck into the middle of the terrine registers 145°F.

5. Remove the pan from the bath and put it on a cooling rack. Allow the terrine to cool to room temperature, then wrap the pan in foil and put it in the refrigerator to thoroughly chill, at least 1 hour or overnight.

6. Remove the terrine from the refrigerator and unmold it: Lay a couple pieces of plastic wrap over your counter. Run a knife (a butter knife is fine) under hot water, then run it along the edges of the terrine. Invert the pan onto the plastic wrap, rapping the pan against the counter if the terrine doesn't immediately release itself. You can use the terrine now or wrap it in the plastic and store it in the refrigerator for up to a week. Or, if you're making this far in advance or don't anticipate making that many sandwiches, cut the terrine into whatever size pieces suit your purposes, wrap well, and freeze. Frozen, the terrine will keep for months. Defrost it as you would any meat, still wrapped and in the refrigerator, allowing at least a couple of hours per pound of frozen terrine.

1½ pounds chicken livers

¼ cup peeled garlic cloves

1 large or 2 medium shallots

1½ pounds ground pork

1½ teaspoons Chinese 5-spice powder

2 tablespoons fish sauce

1 tablespoon plus 1 teaspoon sugar

1 tablespoon plus 1 teaspoon kosher salt

ham terrine MAKES ONE 3- TO 4-POUND TERRINE,

ENOUGH FOR AT LEAST 12 SERVINGS OR SANDWICHES

Fresh ham meat has a lot of fat on it (just like whole hams), but sometimes when you find it in a butcher shop, much of the fat has been trimmed away and you're confronted with a pile of dense pink flesh. If that's the case, buy only 3½ pounds fresh ham and supplement it with an additional ½ pound of fatty pig meat—a slice of raw belly meat, a few good chunks of fat cut from a shoulder, or a brick of fatback, should your butcher have it. The fat is essential to binding the meat together in the terrine. If you can't find fresh ham—which is entirely possible, since many butchers only stock fresh hams around Christmas and Easter—you can substitute a 4-pound piece of boneless fatty pork shoulder or pork butt. It's not the same, but it will work just fine for the sandwich.

4 pounds fresh (meaning unsmoked, uncured) ham meat

2½ teaspoons curing salt (aka pink salt or sel rose)

¼ cup kosher salt

3 bay leaves

2 whole star anise

1 cinnamon stick

5 garlic cloves

1. Cut the ham into 1-inch-or-so cubes. Put the cubes in a large mixing bowl and toss them with the sel rose. Refrigerate for at least 1 day, and up to 3 days.

2. Heat the oven to 275°F.

3. Put the cured ham in a large heavy pot with a lid, like a Dutch oven. Add the salt, bay leaves, star anise, cinnamon, garlic, and enough water just to cover the meat. Bring to a simmer on the stovetop. Cover the pot and put it in the oven for 2 hours, until the meat is very tender.

4. Use a slotted spoon to transfer the ham from the braising liquid to a large mixing bowl; set the pot aside. Break up the meat with your fingers, leaving it in large chunks but removing as much fat as possible. Put the fat in the work bowl of a food processor, piece by piece, as you remove it. (If you've supplemented your ham with another fatty cut you can more or less skip this step, though do harvest any fat from the ham that's there for the taking.)

5. Scoop the garlic cloves from the braising liquid and add them to the braised fat in the food processor. Process until the two come together in a smooth puree, scraping down the sides as needed. (You can loosen the puree with a few spoonfuls of the braising liquid if need be; then discard the braising liquid and spices.) Scrape the garlicky fat into a small bowl.

6. Dip pieces of ham in the garlic fat and line them up neatly in a baking pan with a 6-cup capacity—like a terrine mold or an 8½ by 4½-inch loaf pan. (Alternatively, pour the fat into the bowl with the braised meat, toss the meat well to ensure that all the meat is well coated, and dump that mix into the pan. Doing it that way makes for a less attractive terrine but saves a few minutes.)

7. Wrap the pan in aluminum foil, then set another pan the same size, full of some kind of weight (dried beans, marbles, etc.), on top. (Or, if you don't have a second pan, use anything that fits snugly over the face of the terrine—like a foil-wrapped brick—just so it applies even pressure to the whole meat loaf, which is key for it holding together.) Put the setup in the refrigerator to chill and set overnight.

8. Remove the terrine from the refrigerator and unmold it: Lay a couple pieces of plastic wrap over your counter. Run a knife (a butter knife is fine) under hot water, then run it along the edges of the terrine. Invert the pan onto the plastic wrap, rapping the pan against the counter if the terrine doesn't immediately release itself. You can use the terrine now or wrap it in the plastic and store it in the refrigerator for up to a week. Or, if you're making this far in advance or don't anticipate making that many sandwiches, cut the terrine into whatever size pieces suit your purposes, wrap well, and freeze. Frozen, the terrine will keep for months. Defrost it as you would any meat, still wrapped and in the refrigerator, allowing at least a couple of hours per pound of frozen terrine.

momofuku shortcakes SERVES 8

Shortcakes—first with rhubarb, later with strawberries, and by wintertime, with ham cream in place of fruit—were the first real dessert we made and served at Momofuku. (At Ssäm, we had been serving mochi but they were premade, purchased, and arranged on a plate with sliced apples; at Noodle, we flirted with dessert for a couple of months the first summer we were open and didn't revisit the issue until we bought a soft-serve ice cream machine when Noodle moved into a bigger space.)

But these shortcakes came with Christina Tosi, and after she joined the team, dessert became and will always be a part of what we do. The confectioners' sugar in these cakes make the sweet-salty balance pop a little more than in traditional shortcakes. You'll also find them moister and denser inside with a crisper, crunchier outer shell.

1. Crack the egg into a small graduated measuring cup and whisk it to thoroughly mix the white and yolk. Decant or spoon off half of it (you can discard that part of the egg or reserve it for another use). Add enough cream to the egg in the measuring cup to make ½ cup. Stir briefly, then put the mixture in the refrigerator to chill.

2. Combine the flour, granulated sugar, brown sugar, salt, and baking powder in the bowl of a stand mixer outfitted with the paddle attachment and stir them together. Add the butter and shortening and turn the mixer on to its lowest setting. Mix the fat in until the batter is gravelly, with pea-sized lumps everywhere, which shouldn't take much more than 4 minutes.

3. Once you've got the sandy, lumpy, dryish, short batter together, grab the cream mixture from the refrigerator and stream it into the batter, stirring it in with the machine still on its lowest speed. Do this for as short a time as humanly possible, just until the liquid is barely absorbed; do not overmix. Let the dough rest in the mixer bowl for 10 minutes.

4. Scoop the batter into little balls, using about 2 tablespoons for each (you can assist their shaping lightly with your hands) and line them up on a baking sheet. You should have 8 balls. Chill in the refrigerator for at least 30 minutes, and as long as overnight.

5. Heat the oven to 350°F. Line a couple of baking sheets with parchment paper or Silpats.

6. Pour the confectioners' sugar into a wide shallow bowl. Roll each of the shortcakes through the sugar to coat very lightly, tap off the excess, and place the dusted cakes on the prepared baking sheets, with enough room between them to allow them to double their footprint while baking.

1 large egg

About ½ cup heavy cream

1½ cups all-purpose flour

½ cup granulated sugar

⅓ cup packed light brown sugar

1 tablespoon kosher salt

1½ teaspoons baking powder

8 tablespoons (1 stick) unsalted butter, cut into small pieces and chilled

¼ cup vegetable shortening, at room temperature

About ½ cup confectioners' sugar

Poached Rhubarb (page 212) or Macerated Strawberries (page 213)

Whipped Cream (page 213)

RECIPE CONTINUES

7. Bake for 9 to 11 minutes. The cakes will spread and then rise—the baking powder in it will give them a final, poofy kick and the confectioners' sugar on the outside should crackle when they're ready. Overbaked is preferable to underbaked with these cakes. If their centers fall after you pull them from the oven, bake them for another 60 to 90 seconds. Transfer to a rack and let cool.

8. Serve with either rhubarb or strawberries and a generous dollop of whipped cream.

poached rhubarb
SERVES 8

1½ pounds rhubarb, peeled and cut into 1-inch pieces (4 cups)

1 (750-ml) bottle elderflower syrup (3 cups)

The juice strained from 2 or 3 (10- to 12-ounce) cans of lychees (save the lychees for another use, or just eat them)

2 cups sugar

1. Heat the oven to 225°F.

2. Combine the rhubarb, elderflower syrup, lychee juice, and sugar in a medium oven-safe saucepan and cover with a lid. Poach the rhubarb in the oven for 35 minutes, until tender.

3. Remove the pan from the oven and let the rhubarb cool almost to room temperature, with the lid on.

4. Remove the rhubarb from the poaching syrup with a slotted spoon and serve at once (figure about ½ cup per serving, and make sure to use some of the poaching syrup as part of the dish—drizzle it over the shortcakes and rhubarb), or store the rhubarb in the syrup in the refrigerator for up to 1 week.

macerated strawberries

SERVES 8

One to 2 hours before you intend to serve them, gently toss the strawberries with the sugar; the sugar will draw out the juices from the strawberries. Serve cold or at room temperature, allotting about ½ cup of strawberries per serving. Use the macerating liquid as part of the dish—pour it over the shortcakes and strawberries.

4 cups strawberries, preferably a naturally sweet and not-too-big variety like Tri-star, hulled

¼ cup sugar

whipped cream

MAKES 3½ CUPS

Combine the heavy cream, sour cream, confectioners' sugar, and salt in a large bowl and whisk with an electric mixer or by hand until medium peaks form. The whipped cream can be made ahead of time and kept in the refrigerator for up to a few hours. Rewhisk before serving.

1½ cups heavy cream

½ cup sour cream

¼ cup confectioners' sugar

Pinch of kosher salt

ko

Once we decided that the space that housed Noodle Bar was going to turn into Ko, we needed to figure out what that meant exactly.

Noodle Bar was a mess that turned into a success; it went from a failing ramen bar to a place so busy we needed to triple its size to keep it from imploding. And at Ssäm Bar, we put more thought into where we'd put the oversized John McEnroe poster in the dining room than into who would want to dine on what we were serving in that room. Turning that around meant turning the restaurant's concept on its head.

Fucking up at Ko—getting it wrong and then getting it right, in classic Momofuku fashion—was not an option.

We knew Ko would have fewer seats than Noodle Bar—from twenty-seven down to fourteen or twelve, depending on how it felt when we could get the bar stools in there to try out the new space for ourselves.

If we were going to do a higher-end thing than we had before—the only way we'd make rent with fewer seats—we'd need to take reservations. Making people wait out in the cold to spend $100 on dinner wasn't going to work. My plan was that there would be no servers or waitstaff—that all the tip money coming into the restaurant would go to the cooks—and in order to avoid having to hire someone just to answer the phones, I decided we'd have people make reservations online. First come, first served. No VIPs.

The original idea for Ko was to make it a collaborative effort. I joked that it would be like a sewing circle. We had a few brainstorming meetings, getting all the chefs and chefs de cuisine together at Quino's apartment in Williamsburg and drinking beers and shouting out ideas for dishes.

We struggled with how we'd marry our high-low aesthetic with the demands of a finer-dining setting. We cycled through different scenarios, like serving one sitting of a tasting menu, then serving an à la carte menu until two in the morning so our friends in the industry could come by after work and eat. Some ideas came out of those sessions, like serving breakfast for dinner or serving whole fried chickens (which we ended up doing at Noodle Bar), or focusing on the kind of American food fine dining restaurants don't serve but everybody loves to eat, like chicken-fried steak and fried apple pie.

But I typically left the meetings pissed off. I wasn't satisfied that everyone was taking the idea and the challenge of the restaurant seriously enough. I saw that Peter Serpico and Sam Gelman got it, and I plotted to put them in charge of the kitchen. Christina Tosi was a given.

I wanted Ko to showcase technique, from the very simple and nearly invisible—like cutting fish properly—to roasting scallops perfectly to exploiting more modern cooking techniques in ways that aren't ornate or self-congratulatory. I wanted the food at Ko to look as simple as possible but the ideas and flavors and process that went into the dishes to be as evolved as we could make them. I wanted it to be a place where we could be smart and cook creatively without abandoning the emphasis on deliciousness that connects the first two restaurants.

There are things we say in the kitchen, a codified lexicon, that explain some of the kitchen mentality at Ko. "Make it soigné" means make it right and make it perfect. It's something you hear a lot in traditional French kitchens. No mistakes, no misunderstandings. Make it the best. Do not fuck it up. That was a refrain at the first two restaurants; it became a mantra at Ko.

"Make it nice," said with a slight tilt of the head or a leading tone, means take this thing and cook it right, cook it the best way you know how. Our dishes often evolve from having an amazing ingredient arrive in the kitchen and a cook "making it nice."

Also, the word *chef* can in fact be a derogatory term. What a joke, what a meaningless term it is these days: a fool in a black chef's jacket who has no fucking clue about anything. But when you work in a kitchen, your boss is your chef, and you call him or her that. When they deserve it, it's an honor to call them that. When I meet or talk with or about my mentors, I'm likely to call them "chef": like me and Uncle Choi, I recognize that there's a *si-fu* and a *kung-fu,* and I don't want anybody to think that I don't know the difference.

Serpico, ornery motherfucker that he is, likes calling almost everybody chef. And that became part of the Ko thing: it expresses the deferential humility that the title, properly conferred, should; it expresses the humorous contempt of the term, the way I usually like to use it; and the friction between those two meanings is the challenge at the heart of Ko.

With all that pressure—from me, and from the weight of expectations we had for the place—it fell to me to come up with the opening menu for Ko, the one we'd be judged on. I started road testing some of the dishes by serving them to friends who came into Ssäm Bar months before Ko opened. And, as always, I circulated ideas via our roundtable e-mail:

Thursday, September 20, 2007
10:16 PM
here are opening menu ideas for Ko
that I'd like some thoughts on:
the kimchi consommé seems to be a
real winner, as does the short rib
cooked in a bag. Tosi & I both like the
roasted scallop dish—simple to plate
and real nice, need to work on the
dashi component.

amuse-bouche:
nori cup with uni & caviar
or
seaweed macaroon with caviar—
asked Tosi for some type of macaroon that is savory. maybe a scallion
macaroon with crème fraîche &
caviar
or
rice cracker cup with some type of
tartare

1st
roasted matsutake mushrooms with
pine needle oil, julienne of apple, pine
nut puree (with dashi), chives (cut to
look like pine needles)
or
torched thin sheet of Wagyu, rolled
with shiso & freeze-dried soy salt

2nd
kimchi consommé with oysters,
charred pork belly, chaat, cabbage
or
steamed giant oysters (Chinatown
style) with julienne of ginger scallion
sauce
or
braised Tokyo turnips with squab
broth & black trumpet mushrooms
or
Santa Barbara uni set in dashi jelly
or
chawan mushi with black truffle, beef
jus, snails

3rd
roasted day-boat scallops with nori
puree, candied sea beans, whipped
dashi
or
pork dumpling agnolotti

4th
short ribs with braised daikon &
pickled mustard seeds

Sweets
fried apple pie

other ideas I like
torchon of foie with ???
barley risotto
really like Tosi's chicken-fried chicken
Serpico's fluke with charred lily bulb
tuna with kohlrabi, apple & mustard
oil
coddled hen eggs with mushroom
ragout
roasted squab, five-spice, savoy
cabbage

Wednesday, September 26, 2007 2:10 AM
some more notes and testing . . .

Tosi, I know we spoke about doing less with nori with the amuse, and although I'm still optimistic for a savory macaroon that will sandwich caviar, I keep on thinking that an irregular nori chip with your buttermilk thickened with ultrasperse topped with caviar might be delicious.

Canapé—change the matsutake mushroom dish to roasted, halved, a savory pine nut brittle (very thin sheet), pine nut oil, chives cut to look like pine needles—the original simmered matsutake might work better on another menu. Or we do a simple crudo.

egg course—I think this might be a great egg course, as it requires simple à la minute assembly: soy sauce soft eggs—4-minute egg, boiled, ice bath, peeled, and stained in flavored soy, ginger, star anise. Use fish tippet to cut eggs in smooth halves, fines herbes, pecans, country ham dust. We will try tomorrow.

kimchi consommé with oysters, charred pork belly, chaat—finished, ready to roll out—need hot sake carafes.

roasted day-boat scallops with nori puree, pickled chanterelles, whipped dashi— almost ready, 1 week out—need to get granny hand mixer and start timing when the methylcellulose f50 begins to break down and conditions that might help the process, like hot plates.

beef short rib with braised daikon, pickled mustard seeds & baby carrots—ready to roll out—all we need is a nice shallow bowl/plate.

dessert—Tosi, I still like fried apple pie.

Pete, I really like the sweetbreads with yuzu lemon puree, but didn't really like the scallop with it, as I think that it was lost in the whole thing and actually had the mouthfeel of an uncooked scallop. But maybe we keep it really simple and do a classic roasted sweetie with citrus puree.

I think the duck is the way to go.

I think we made great progress on the scallop course—we are going to make a mockery of foam by dumping it all over a very pretty scallop dish. However, the foam will be unstable with methylcellulose f50, so when we scoop it over the dish, the foam burps and disappears by the time the customer eats it. Hard to describe, but I think that Pete, Tosi, and I were really excited by the results. Needs tweaking, but it's a great way to make a statement about the food at Ko, and at the same time it's sort of a tongue-in-cheek jab at foam. Basically, it's there and then it disappears. I hope that it mimics the low tide at the beach.

Everything was so fluid, so changeable. We had no idea what we were doing. But at least we had parameters for once. We wanted to make good dishes. Dishes that were outwardly simple and inwardly complex. Dishes that would make people slap themselves on the forehead, like, "Holy shit, that's so simple and so good."

There was plenty else going on at the time to distract us from turning Ko into something cool.

I was flying around the country, exploring opportunities to expand Momofuku. Vegas was interested. Saying no to some of the deals I was offered out there kept me up at night. I imagined goons with crowbars hunting me down afterward to make me "reconsider."

I flew to Dubai, which cleared up any cobwebs that might have been in my eyes about American hegemony. "America is fucking over," was what I thought after going there. I was told that 70 percent of the world's cranes were there building a new supercity, and the skyline, a thicket of Erector set spires, made that figure seem likely.

Christina Tosi and I looked into converting an old gas station in northern Virginia, where we're from, into a Dairy Queen–like confectionery palace we would call Momofuku Milk Bar.

And, of course, the new Noodle Bar ran behind schedule. We only complicated matters by trying to open it under cover of night, like a bunch of fucking ninjas. I even made a fake menu for "Paul's Grill" and posted it in the window of the space to throw people off.

Then somebody got drunk and let our plans slip to a food blogger, so that was an additional distraction, because everybody wanted to ask questions and speculate about what Ko was going to be, which I didn't have answers to. The media's fascination with Momofuku and me personally didn't end, and I got used to being the asshole in the magazines, even if it wasn't something I ever sought out. For me, the amount of early press we got seemed surreal simply because it was like, "Why does anybody care about us?"

STARTERS

MOZZERLLA STICKS
Marinara Sauce, Parsley   5.95

TUNA TARTARE
Avocado, Wasabi Flying Fish Roe   12.95

KOBE SLIDERS
Shoe String Fries, Trio of Ketchups   11.95

CHICKEN TENDERS
White Meat, Cornbread Crust, Ranch Dressing 10.95

GARDEN SALAD
*Red Onions, Cherry Tomatoes, Blue Cheese
House Dressing*   8.95

ENTREES

GRILLED SWORDFISH
Sauteed Spinach, cherry tomatoes   18.95

BRAISED BERKSHIRE PORK BELLY
Braised Pork Belly, Foie Gras Sauce, Orange 22.95

ROASTED CHICKEN
French Fries or Baked Potato, Garden Salad   15.95

GRILLED TUNA BURGER
*Fresh Sashami Grade Tuna, Wasabi Mashed Potatoes,
Cole Slaw*   17.95

PAUL'S MOM'S MAC & CHEESE
Four Types of Cheeses, Truffle Oil, Fresh Mushrooms
small 8.95 / large 15.95

LOBSTER ROLL
French Fries or Baked Potato, Cole Slaw   M/P

KOBE NY STRIP
Wasabi Bernaise Sauce, Fresh Pasta   38.95

SWEETS

WARM FLOURLESS CHOCOLATE CAKE
dark chocolate cake with vanilla gelato   8.95

PAUL'S

PAUL'S GRILL W/ 24 JUMBO FLAT SCREEN TV'S COMING SOON

COMING SOON!!!

171 First Avenue, New York, NY 10003

By the time Ko was opening it was very literally surreal: one afternoon Kevin Pemoulie and I and a couple of guys from Noodle Bar drank a case of PBR in a glass cube on Sixth Avenue in Midtown as part of an art project somehow connected to an article that I was featured in in *Esquire*. Good or bad, big or small, whatever we did got ink. It was great for business and terrifying for me. People, particularly bloggers, chronicled anything and everything that happened at Momofuku: Ssäm Bar served Diet Dr. Pepper and not Diet Coke, and that was news. It put the pressure on to push myself and my guys harder and harder, always.

So when I was at the restaurants, I didn't see a full dining room or a menu with a bunch of stuff on it that people thought was awesome. I saw fish stored in a way that made my blood boil. I'd find pepper grinders with no pepper in them. See some idiot slicing fish cakes carelessly right in front of me. I went nuts because some dishes had been on the menu too long; I did the same when I saw new dishes on the menu that hadn't been developed enough and weren't ready to go on. I saw everything that could possibly have been wrong going wrong, and I yelled and tossed dullish knives into trash cans and threw temper tantrums and had meetings where I'd castigate the staff for not caring as much as they should or they could.

I knew it from the beginning, from when Quino and I did everything ourselves, but by this point I knew the difference between Momofuku and McDonald's: caring. Caring about every detail. When you start to cook on autopilot, when you buy into bullshit people write about you, when you stop paying attention to details—not to mention big things, like seasoning—no amount of press in the world will make up for it. I preached this to my crew. What is the point of cooking at all if you're not gonna do it right?

And even that sentiment ended up packaged like a ready-for-TV sermon in a story about me in *The New Yorker*. Being Dave Chang was beginning to be like being in *The Truman Show*. The only outlet I had to deal with any of it was getting Ko right.

A couple of months before Ko opened, Tosi and I went to Deauville, France—which is like Paris's Hamptons—to participate in the third annual Omnivore Food Festival. (I was invited because Wylie Dufresne was getting married and Grant Achatz was battling tongue cancer at the time. Still, I've never been so stoked about third place.) I knew René Redzepi, the chef of Noma in Copenhagen, was going to be there—his book and his food are hugely inspiring to me—but I had no idea how cool the whole thing would be: at one point over the weekend Michel Bras cooked staff meal for a kitchen full of chefs. I got to eat it. Insane.

But it was a meal that we ate during a few hours passing through Paris on our way to Omnivore that was the highlight of the trip. It was at a restaurant called L'Astrance run by a chef named Pascal Barbot.

L'Astrance was so strong: no flash, no bullshit, no smoke and mirrors. All pure technique. The kitchen has a dishwasher, two burners, a tiny triangular flattop, and a cramped oven stuffed under those burners. The room is awful—weirdly eighties, very bright, no music. The desserts were non-events. And the savory courses? Perfection.

The meal started with a whole-grain brioche, fresh cheese, and sea salt. Dead simple and absolutely perfect.

A couple more bites, then Barbot unleashed his signature *galette de champignons de Paris et foie gras mariné au verjus, huile de noisette, citron confit* on us. He shaved raw button mushrooms and marinated raw foie gras and layered them into a little tower that was anchored with a disk of pastry. The hazelnut oil added bass, the lemon sparkle and brightness. It was the lightest foie gras course ever. While I was eating it, I thought to myself that I would travel around the world just to eat another dish like it, something so revelatory and delicious. It was the best single plate of food I've ever eaten. And it was made from button mushrooms and raw duck liver. That is badass.

From there, it was something straight out of the Alain Passard or Michel Bras playbook: a bright yellow foam—like something Jean-Georges would do—over a scallop and a prawn, each exceptionally fresh. They were in a reduced fish fumet mounted with curry and coconut milk and surround by petite peeled vegetables: red and green radishes, carrot slivers, snow peas, edible flowers. It could have been so lame, but it was one of the best dishes I've ever had. A perfect mix of spices—every one of them pinpointed to hit you just the right way—made it stand out.

When we were almost done with that dish, they brought out a quenelle of scallop tartare with black truffles in something earthy, like mushroom stock but with lemongrass. And they dropped it right when we were about to be finished with the first scallop dish, and like that, we were totally transported to another planet, another country, while eating that dish. So, from the floral, aromatic flight of fancy to this impossibly earthy dish—both takes on scallops, timed so you don't even have time to recover.

After that, a custard, a parfait of yogurt with Espelette pepper, saffron; it was not seasoned well at all. I was like, "What the fuck is this?" It was good but not insane. Then I figured out what he was doing: resetting our palates. It went on from there: amazing mackerel dish; amazing pollock dish; buttery, cheesy truffled celeriac soup; Chinese-style braised pork belly; fat, rich clams with buttery greens; *tranche* of duck with salsify. Just an all-out assault.

And the service was killer: they did great wine pairings, and they handled all the plate dropping and clearing with amazing grace, but they weren't wearing ties, and there wasn't anything stuffy about how they carried themselves or represented the kitchen. The menu is called "Le Menu Surprise," and you can't ask what's on it or what you'll be served when you order it.

After eating at L'Astrance, I knew I'd rather be like Barbot than anyone else. Because anybody could do what he does, but it's just so hard to do. The difference between à la carte steak on a plate and an orchestrated attack like that—he's like a sniper: one shot, one kill. Superclean, superexact, all about flavors, all about setting you up—each course anticipated the next. He was playing on another level. And despite the dining room and the tiny staff and the fact that he's closed on weekends, he's got three Michelin stars.

My experience at L'Astrance was less an influence than an assurance. It made me feel confident that we could pull off something in a similar spirit—

no printed menu, no coddling, just pure cooking. It could work and succeed and get recognition in Paris. We'd test out the theory in New York.

Eventually we got to fire up the kitchen at Ko and try cooking in it. We'd installed an inferno-hot grill outfitted with a Korean braising grill (tilted, with a gutter to collect the marinade and cooking juices that run off the meat) that we were excited about—we thought we'd run whole côtes de boeuf every once in a while, along with all kinds of other big pieces of meat that two to four diners could share. But the first time we cooked one, everybody and everything in the place smelled like hot meat, and not in a good way. So then we had another restriction: a minimum of à la minute cooking, no huge pieces of meat flaring away on the grill, or our diners would smell like they'd been working in a kitchen by the time they left. We had to cook just enough to make it work. In that way, the space helped dictate and further restrict our menu.

I remember marveling at the coffin-like claustrophobia of the space and the limitations it imposed. It was unbelievable that Noodle Bar came out of that space. To me, it's the most absurd thing ever. One in a billion.

But now we needed to take that space and turn it into a place that would upend expectations about Momofuku, that would earn us stars without flowers or linens or anything in the way of creature comforts.

A couple of weeks before we were going to open, Cory Lane, our GM and wine guy, was trying to teach the crew about wine—how to talk about it, present it, open it, and pour it. I was excited about the idea of putting all the service in the hands of the kitchen, but even on dry runs with nobody in the restaurant, it was clear that wasn't going to work. It's hard enough to figure out who's cooking what without having to remember which side to clear a plate from or make sure that wine is properly presented.

Yet even when we saw that the serverless formula wasn't going to pan out, it started to get exciting: every day we worked on the dishes that would make up the opening menu. We'd make a plate or two, pass it around, critique it, poke it with chopsticks, decide how to refine it, and then repeat the whole process. The first menu—when we finally settled on it—was an interpretation of kaiseki cuisine through an American lens, hence the miso soup dish at the end of the savory courses. It went like this:

Chicharrón with togarashi
English muffin with bay leaf butter
Fluke with whipped buttermilk, white soy, poppy seeds
Kimchi consommé, grilled pork belly, Beau Soleil oysters
Scallop with foaming dashi
Shaved foie gras, lychee, pine nuts, Riesling gelée
Deep-fried short rib, pickled mustard seed, daikon
Miso soup, pickled vegetables, grilled rice
A dessert amuse, either pineapple sorbet (on days the freezer worked)
    or cereal milk, a custard, on days when it didn't
Fried apple pie

We got it to the point where we—Peter Serpico and Sam Gelman and Christina Tosi and I—knew there was no way anyone could say the menu sucked. It didn't. And Peter and Sam kept tweaking and refining it, making it better and better.

It became clear to me and to all of us that we had an opportunity—if everything worked, that is, if we cooked the most beautiful and delicious food—to destroy the notion of what it means to eat in a fine dining restaurant in New York. If it worked, we could open doors for other people to do

something awesome without needing to spend millions on floral arrangements and fancy linens and underpaid illegal busboys.

We planned for two weeks of friends-and-family dinners—giveaways, essentially, for friends and cooks and people who had written about us and would raise hell as soon as the place was officially open, because the online reservation system has no back door. We'd never done anything like it with the first two restaurants, but it made sense: we were going to tweak it for two weeks, so when we opened, we'd know we were on our A-game. There was no back-up plan—if it flopped, we were screwed.

Extended friends and family was the right move. We worked out service, how to cook in the space, how to space out reservations, all that back-end crap that's as boring as wallpaper but important as running water to the experience of eating in a restaurant. We tweaked dishes: the kimchi consommé with oyster and pork belly needed a second oyster slipped into the shell of the first to make it more substantial. There was no way to know that before we watched a few people fumble with eating the dish. The scallop dish with disappearing foam I'd been so psyched about was staying on the menu only because I came up with it, and within a couple weeks of opening, it was gone.

But the feedback from the people we had in to eat was pretty goddamn good. Ruth Reichl wrote a glowing review of us for *Gourmet* before we were even open. Not everybody got it, or got every dish—even the frozen foie gras, which is like the beloved pork bun of Ko, pissed off some people—but in general, we knew we could feel good about what we were doing and continue to push ourselves to push it further. That for as many haters and detractors that were out there—and they are legion—that Ko worked. It did: no flowers, no vests and ties, no starched chef jackets or toques. Just solid cooking. We got the three stars we hoped for from the *New York Times*.

Later, in a very surprising turn of events, we got two stars from the

Michelin Guide. But by that point I was almost out of the equation. Peter Serpico and Sam Gelman, leading a squadron of badass cooks, kept the menu moving forward, taking it to places I couldn't. The opening process and menu had left me winded. I felt like I didn't have any more good ideas left in me, so I pushed Gelman and Serp.

I stepped back into something like an editor's role: we taste new dishes collectively and then just rip them apart. The first question: "Is it fucking dericious? Does it taste awesome?" The best dishes are the ones where you're like, "Man, why didn't I think of this? It's so goddamn good." So it has to taste good.

From there we just continually destroy and rebuild. Anticipate how it will be received. Rework it. We edit new dishes to the point where a person with a normal palate—which to us, means a cook—is going to be like, "That's right on." To the point where there's no way somebody's going hate on it. They may dislike it—a lot of people who come to Ko who might be coming more because it's a hard restaurant to get into than because they're into food—but they can't say it sucks. We want every dish to be well thought out, the sort of preparation that you couldn't argue the effort wasn't there.

There's an apocryphal story about Ben Hogan, my childhood hero. He had just won a tournament, hitting impossible shots one after another on the last three holes.

A reporter asked him, "Mr. Hogan, how is it you can keep making these spectacular shots under such pressure?"

Hogan thought for a minute. "Well, I guess I'm just lucky."

The reporter retorted, "But, Mr. Hogan, you practice more than any golfer in the world."

Hogan thought for a minute more and said, "Well, the more I practice, the luckier I get."

I opened Noodle Bar in 2004 to see how far I could push myself mentally and physically. I saw it as a battle against certain failure. All I knew was that we would work harder than the next guy (I personally wasn't going to leave anything in the tank for the swim back home), and pray to the gods for luck to rain down on us. Strangely, it did.

Winning awards and all the success was never part of the plan. It was about trying to do something honest, a journey of personal growth. But somehow we caught lightning in a bottle.

And looking back, it's amazing to me to see how we've grown. To be a part of a group of talented people—from those who were there at the outset to those who are now trying to push the culinary envelope—all working together and creating this living Momofuku thing.

Part of the reason to write this book was to document what happened over these crazy hyperactive years. But Momofuku isn't about looking backward. If you make it to the restaurants, I'll be happiest if you never see any of these dishes on our menus. It's my belief that everything can be replaced. That there's nothing so sacred it can't be improved upon.

Five years is not a long time, but during these five years we've moved at a ridiculous pace—five openings (we did Noodle Bar twice) that we've poured everything we had into. We found success that we never could have expected or even imagined.

But that's all behind us. We're going to open more restaurants, we're going to work constantly to improve the restaurants we have now, and we're going to keep training new talent and trying to come up with new concepts. We're going to keep our heads down and try to be the most disciplined, knowledgeable, and accountable cooks ever.

And me, I'm burnt out. Fried. At some point "me" evolved into "we." My life stopped being mine and the restaurants' needs replaced any I might have had. I got into the kitchen to get away from sitting at a desk and having to be nice to people, and here I am with a calendar full of events and meetings and food conferences. I opened a noodle bar so I wouldn't have to deal with the expectations of the starred restaurant world and that plan fell flat on its face. (Living up to high expectations sucks.)

But for all that, I know this: I am one very lucky bastard.

chicharrón

A chicharrón to start the meal. I'm sure some people saw it as a little "fuck you" to kick off an $85 menu, and I can't say that there wasn't some of that in serving a fried pork rind to start a fancy dinner; it's not an amuse-bouche in the traditional sense. But, really, chicharrones have what it takes to be a great amuse: fat, salt, spice, and crunch all in one bite.

And even more than that, we were really excited about pork rinds at the time. I'd been involved in many failed attempts to make them over the years at Noodle Bar and at Ssäm Bar. We'd had a copy of chef Brad Thompson's chicharrón recipe kicking around the restaurants for years, but we couldn't ever get it to work. Why? Because we are idiots.

All we had to do was follow the directions to the letter: boil and chill, scrape and dry, shatter and fry. It's not hard, but it requires discipline if you want a great product, and we never had enough discipline until Ko. (Once we got them right, I called Brad at Mary Elaine's at the Phoenician in Arizona, where he was the chef at the time, and got permission to cop it for our menu.)

If you undertake the making of chicharrones, allow enough time to thoroughly dedicate yourself to the task. Boil the skin and chill until cold—don't go at it when it's hot or warm or at room temperature. Be patient. Make sure to scrape all of the fat off. Everything but the skin should be gone, or the chips won't fry up right. Dry the skin out in a food dehydrator. While it is possible to press it against a baking sheet and park it in a 150°F oven overnight or something, we have not found that to be anywhere near as reliable a method. The dehydrator is the engine of certain success.

Quantities don't matter much for this recipe. The skin cut from a 3- to 4-pound piece of pork belly will yield about 12 chicharrones (which would be 12 amuse servings or one nice bag of pork rinds), but you can do it for as much or as little skin as you like.

Pig skin, nipples (if present) trimmed off

Shichimi togarashi (Japanese 7-spice powder)

Kosher salt

1 to 2 quarts (liters) rendered pork or duck fat or grapeseed or other neutral oil for deep-frying

1. Put the pork skin in a pot that accommodates it with room to spare and fill the pot nearly to the brim with cold water. Bring the water to a boil over high heat and boil it hard for 1½ hours, replenishing the water as necessary to keep the skin submerged. At the end, the water will be milky with fat and the kitchen will smell piggy.

2. Remove the skin from the water and, handling it gently as not to tear it, unfurl it onto a cooling rack (perhaps set over a rimmed baking sheet to collect any runoff). Discard the water and put the skin, uncovered, in the fridge to chill thoroughly. After the skin is cold, you can wrap it in plastic and chill it for up to a week before proceeding with the recipe.

3. Clean the pork skin: Lay it out fat side up on a cutting board. Using the side of a spoon, scrape all of the fat off the skin. Scrape gently but with determination. Take care not to rip the skin, and do not leave any but the most stubborn fat behind. Any patches of fat that refuse to detach from the skin will need to be cut out or off, since they'll have the texture of soggy packing peanuts if fried.

4. Arrange the scraped skin in the trays of a food dehydrator. Dehydrate the skin for 12 hours. It should be dry, crisp, and shiny, like a piece of brown plastic.

5. Break the skin up into rough 1-by-2-inch rectangles (or disks the size of a casino chip) with your hands—they will expand to about twice their size when fried. At this point, you can store them at room temperature in a sealed container with a little packet of silica gel dessicant (like the kind that might come in the box with a new pair of sneakers or a packet of Japanese snack crackers, and which says "DO NOT EAT" on it for a very good reason) for days, if not weeks.

6. Mix together a couple of tablespoons of shichimi togarashi and salt.

7. Heat the fat to between 390° and 400°F in a smallish pot with high sides. When the oil reaches temperature, drop in a chip of pork skin and gently agitate it in the oil with a slotted spoon until it blows up and gets crisp, 10 to 12 seconds. (It's unwise to try and fry more than one at a time unless you're frying in a really huge pot, because the chicharrones will stick together.) Remove the chicharrón from the oil; drain it on a paper towel set on a cooling rack and season it while hot with the togarashi and salt mixture. Fry the remaining chicharrones. Serve the chicharrones hot or at room temperature.

english muffin

MAKES ABOUT 4 DOZEN MINI OR 2 DOZEN FULL-SIZE ENGLISH MUFFINS

After the chicharrón, while you're nursing a glass of champagne or sparkling wine or whatever, comes the English muffin, our "bread service." It's filling enough to stave off any serious hunger, but not so imposing that it's going to threaten the appetite you'll need to finish off the whole meal.

As for how it got on the menu: it just happened.

At some point in the menu development process, we realized we needed a bread course. Bread service is one of the ways haute cuisine restaurants differentiate themselves from their peers.

Whatever we did had to fit into the streamlined menu at Ko—a bread course, not a bread basket. I asked Christina Tosi to come up with something for it, something that checked off the bread requirement, something warm and comforting. I wanted a "fat bomb," something salty and buttery and rich.

We talked through a lot of possibilities—savory macaroons, bread with unmelted butter baked inside of it (which we ultimately figured out, though it took months and months of tinkering)—but one day shortly before we opened Tosi made these muffins and it was just, like, yep, these are going on. They have that familiar thing in common with chicharrones and the fried apple pie, but by making them ourselves, we were able to elevate them.

Ko English muffins are about half the size of store-bought English muffins, loaded with nooks and crannies, and the schmear of bay leaf–infused lard-butter is as delicious as it is subtle. They also fit soundly into the technique-driven rhythm of Ko: they're not hard to make (like, you're not carving a swan out of a melon), but they demand focus and attention if they're to come out right.

2 tablespoons plus 1 teaspoon (12 grams) active dry yeast (a little less than the contents of two ¼-ounce packets)

¼ cup (50 grams) lukewarm water

1¾ cups (400 grams) buttermilk

4 cups (600 grams) bread flour, plus more as needed

¼ cup (50 grams) sugar

1 tablespoon plus 2 teaspoons (22 grams) kosher salt

5 tablespoons (70 grams) unsalted butter, at room temperature

Nonstick vegetable oil spray

Cornmeal as needed (or yellow grits, in a pinch)

Bay Leaf Butter (page 238) as needed

Maldon salt

Chives, cut into 1-inch-long batons (2 per English muffin)

1. Combine the yeast and water in the bowl of a stand mixer outfitted with the dough hook and whisk together to dissolve the yeast.

2. Nuke the buttermilk in the microwave for 20 to 30 seconds, or warm it over low heat in a small pan on the stovetop just until it loses the refrigerator chill; you're not really heating the buttermilk, but ensuring that chilly milk won't retard the dough's rise. Stir the no-longer-cold buttermilk into the yeast and water.

3. Add the flour, sugar, and kosher salt to the bowl, turn the mixer on to low/medium-low speed, and process just until it comes together as a shaggy, droopy dough, 3 to 4 minutes.

4. With the mixer still running, add the butter to the dough a tablespoon at a time. (Make sure it's at room temperature—you'll overwork the dough trying to incorporate cold butter into it.) The dough will look as if it is separating, and from this point on it will hang out at the bottom of the bowl, reaching up the dough hook like an appendage of the sandman but never fully coalescing into a ball again. Knead it for 7 to 8 minutes, by which time it should be tacky but no longer sticky and hold its shape.

5. Lightly spray a large mixing bowl with oil. Using a rubber spatula, scrape the dough from the mixer bowl into the greased bowl. Cover with plastic wrap and leave the dough to rest, relax, and rise (though it doesn't rise so much as it expands in the bowl) for 1 hour.

6. After the dough has risen, put it into the refrigerator for 30 minutes to 1 hour to chill, to make it easier to handle.

7. While the dough's resting, line a couple of rimmed baking sheets with parchment paper and cover them each with a ¼-inch-deep layer of cornmeal, into which you will nestle your muffins. (That's way more cornmeal than will stick to the muffins, but whatever's left over will be fine to use in another recipe.)

8. Scatter your work surface with a very, very fine dusting of flour, and very lightly flour your hands. Turn the dough out onto the work surface and knead it a few times to deflate it. Shape it into a fat, smoothish log. For Ko-sized mini English muffins, pinch off clumps the size of Ping-Pong balls (if you're working with a scale, they should weigh 30 grams). For traditional-size English muffins, pinch off pieces about the size of a handball (which should weigh about 60 grams). With lightly floured palms, roll the pieces of dough into neat balls, applying as little pressure as possible. The dough should be pillowy and tender and delicate and have the tiniest bit of spring to it. As you shape them, transfer the balls of dough, one by one, to the baking sheet: Nestle each ball of dough into the cornmeal, then pat it down gently so some of the cornmeal adheres to the bottom of the future muffin, grab the ball very gently by its sides (the parts you don't want cornmeal on), and flip it over, gently patting the cornmealed top so the bottom picks up some of the cornmeal. Leave about an inch between the muffins, giving them enough space to stretch and rise as they may need. You can proceed with the recipe directly, or you can wrap the baking sheets of proofing dough in plastic wrap and put them in the fridge to chill for 30 minutes, after which time the muffins will be easier to handle. You can also take a longer break: wrapped and refrigerated, the muffins will keep (and improve) for up to 3 days.

9. Turn the oven on to 250°F. Warm a cast-iron skillet or griddle over the lowest heat setting possible for 5 or so minutes. You should be able to comfortably hold your hand very close to the pan and just feel some radiant heat—nothing that would make you want to pull your hand back. Scatter the pan with a thin, even layer of cornmeal and warm for a minute more.

10. Grab the proofed muffins one by one by their uncornmealed sides, dust off any excess cornmeal clinging to their tops and bottoms (you want a thin even coating, not a thick jacket), and transfer them to the pan, working in batches. This is the all-important nooks-and-crannies-forming stage of English muffin cookery: you want the muffins to rise and griddle-bake *slowly*. You almost can't take enough time with this stage. (And if at any point before the final couple of minutes of cooking you smell cornmeal toasting or browning, instead of just warming, turn the heat down.) After about 4 minutes, their tops will begin to puff and dome: that's your cue to flip them. Use a small offset spatula to flip them if you have one (and buy one to do so the next time if you don't—your fingers will leave prints). After 4 or 5 minutes on the second side, the bottoms of the muffins should be forming delicate but noticeable skins. Flip them again, cook for another 5 to 6 minutes, and then flip them again. The tops and bottoms of the muffins should be firm, but the muffins should still feel airy and light. Once they're at that point (you may have to gently cook and gently flip them one more time before they get to the handleably delicate stage), you can nudge up the heat slightly, and, turning them every 2 to 3 minutes, toast their tops and bottoms. (Here the smell of toasting cornmeal is okay.)

11. When the muffins are toasted—tops and bottoms mottled with brown, but mainly golden—transfer them to a baking sheet, and put them in the oven for 10 minutes to finish baking. Remove from the oven and let them cool on the baking sheet until they reach room temperature.

12. Use the tines of a fork to puncture an equator of tiny holes around the middle of each muffin, and then pry them apart into two halves. Spread

RECIPE CONTINUES

each half with a generous teaspoon of the bay leaf butter. Heat a cast-iron or other skillet over medium-high heat for a minute or two, until good and hot, and then sear the muffin halves fat side down for 30 or so seconds, until browned and crisped. Sprinkle the muffins with Maldon salt, arrange a couple of chive batons on each, and serve hot.

bay leaf butter
MAKES ABOUT ½ CUP

SOS Chefs, a specialty store near the restaurant, had these beautiful fresh bay leaves one day that I couldn't not buy. And as a company we are always looking for ways to use up pork fat. The math is pretty simple from there.

8 fresh bay leaves

¼ cup plus 1 tablespoon (60 grams) rendered pork fat, chilled

4 tablespoons (½ stick; 50 grams) unsalted butter

Scant 1 teaspoon (3 grams) kosher salt

1. Roughly chop the bay leaves, then give them a good mashing in a mortar and pestle.

2. Combine the pork fat and butter and warm in a small saucepan over low heat or in a bowl in the microwave until melted and melded. Remove from the heat, add the bay leaf mush to the warm fat, and let it steep for about an hour, stirring it occasionally for good measure, and lightly rewarming the mixture if the fat threatens to congeal.

3. Strain the bay leaf mess out of the fat by passing the fat through a fine-mesh strainer. Discard the bay, and put the strained fat in the refrigerator to chill until it firms up.

4. Put the chilled bay-scented fat and salt in the bowl of a stand mixer outfitted with the paddle attachment. Paddle it on medium-high speed for 5 to 10 minutes—it should have a superglossy sheen to it like you've never seen before. Scrape it out of the bowl and store it in the refrigerator until needed; it will keep for up to a month, though it's best shortly after it's been made.

fluke buttermilk, soy & poppy seeds SERVES 8

You've had the salty pig chip. And the buttery English muffin. Now it's time for raw fish. We cycled through a few ideas before this one, but when it came together, it was a clear winner: not too weird (in fact, the buttermilk and hot sauce have a Buffalo wing kind of thing going on—the night we made it for the first time, a couple weeks before Ko was set to open, we ate all the extra buttermilk dressing drizzled onto baked potatoes) and very simple looking. We had talked about the dish for months—Serpico and I pirated the poppy-seeds-with-fish idea from the langoustine carpaccio with roasted poppy seed dressing we ate during a research lunch at L'Atelier de Joël Robuchon in Midtown—but we never tried to make it until just before we opened, because we knew it would work.

If you can't find great fluke for the dish, substitute similarly sliced diver scallops. Some nights, we mix up the menu and alternate fluke and diver scallops between diners.

Buttermilk Dressing (recipe follows)

Two 10- to 12-ounce (280- to 360-gram) skinless fluke fillets

4 teaspoons (12 grams) Shiro Shoyu Vinaigrette (recipe follows)

2 teaspoons (7 grams) poppy seeds

2 tablespoons 1-inch-long chive batons

Maldon salt

1. Put a tablespoon or so of the buttermilk dressing in the bottom of each of eight chilled shallow bowls.

2. Thinly slice the fluke a little less than ¼ inch thick. (Bonus points for slicing the fluke on a 30- to 35-degree bias—not so exaggerated as a traditional 45-degree bias cut, but with a little more finesse than the slices will have if you just cut with your knife perpendicular to the cutting board.) Fan the slices out over the buttermilk dressing.

3. Add ½ teaspoon of the vinaigrette to each plate, around the rim of the buttermilk sauce. Scatter ¼ teaspoon poppy seeds over each serving, and follow with some chive batons and a tiny pinch of Maldon salt. Serve at once.

buttermilk dressing
MAKES ½ CUP

⅓ cup (100 grams) buttermilk

2½ tablespoons (30 grams) sour cream

Scant ½ teaspoon (1.5 grams) kosher salt, or more if needed

Generous ¼ teaspoon (1 gram) sriracha (Asian chile sauce), or more if needed

Whisk together the buttermilk and sour cream in a small bowl. Whisk in the salt and sriracha, and taste: it should have some heat but it shouldn't be "spicy." Add more salt or sriracha to taste. Refrigerate until ready to use, or for up to a few days.

shiro shoyu vinaigrette
MAKES ABOUT ¼ CUP

¼ cup (70 grams) shiro shoyu (white soy sauce)

⅛ teaspoon (2 grams) bottled sudachi lime or yuzu juice

1½ teaspoons (7 grams) mirin

A tiny dot (0.5 gram) green yuzu kosho (jarred yuzu and chile paste)

Stir together the soy sauce, lime juice, mirin, and yuzu kosho in a small bowl. Store for up to a month in the fridge.

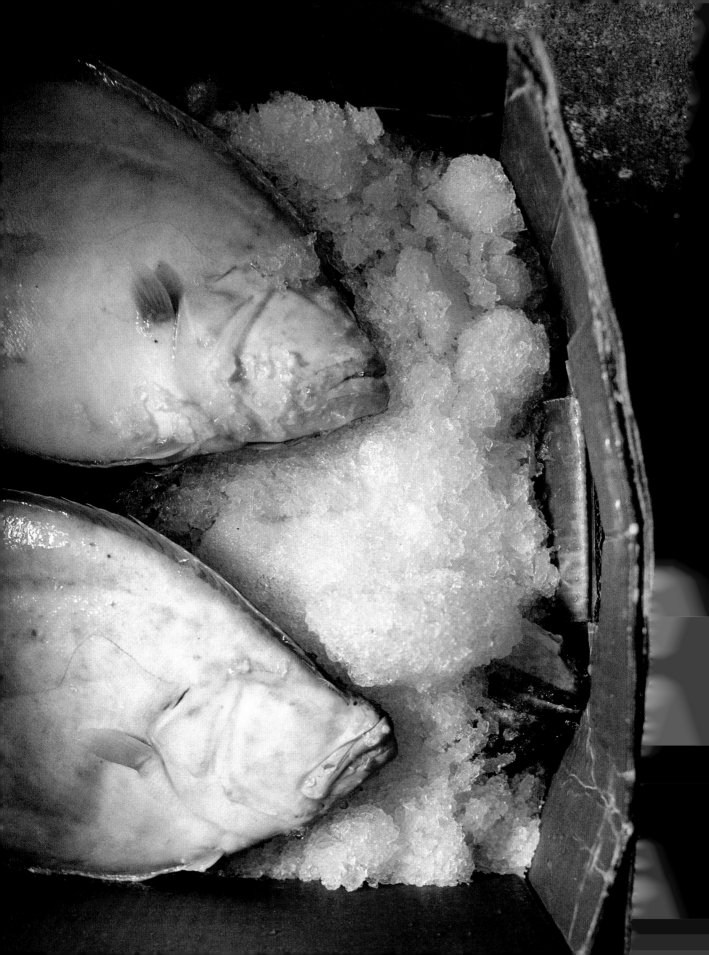

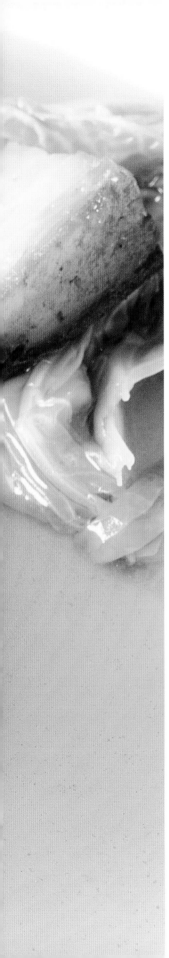

ko kimchi consommé
pork belly, oysters & napa cabbage SERVES 8

So the bo ssäm at Ssäm Bar is our revision and interpretation of classic Korean bo ssäm. This is bo ssäm taken to another place, further from the source material but still recognizable. The kimchi becomes kimchi consommé, the oyster takes on prominence, and the pork and the "wrap"—in this case, cabbage—recede into the background. In the progression of the menu, it is like a second raw seafood course, though one that includes more pork belly than most.

Kimchi consommé was already a standard preparation at Ssäm Bar, so to take the idea somewhere else, we ditched the gelatin clarification and went back to the traditional consommé clarification technique, and we used pork stock in addition to water to thin out the kimchi puree. The result is a more muscular, more deeply colored, more robust kimchi consommé. At the restaurant, we heat up the consommé in little sake carafes and pour the consommé into the bowl in front of the diner to make it even more soigné.

Otherwise, the dish is very straightforward. The belly is prepared in a similar fashion to the way it is at our other restaurants; the cabbage is trimmed and simply blanched. After a few nights of friends-and-family, we realized that one oyster wasn't enough but two shells in the bowl were a pain, so we started doubling them up in one shell. We use East Coast oysters for this dish—East Coast oyster shells are less brittle than those from the West—and we prefer smaller oysters, like those from Beausoleil or La St. Simon.

8 nice big leaves of Napa cabbage

16 oysters, very, very well scrubbed, shucked (see page 132), and left in the half-shell

Pork Belly for Ko Kimchi Consommé (opposite)

2 cups (400 grams) Ko Kimchi Consommé (page 248), hot

1. Put a large pot of water on to boil and salt it well. Prepare an ice water bath in a large mixing bowl.

2. Make a triangular incision in each of the cabbage leaves to cut out the large, tough white rib. Blanch the cabbage leaves in the boiling water for 10 seconds, just until they begin to soften. Use a large slotted spoon or spider to transfer the blanched leaves to the ice bath. Drain them well and reserve until ready to use. We typically reheat them in a low oven just until warm to the touch.

3. Fold each cabbage leaf over onto itself—make it look nice, but make it into a convenient shape for the oyster shell to lean against, so it stays upright. Place a cabbage leaf just off the center of each of eight small shallow bowls, and nestle a shucked oyster in its shell right next to it. Slide a second oyster out of its shell onto the oyster already in each bowl. Arrange the pork belly next to the oyster and pour enough kimchi consommé into each bowl to fill it up by a few millimeters—not enough to even get close to the brim of the oyster shells. Serve hot.

pork belly for ko kimchi consommé

SERVES 8

This is a lightly modified version of the way we make belly for buns and ssäm and everything else—it's pressed after it's cooked, so it's denser and easier to cut. If you have it on hand, you can substitute belly prepared for those other recipes.

1. Nestle the belly into a roasting pan or other oven-safe vessel that holds it snugly. Mix together the salt and sugar in a small bowl and rub the mix all over the meat; discard any excess salt-and-sugar mixture. Cover the container with plastic wrap and put it into the fridge for at least 6 hours, but no longer than 24.

2. Heat the oven to 270°F.

3. Discard any liquid that's accumulated in the pan, then put the belly in the oven, fat side up, and cook for 3 hours, basting it with the rendered fat every hour, until it's yieldingly tender.

4. Sandwich the belly between two rimmed baking sheets, wrap them in plastic, and put something heavy on the top pan to weight and press down the belly. Put the whole setup in the refrigerator to chill overnight. You can complete the preparation through this step a couple of days in advance.

5. Unwrap the belly and cut it into scalene triangles: long, narrow, and tapered. You need two per dish.

6. Light a good hot fire in a grill, or get a cast-iron pan or grill pan scorching hot.

7. Grill the pork belly slices for 2 to 3 minutes, until you've got grill marks running one way on the meat, then rotate it 45 degrees to mark the meat with a nice crosshatch and warm it through, no more than 4 to 5 minutes total. Use at once.

One 1-pound (450-gram) slab of skinless pork belly

2 tablespoons (24 grams) kosher salt

2 tablespoons (30 grams) sugar

ko kimchi consommé

MAKES ABOUT 1 QUART

2 large egg whites

¼ pound (115 grams) ground pork, preferably very lean

1 very small onion, chopped

1 cup (260 grams) Napa Cabbage Kimchi (page 74)

2 cups (420 grams) Ramen Broth (page 40), cold, skimmed of as much fat as possible

2½ cups (500 grams) cold water

1. Whip the egg whites to soft peaks in a large mixing bowl. Add the pork and onion and mix well.

2. Put the kimchi in a blender jar and puree it until smooth, just a minute or two. Pour it into a small stockpot, add the broth and water, and top with the pork-egg-onion cloud. Bring to a slow simmer over medium-low heat, gently stirring the contents every once in a while so they don't stick to the bottom or sides of the pot. The meat and egg white mixture will eventually coagulate into a "raft," a disk of egg and meat floating on top of the liquid, which will capture any loose bits or impurities in the broth. Keep it moist: use a large spoon to baste the raft regularly—like every couple of minutes—with the broth.

3. A couple of minutes after the raft forms—after maybe 25 to 30 minutes total simmering time—carefully remove it from the pot, then use a ladle to transfer the clarified broth to a clean container, passing it through a strainer lined with cheesecloth, paper towels, or a coffee filter at least once, twice if there is any fine debris in it. Note that you *do not* want to cook the consommé longer than needed during either clarification or reheating, or you will cook the kimchi flavor out of it and possibly make it cloudy. *Do not* boil it to reheat it, or reheat it for longer than necessary when plating the dish. It will turn to shit. The kimchi consommé will keep in the refrigerator for up to 1 week.

soft-cooked hen egg
caviar, onions & potato SERVES 8

Almost every great French restaurant has a signature egg dish. Alain Passard's L'Arpège serves his *chaud-froid d'oeuf fermier, sirop d'érable,* a warm, runny egg topped with a cold cloud of whipped cream flavored with maple syrup. It's an amazing eating experience. Or Jean-Georges Vongerichten's signature "Oeuf au Caviar": an eggshell cut open with Fabergé-like precision and filled with perfectly scrambled eggs, with vodka-flavored whipped cream and a huge dollop of beluga caviar on top. This dish takes its inspiration from that juxtaposition of humble and decadent, playing the creamy richness of hen eggs against the salty pop of fish eggs.

It took us a while to get an idea that we all felt worked. One of the first drafts of the menu we passed around mentioned coddled hen eggs with a mushroom ragout. Around that time, I was playing with the idea that we should soak and stain the egg in a way inspired by but not at all technically related to the way the Chinese make 1,000-year-old eggs (which are "cooked" in an alkaline solution).

The first iteration of the Ko egg course that we actually made included a "soy sauce soft egg" (4-minute eggs, chilled in an ice bath, peeled, and soaked in soy sauce flavored with ginger and star anise), a fines herbes salad, roasted pecans, and country ham dust. We sliced the eggs in half neatly and cleanly with a strand of fly-fishing tippet. Eventually we reeled back on the soaking of the egg, deciding that the soy sauce egg was too blunt of an instrument at that juncture in the meal, as was the country ham, and that the dish needed finesse, not bombast.

But I wasn't over that soaked-egg idea. Somehow I got it in my head that we should use a smoked egg. We tried using a few drops of Liquid Smoke in a large quantity of water and then soaking peeled 5-minute eggs in it, but, even highly diluted, the Liquid Smoke discolored the eggs in a way that wasn't quite right. Eventually we started cold-smoking water—literally putting a big container of cold water in the smoker in the kitchen at Noodle Bar—and soaking the eggs in that, so they stay perfectly white but have a faint trace of smokiness to them.

Soon enough we got around to this combination. It's a harmonious mix of things that are delicious to eat on their own and are even better together: a runny egg, caviar (we use American, because it's delicious, affordable-ish, and isn't emptying the Black Sea of sturgeon), onion soubise (about as luxurious as onions can be, plus they make a perfect nest for holding the egg), freshly made potato chips (which add crunch), a little fines herbes salad mix (the anise-like flavor of the chervil complements the smokiness), and the secret weapon, sweet potato vinegar, which adds color and acid to help balance the dish and bring everything together.

Onion Soubise (recipe follows), warmed

Fingerling Potato Chips (opposite)

½ loosely packed cup (9 grams) Fines Herbes Salad (opposite)

8 "Smoked" Eggs (page 256) or 5:10 Eggs (page 256), warmed

2 ounces (50 grams) American hackleback caviar

Smoked salt

4 teaspoons (20 grams) sweet potato vinegar or, failing that, top-quality sherry vinegar

We serve this dish in a very wide, very shallow bowl, almost like a concave plate. Putting together the dish, we imagine the middle of the plate as a circle: the right half of the circle should be onion soubise, two-thirds of the left half should be potato chips, and the remainder—the part of the circle that will face the diner—a little pile of fines herbes salad. Make a small indentation into the onions on each plate, using the back of a spoon, and nestle an egg in it. Split the egg open a little more than halfway with a small knife, and then use a small spoon to sneak the caviar into the egg and settle it into the yellow river of yolk spilling out onto the plate. Add a few grains of smoked salt on top of each egg and a tiny splash of sweet potato vinegar over by the onions. Serve immediately.

onion soubise
MAKES ABOUT 1¼ CUPS

Tender, tender onions in an emulsified sauce of butter, onion juice, and water.

¾ pound (340 grams) yellow onions

4 tablespoons (½ stick; 58 grams) unsalted butter, preferably at room temperature

½ cup (100 grams) water

1 teaspoon (4 grams) kosher salt

1. Peel the onions. Cut them in half through the root-stem axis, and then, working in the same direction, slice the halves into ¼-inch-or-so-thick slices—they should be thin but not too thin—with a knife or on a mandoline. You should have 2½ to 3 loosely packed cups sliced onions.
2. Combine the onions, butter, water, and salt in a saucepan large enough to accommodate them snugly. Turn the heat under the pan to its lowest setting and cook, keeping the heat immoderately low and gentle, for 2 hours, stirring occasionally. Remember that you are trying *not* to color or brown the onions at all.
3. After 2 hours, the onions should be tender and sweet and the butter and water should have quietly reduced into a satiny sauce that cloaks the onions (if it's still loose and watery or the onions are not completely yielding, continue cooking). Use the soubise immediately, or let it cool and then store, covered, in the refrigerator for up to a week. Warm through just before serving

fingerling potato chips

MAKES ABOUT 2 CUPS

1. Scrub the potatoes clean. Then, working over a small mixing bowl nearly full of cold water, slice the potatoes into thin-as-possible disks using a mandoline. The slices should be see-through thin. Remove excess starch from the potatoes by rinsing them in one or two changes of water, until the water is clear.

2. Pour about 1½ inches of oil into a deep saucepan (the oil will sputter and violently bubble up when you add the potatoes, and you don't want it bubbling over the rim of the pan—nobody wants to deal with a grease fire). Heat the oil to 360°F, using a thermometer to monitor its temperature. (Oil that's too hot can impart a nasty flavor; oil that's too cool won't crisp the potatoes.) Have a plate covered in a double thickness of paper towels near at hand.

3. Wring out a couple handfuls of potatoes, blot them even drier on a paper or kitchen towel, and pile them in a spider or slotted spoon with a long handle. Plunge the potatoes into the hot oil and immediately stir them, agitating the contents of the pan until the bubbling subsides. Fry them for 3 to 3½ minutes, stirring regularly to prevent the potatoes from sticking to each other, until crisp and very lightly browned. Remove the fried potatoes to the paper towels and season immediately and heavily with salt. Wring out another handful of potatoes and repeat, replacing the paper towels you're draining the chips on as necessary and keeping an eye on the temperature of oil. When all the potatoes are cooked and cooled, remove them from the paper towels and reserve until ready to use, or eat straightaway.

4 finger-sized fingerling potatoes, very well scrubbed

Grapeseed or other neutral oil for deep-frying

Kosher salt

fines herbes salad

This one is pretty loose and easy, depending on what's available to you. We mix two parts chervil leaves to one part parsley leaves and one part chives cut into inch-long batons. Tarragon is a soigné substitute for the parsley or a good stand-in for the chervil if you can't find it.

5:10 eggs

MAKES AS MANY AS YOU CHOOSE TO COOK

This is simply a soft-boiled egg, though we've honed in on 5 minutes and 10 seconds as the perfect length of time for the ratio of runny yolk to firm white we want for the dish. Make sure to boil more eggs than you need for this preparation—not all of them will peel perfectly. I'd boil a dozen eggs, hoping to get eight perfect ones for the dish. If you end up with extra eggs, it's easy to find other uses for them—like sandwiched between the halves of an English Muffin (page 235) for a Ko Egg McMuffin.

Large eggs, as many as you like

1. Bring a large pot of water to a boil. Gently lower the eggs, in their shells, into the boiling water with a slotted spoon or spider. (Some will crack, though they should still be usable even if they're not beautiful.) Set a kitchen timer for 5 minutes and 10 seconds from the moment the eggs go into the water, and prepare an ice water bath for the eggs in a large deep mixing bowl.

2. When the timer rings, use the spoon or spider to transfer the eggs to the ice water. Peel the eggs when they are cool enough to handle, cracking them open on a cutting board and then peeling them underwater, in the bowl. (We've found that the little bit of water that sneaks in between the shell and the white as you work helps with the peeling.) Reserve the eggs in the fridge until ready to use, or for up to 8 hours. Warm them for a minute under hot running tap water before serving.

"smoked" eggs: Soak peeled 5:10 eggs in the fridge in smoked water, which is water that's been parked in a cold-smoker for an hour or so, just until it's picked up the flavor of the smoke. Or, if you're not going to be smoking water—and I can't say I blame you, I'm just putting it out there as this is how we serve the dish at Ko—you can do a couple drops of Liquid Smoke in a couple gallons of water and soak the eggs in it for a couple hours in the fridge (or just omit the smoke soak all together and serve 5:10 eggs).

roasted new jersey diver scallop
kohlrabi puree & iwa nori SERVES 8

While we were developing dishes for Ko, Tosi and I were making nori puffs and dashi puffs and foams with a hydrocolloid called methylcellulose f50—Dave Arnold gave us a big batch. During one of my many accidents with f50, while trying to make a foam, I learned that if you add too little f50 to a certain amount of liquid, it becomes very unstable—that the foam pops and vanishes, like the way waves lapping at the shore hit, bubble, and then retreat into the sea. Hey, you work in stainless-steel-walled rooms long enough, and your imagination starts doing strange things.

I decided I wanted to highlight this "technique." I thought it would help us capture the essence of the sea while, even if it was only apparent to me, sending up the whole idea of "foam" as a culinary concept. If we timed it right during service, we could exaggerate the entire foam experience—put way too much foam on the dish and then have it disappear in seconds. We'd make it with dashi, which tastes like seaweed and fish, and the foam would revert to a liquid state and mingle with nori puree to make it look like a plate of seafood garnished with algae-laden seawater at low tide.

So when we started out, the idea was to do a roasted rouget or scallop, depending on what was fresh, with sea beans, pickled chanterelles, nori puree, and the finishing tidal wave of dashi foam.

It was a very calculated dish. Most people hated it. Gradually Serpico and Gelman defected to the haters' side too: having to whip up foam with a granny-style hand mixer twenty-four times a night got to be tiring, and the noise it generated didn't ultimately pay off on the plate.

So the dish was almost constantly in flux during the early months. This recipe is for version 1.5. Depending on what is in the market or available, the puree can be mushrooms—like black trumpets—and the pickles can be fennel instead of chanterelles. Version 2.0 saw scallops replaced with local trout, and Serpico changed the kohlrabi puree to bacon puree; for 2.5, late-spring wax beans replaced the already-gone sea beans. The dish kept on changing until it had nothing to do with the original bad idea. Sometimes that's how it goes.

Note that the pickup and assembly on this dish is very quick. Have small dishes or pans of bacon dashi and kohlrabi puree hot and in close reach; have the mushrooms, iwa nori, scallions, and finishing salt near, and eight shallow bowls near at hand too.

Grapeseed or other neutral oil, as needed

8 large diver scallops

Kosher salt and freshly ground white pepper

8 tablespoons (1 stick; 115 grams) unsalted butter

Kohlrabi Puree (opposite)

Pickled Chanterelles (opposite)

1 scallion, cut into incredibly fine 1-inch-long julienne, soaked in cold water for a few minutes, and drained

½ cup (3 grams) iwa (or unpressed) nori

1 cup (200 grams) Bacon Dashi (page 45), hot

Maldon salt

1. Heat the grapeseed oil in a wide cast-iron skillet over high heat for 1 minute, until it's good and hot. While the oil's heating up, pat the scallops dry with a paper towel and season them on both sides with salt and white pepper. Add the scallops to the pan one at a time, leaving space between them, and lightly press down on each with the back of your hand when you do so, to ensure the entire face of the scallop browns evenly. After a minute and a half, once the scallops have begun to color, add the butter to the pan. Tilt the pan back toward you and use a large spoon to scoop up the melting butter and baste the scallops with it. Cook them on the same side for another 1½ minutes, or until the side facing the pan is deeply browned but the scallops are not entirely cooked through. Remove the scallops from the pan to a paper towel–lined plate to rest, browned side up, while you put together the rest of the dish.

2. Plop a generous tablespoon of kohlrabi puree down in the middle of each shallow bowl, then use the back of the spoon to draw it out from the center and up the side of the bowl. Place a scallop in the middle of each bowl, on top of the kohlrabi smear. Arrange a few pickled chanterelles on and around each scallop, then a few strands of julienned scallions on top of the mushrooms. Arrange a few pieces of iwa nori in the kohlrabi puree. Finish with a few tablespoons of hot bacon dashi per bowl, added gently so as not to disturb everything else in the dish. Put a pinch of Maldon salt on each scallop, and serve at once.

kohlrabi puree

MAKES ABOUT ½ CUP

Put the kohlrabi in a small saucepan, add the salt, and pour in enough water to barely cover. Simmer the kohlrabi over medium-high heat until it offers no resistance to the tip of a sharp knife, about 20 minutes. Drain it, mash it, and pass it through a fine-mesh strainer or a tamis. Taste, add salt as needed, and reserve until ready to use, up to a few hours. Warm gently before serving.

1 medium or 2 small kohlrabi (500 grams), peeled and cut into rough chunks

1 teaspoon (4 grams) kosher salt, or more to taste

pickled chanterelles

MAKES ABOUT ½ CUP

1. Put the chanterelles in a strainer and rinse clean under cold tap water. (Don't buy into that whole line about never washing mushrooms; it's bullshit for most mushrooms.) Wash them well, just handle them delicately so they don't crumble.

2. Combine the hot water, vinegar, sugar, and salt in a container with a lid and shake until the sugar dissolves, then add the mushrooms. Seal the container and put it in the refrigerator. The chanterelles can be used after a few hours and will keep for up to a week.

½ cup (35 grams) chanterelles

½ cup water (110 grams), piping hot from the tap

¼ cup (50 grams) rice wine vinegar

3 tablespoons (45 grams) sugar

1 teaspoon (4 grams) kosher salt

foie gras

There is a growing movement in the United States to demonize foie gras as the product of some kind of perverse abuse of animals perpetrated exclusively in the name of oligarchs who pay top dollar for it. All I can say to that is this: bullshit.

I'm sure there are absolutely fucking horrible places around the world doing terrible things to ducks in the name of foie gras. But that's not the case at Hudson Valley (our local producer, and one of very few foie gras farms in North America) and I very, very strongly doubt it's the case at any top-flight foie gras operation. Just after we'd opened Ko, after we'd decided we'd be serving foie gras, we got a bunch of the guys together and took a trip up there to see and learn more about foie instead of just buying into an opinion about it.

This is the building at Hudson Valley Foie Gras where the ducks live—a large, well-ventilated building with lots of fresh air and daylight and drinking water for the ducks. The ducks have plenty of room to waddle about.

Hudson Valley handles every aspect of the foie gras making process, from duckling to carcass (and the meat of their ducks is excellent, too). We went there as a crew to see the whole process firsthand, so we'd have a more complete knowledge of the ingredient we were working with and a deeper understanding of what a duck's life and death were like to help us in striving to respectfully honor its gifts.

For the last few weeks before slaughter, ducks that are raised for foie gras are fed huge helpings of grain to fatten their livers to a few times their normal size. The ducks we saw getting fed didn't seem to mind at all and the ducks around the farm all seemed pretty happy—I mean, I'm not a vet, and I don't think I'd want to be an animal that was raised for meat, but as far as farm animals go, they seemed to be pretty cool with things.

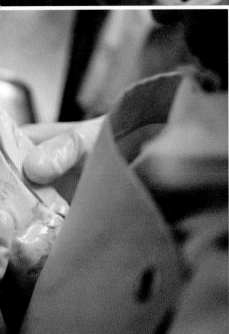

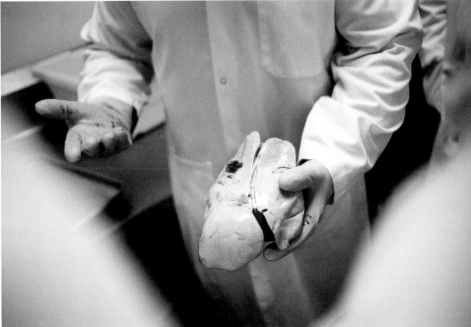

This is the thing—the foie gras, the fattened liver. It takes an enormous amount of care and work and expense to produce it. It is super delicious and it should be handled and cooked with care. The torchon recipe on page 270 is the most delicious way we know to prepare it.

shaved foie gras
lychee & pine nut brittle SERVES 8

We were grabbing for stars with Ko—we wanted to be taken seriously; we wanted our customers to feel like they were getting some luxury for the coin they were dropping on dinner. All those wants pointed in one direction: we needed to serve a foie gras course.

The genesis of this dish was a happy accident: I came across a torchon of foie gras in the freezer. I don't know why it was there—we'd probably made some for a special event, had not used all of it, froze it for future deployment, and then forgot about it. I thought I'd give grating it a try, just to see what it was like or if it worked.

It did: it avoids the overtly creamy, typically fatty assault of most foie gras dishes—it tastes almost light when you spoon it into your mouth, but as soon as it hits the back of your tongue—boom! Creamy, fatty, sweet, and cold. Delicious.

The composition of the rest of the dish was gradual. We got into eating and cooking with canned lychees through the Chinese guys who worked for our architects Swee and Hiro (and who built our restaurants)—they'd always eat cans of them for dessert after their lunches. It didn't take us long to jump on that train—we started by using them in an early version of the Ssäm Bar apple salad and tried them out in a couple other places before matching them up with the foie gras. Perfect. Plus a nice contrast: expensive foie gras and dirt-cheap canned lychees. (And, unlike foie gras, the cheaper the can of lychees, the better. I don't know why this is, but the flavor of cheap canned lychees versus fresh or fancy canned ones is vastly superior and more deeply lychee-like.)

The pine nut brittle came on board to add more textural contrast than the lychees did alone. The first time I made it with honey, but it eventually evolved into the version on the following pages, with isomalt and sucrose, because those sugars make for a less sweet and less cloying brittle. The Riesling gelée was the last component; it just rounded out the dish.

The final refinement was Sam Gelman's: he switched us over to curing the torchan instead of a cure-then-poach technique. It produces a more aggressively salty torchon that works even better with all that sweet shit.

And what started as a forgotten thing in the back of the freezer became our signature dish, the pork bun of Ko, the dish I think we'll never be able to take off the menu. Go figure.

One 12-ounce can lychees in syrup

½ cup (35 grams) Riesling Gelée (recipe follows)

½ cup (90 grams) Pine Nut Brittle (opposite)

⅓ to ½ Frozen Foie Gras Torchon (page 270)

1. Open the can of lychees, drain off the syrup, and quarter the lychees. Chill in the refrigerator until ready to use.

2. Place 2 tablespoons of the quartered lychees in the bottom of each of eight smallish serving bowls. Top the lychees with a tablespoon of Riesling gelée per bowl and top the gelée with a tablespoon of cracked brittle. Use a Microplane to shave a mound of the frozen foie gras onto the ingredients in the bowl; be as generous as you like.

riesling gelée
MAKES 1½ CUPS

Halve this recipe if you'd like (you only need about ½ cup for eight servings of Shaved Foie Gras, page 267), but the extra gelée is splendid with any leftover foie gras torchon.

2 sheets (4 grams) gelatin

1¼ cups (250 grams) decent Riesling, sweet or dry

1 teaspoon (4 grams) rice wine vinegar

1. Combine the gelatin, Riesling, and vinegar in a medium saucepan and bring to a simmer. Remove from the heat and pour into a small mixing bowl.

2. Put the bowl in the refrigerator to chill for 6 to 8 hours, using a long-tined fork to stir and break up the gelée thoroughly once an hour, to give it the look of shattered glass. The gelée keeps for up to a week, covered, in the refrigerator.

pine nut brittle

MAKES A SCANT 2 CUPS

Can you make a brittle for this dish without all these fancy sugars? Sure. But this brittle, developed by Christina Tosi, is easier to break, easier to eat, and easier to crush than your average brittle. The isomalt, which, along with the glucose, you can buy from Le Sanctuaire in Santa Monica, California, helps to keep the sweetness down, which is important to us, because the overall dish is sugary already. Ergo: a better brittle. Incidentally, this better brittle is excellent over ice cream too.

1. Heat the oven to 300°F. Cover a baking sheet with parchment paper or a Silpat or other nonstick baking sheet liner.

2. Combine the sugar, glucose, and isomalt in a medium heavy-bottomed saucepan over medium heat. Cook the sugars to a caramel without stirring or disturbing: the sugars will liquefy and then gradually take on color. After 12 to 15 minutes, the caramel should be light brown, not deep brown, and nutty smelling.

3. While the sugars are caramelizing, spread out the pine nuts on a baking sheet and put it in the oven. (They should warm through and only lightly toast.)

4. Add the warm pine nuts to the caramel and cook, stirring to incorporate them, for 1 minute. Add the butter and salt and cook, stirring, for 30 seconds more. Immediately pour the caramel out onto the prepared baking sheet and allow to cool to room temperature.

5. Use a mallet to break the brittle into small—bite-sized—pieces. Stored in a covered container at room temperature, pine nut brittle will keep for at least a week.

½ cup (100 grams) sugar

¼ cup (100 grams) glucose

¼ cup (100 grams) isomalt

⅔ cup (400 grams) pine nuts

5½ tablespoons (75 grams) unsalted butter, at room temperature

Pinch of kosher salt

frozen foie gras torchon

MAKES APPROXIMATELY ONE 1²/₃-POUND (750-GRAM) TORCHON

This recipe makes more than you will need for the shaved foie gras dish for eight—it actually makes two to three times as much as you need—but you can't buy less than a whole lobe of foie gras, and, like, leftover foie gras is such a problem? Bust out the brioche points and serve thick slices of the torchon topped with extra Riesling gelée or ripe seasonal fruit. You could do a lot worse. One more thing: you need a scale for this recipe, but I'm thinking that if you're going to shell out the cash for a lobe of foie gras, that isn't a problem—and you definitely don't want to fuck it up.

But, seriously, I really have no idea why anyone would try to make a torchon of foie gras at home. I could write a million words about doing it—Thomas Keller's got a longer recipe than we do in his French Laundry cookbook—but cleaning foie gras is ineffable. Track down a torchon from a specialty foods shop, freeze it, and then go to town. But for those who won't be deterred by common sense, here's our recipe.

1 lobe foie gras (2 to 2½ pounds; 907 to 1130 grams)

2 liters seltzer

per each 1.1 pounds (500 grams) of cleaned foie gras

2 teaspoons (8 grams) kosher salt

⅛ teaspoon curing salt (aka pink salt or sel rose)

¼ teaspoon (1 gram) sugar

2 tablespoons (25 grams) bourbon

2 tablespoons (25 grams) sweet dessert wine, such as a late-harvest Riesling or Muscat

¼ teaspoon (1 gram) finely ground pepper mix (one part white pepper to two parts black)

Kosher salt to cover (approximately 2 pounds, or 907 grams)

1. Soak the whole liver in the seltzer for 1 hour at room temperature.
2. Remove the foie gras from the water and allow it to sit on a clean, dry towel for 10 minutes. Then separate the lobes: With a small pair of tweezers and a butter knife, remove all visible veins, blood, and surface fat from the foie gras. Use the tweezers to pinch out green bile spots. Pinch or cut the foie gras into finger-sized pieces as you work, and inspect the pieces to make sure they are free of discoloration and veins. Transfer the cleaned foie gras to a large mixing bowl.
3. Weigh the cleaned foie gras and return it to the bowl. Using the ratios at left, prepare the marinade: dissolve the kosher salt, pink salt, and sugar in the bourbon and wine, add the pepper, and pour the mixture over the foie gras. Gently toss to ensure even distribution, then cover the bowl with plastic wrap and put it in the refrigerator to marinate for at least 4 hours, and as long as 24.
4. Put a large piece of parchment paper on your work surface. Mound the marinated foie gras chunks together in a neat long, rectangular pile on the paper and use the paper to help guide the foie gras into a neat, even log. Stack three 2½-foot-long pieces of cheesecloth atop one another on your work surface, with a long side of the rectangle facing you. Transfer the

foie gras from the parchment to the cheesecloth. Wrap the cheesecloth around the torchon and twist the ends tightly, using the torque of the twisting to help squeeze and shape the foie gras into a compact cylinder that's about 2 inches in diameter. Tightly tie one end with kitchen twine; twist the untied end again, and tie it. Put the torchon in a shallow pan and bury it in kosher salt. Cure it in the salt in the refrigerator for 18 hours.

5. Remove the torchon from the salt, brush off any salt still clinging to it, and hang it in the refrigerator for 24 hours, using the twine at one end to suspend it. (It doesn't matter which end is up or down, you just want to make sure air circulates around it.)

6. Remove the cheesecloth and wrap the foie gras in plastic wrap. Freeze for at least 8 hours, or for up to a few weeks. Unwrap and shave the torchon immediately after removing it from the freezer. Rewrap tightly and return to the freezer or thaw (which will take 1 to 2 days in the refrigerator) before slicing and serving chilled.

48-hour short rib braised daikon,
pickled carrot & mustard seeds SERVES 8

Time for some meat in the meal. This preparation of short ribs appeals to me because it's a superrefined version of some of my favorite rustic, simple meat dishes.

In the primordial days of Momofuku, when the space that is Ko was Noodle Bar, back when we started our slog from cooking whatever we could pull off to cooking whatever we wanted, a short rib braised in my mom's *kalbi* marinade was a staple on our winter menu. We'd also do a braised slab of pork belly with braised daikon that I'd copped from Kozue, the kaiseki restaurant where I had the pleasure to work when I trained in Tokyo. This dish is an amalgam of those two, with a goodly and corrective dash of sous vide cooking thrown in.

Back when I was a *stagiaire* at the Park Hyatt there in Tokyo, I worked at two of the restaurants in the hotel: Kozue, the fancy kaiseki place, and New York Grill, a popular, high-volume steak house. The meat guy—the *only* meat guy on the line at a 400-seat *steak* restaurant—had all of his meat parcooked in vacuum-sealed plastic bags, and he'd take out a piece of meat when it was ordered, slice it out of the bag, char it quickly on the grill, and get it onto the pass to go out to the dining room. Despite the fact that one guy was cooking hundreds of pieces of protein—from all kinds of different animals—at the same time and all to a perfect state of doneness, I thought that kind of cooking was a total cop-out. I thought he couldn't cook and the parcooking was a crutch for his weakness. Then, in the intervening years, I got some more experience and grew up a little bit and came to realize that sous vide cooking is amazing magic. (Or at least it can be; all good techniques can be poorly used.)

Sous vide cooking was invented in the 1970s in France. Boiled down to the nuts and bolts, it is ingredients (meat or vegetables or whatever, plus seasonings) vacuum-sealed in a plastic bag and cooked in a large tub of water that is heated to a precise temperature. At the restaurant, we use an immersion circulator—a piece of lab equipment with a heating element that is submerged in the water and a mechanism that circulates the water in the bath gently and constantly—to keep the water at a constant temperature. Sometimes the vacuum-packing is part of the "cooking" process—it can help infuse flavors (Dave Arnold vacuum-packs vegetables and booze like vodka to make almost instantly flavored alcohol), but *most* of the time, it's the low-temperature cooking aspect that cooks are after when they employ sous vide techniques.

That's because low-temperature cooking affords cooks an accuracy and a measure of control over the doneness of meat that we have only dreamed about since humans first witnessed the marriage of meat and fire. In its most basic and common application, you can cook an entire steak from tip to tail and all the way through to 125°F, say, without any under- or overdone parts, the way there always are when you cook a piece of meat with more traditional means. Give it a deep, quick browning over high heat—because the flavor of seared meat is part of what makes it so delicious— and that's it. No poking, no prodding, no thermometer: you know it's perfectly cooked.

This dish takes low-temperature cooking a little further, to turn a shoe leather– tough piece of beef into one that is marbled and textured like a sirloin. (Some customers at Ko think the rib is undercooked, because they're used to getting a sloppy soft braised thing when they get a short rib.) Cooking the short ribs at a really low temperature for a really long time—two days—breaks down certain, tough connective tissues and some fibrous structural proteins. It's a technique that was first made popular by Andoni Luis Aduriz at Mugaritz, outside San Sebastian. We Momofuku-ed it by braising it in a take on my mom's *kalbi* marinade and pairing it with braised daikon and pickles.

A little reality: This recipe is not a reasonable proposition for the home cook unless you are willing to buy a vacuum-sealing machine and fabricate a water circulator situation. And even then, 48 hours is a world of time to cook something. There's almost always somebody a couple of feet away from the ribs at the restaurant to keep an eye on things and make sure that the circulators don't die or anything, but there probably isn't (and probably shouldn't be) in most homes. But here's how to do it anyway.

short ribs

2⅔ cups (600 grams) water

½ cup plus 2 tablespoons (150 grams) usukuchi (light soy sauce)

3 tablespoons plus 1 teaspoon (42 grams) pear juice

3 tablespoons plus 1 teaspoon (42 grams) apple juice

2½ tablespoons (23 grams) mirin

1 tablespoon (13 grams) Asian sesame oil

1¼ cups (250 grams) sugar

10 grinds black pepper

½ small onion

1 small carrot

3 scallions, whites only

2 garlic cloves

8 pieces bone-in short ribs (5 to 6 ounces each; 140 to 170 grams each), trimmed of any silverskin and cut into individual ribs

Grapeseed or other neutral oil or rendered pork or duck fat for deep-frying

1. Make the marinade for the short ribs: Combine the water, soy, pear and apple juices, mirin, sesame oil, sugar, pepper, onion, carrot, scallions, and garlic in a large pot and bring to a boil over high heat. Reduce the heat so the liquid simmers gently and cook for 10 minutes. Strain the solids out of the marinade and cool it in the refrigerator. It can be stored, covered, for up to a few days.

2. Combine each short rib with ½ cup marinade in a vacuum-sealable bag and seal it, then seal the bagged rib in a second bag. (If one of those bags pops, your rib is toast, and it'll make a mess of everything, so better safe than sorry.) Put the bagged ribs in a water bath and set your immersion circulator to 60°C (140.2°F). Cook the ribs at that temperature for 48 hours.

3. When the ribs are cooked, remove them from the warm water bath and plunge them—still in their bags—into a large bowl of ice water. After they've been cooled, they can be stored in the refrigerator for up to a few days or frozen for a few weeks (defrost them overnight in the refrigerator).

4. Cut the ribs out of their bags over a mixing bowl to catch the braising liquid; set the ribs aside. Strain the braising liquid through a fine-mesh strainer into a small saucepan. Bring it to a boil over high heat and reduce it until you have about 2 cups, no more than 10 minutes. Reserve, covered (in the pan is fine), until you're ready to plate the dish.

5. Meanwhile, slide the bones out of the short ribs. Trim off any large obvious pieces of fat, and trim the ribs into neat cubes (or rectangles) that weigh about 3 ounces each.

6. Blanch the scallions for the garnish: Bring a small saucepan of salted water to a boil. Add the scallions and blanch for 10 seconds, then drain and cool in an ice bath or under cold running water. Drain well and reserve.

7. Heat a quart or two of oil to 365°F in a high-sided pan over medium-high heat. Line a plate with a double thickness of paper towels on which to drain the beef. Fry the short rib chunks in batches as necessary, so as not to crowd the pan, for 3 to 4 minutes; they should be mahogany brown outside and warmed all the way through. Remove the fried ribs from the oil and drain on the paper towels for a couple of minutes.

8. Put a couple of tablespoons of the reduced braising liquid in the center of each of eight large white plates. Lay a pickled carrot down across the pool of liquid (cut the carrots lengthwise in half if they're thick) and nestle a braised daikon disk up against it. Lay the green part of the blanched scallion across the carrots (the white should be sticking out like the minute hand on a clock). Slice the chunks of short ribs into three or four ⅜-inch-thick slices each, and shingle them over the scallion green. Fold/wrap the scallion back around over the meat, carefully perch the mustard seeds atop the daikon, and sprinkle the meat with Maldon salt. Serve at once.

garnish

8 scallions

8 medium Pickled Carrots
(page 177)

Dashi-Braised Daikon (recipe
follows)

¼ cup (70 grams) Pickled
Mustard Seeds (page 72)

Maldon salt

dashi-braised daikon
MAKES 8 PIECES

In Korean and Japanese cuisines, braised *mu* (Korean) or daikon (Japanese) is very common in stews and braised dishes. It's amazing, because it doesn't ever break down; it just turns into a tender flavor sponge.

1. Scrub the daikon, peel it, and cut it into 1-inch-thick disks.
2. Bring the dashi to a steady simmer in a small pot on the stove. Add the daikon and simmer for 30 minutes, until it is tender but not falling apart. At this point, you can cool the daikon in the dashi and store it in the refrigerator for up to a day, until ready to use.
3. When you're ready to serve, bring the dashi back up to a simmer and hold it there until the daikon is warmed through, 5 or so minutes. Scoop the daikon out of the dashi to serve. (The dashi can be reserved for another use or discarded.)

2 medium daikon, each a little
more than 1 inch in diameter

4 cups (1 liter) Traditional Dashi
(page 44) or instant dashi

rice with miso soup SERVES 8

This was a short-lived dish at the restaurant, but one that signaled our early commitment to a kaiseki-style meal, in that it concluded the savory portion of the menu with rice and pickles and miso soup, just as it would be done in a traditional kaiseki restaurant.

It was a perfectly fine dish, if maybe a little boring. There are a million ways a dish can fail—poor conception, poor execution, and so on—but this one fell off the menu fast because it demonstrated a too-literal commitment to an idea—to the idea of reinforcing that kaiseki connection to the first Ko menu. It was the same case with the foaming dashi scallop dish. The scallop was a send-up of foam; this dish was a way to say "Hey, this is kind of like kaiseki." The thing is, both were better ideas than they were dishes. Coming up with the first menu at Ko, wading out deeper into the uncertain waters of a more cerebral style of cooking, I stumbled into traps I hadn't confronted before, at least not as a chef.

Going forward, once we'd scrapped both the scallops and the miso soup, it became really important that whenever I or Gelman or Serpico was coming up with a new dish that it clear one hurdle for sure: Is it delicious? Good. Then the whole analytic thing can kick in: Is it a good idea, is it new, is it creative? And if it starts with an idea, no matter how dearly held or trailblazing the idea is, it still has to pass the test. No delicious, no go.

soup

2¼ pounds (1 kilo) white button mushrooms

1 small carrot, peeled and trimmed

1 small onion

2 garlic cloves, lightly crushed and peeled

8½ cups (2 liters) water

3 tablespoons (40 grams) whole-grain barley miso, or more to taste

Usukuchi (light soy sauce) if needed

garnish

About 1 tablespoon 1-inch chive batons

Pickled Napa Cabbage (page 69), made using whole leaves, cut into strips ½ inch wide and 2 inches long

8 Pickled Tokyo Turnips (page 69), quartered, or cut into sixths if particularly large

Nori Powder (recipe follows)

8 cylinders Grilled Rice (opposite)

1. Make the mushroom stock: Combine the mushrooms, carrot, onion, garlic, and water in a medium stockpot. Turn the heat under it up to high and bring the water to a steady, persistent simmer. Lower the heat and simmer the vegetables for 1 hour.

2. Strain the stock; discard the vegetables. Once cool, the stock can be kept, refrigerated and covered, in the refrigerator for up to a couple days, but it is best the day it is made.

3. When you're ready to serve the soup, heat the mushroom stock to a near-boil in a saucepan over high heat, then turn the heat off. Stir the miso into the broth and taste: it should taste identifiably of miso—the mushroom flavor should be in the background, adding depth and round-ness. If there's not enough miso flavor, add more miso by the tablespoon until it's right. Depending on your palate and your miso, the soup may need a little salt even after you've gotten the miso flavor right. Add soy sauce by the teaspoon, stirring and tasting after each addition, if that's the case.

4. Pour the miso soup into eight hot small bowls and float 4 chive batons in each. Put the bowls on large serving plates, then place a few strips of pickled cabbage in a small pile on each plate, flank it with a portion of pickled turnip, and sprinkle the assemblage with nori powder. Nestle a grilled rice cylinder alongside.

nori powder
MAKES 2 TABLESPOONS

2 tablespoons (26 grams) mirin

2 tablespoons (32 grams) usukuchi (light soy sauce)

Two 6-by-6-inch sheets nori

1. Stir together the mirin and soy sauce in a small bowl. Brush a very light coating of soy and mirin on both sides of the sheets of nori and dehydrate the nori in a dehydrator for 1 hour.

2. Crumble the seaweed, transfer to a spice grinder, and pulse on and off a few times: the nori powder should be a mix of flakes and dust. Stored in a covered container away from sunlight, it will keep indefinitely.

grilled rice

MAKES 8 RICE BALLS

At Ko, we use a mold to shape the rice for this dish into cylinders—the same kind of rice molds a Japanese mom might use to shape rice, or *onigiri,* for a kid's bento box lunch. Just before serving, we slick the cylinders with warmed rendered pork fat, sprinkle them with Maldon salt, and char them on the grill. Without a rice mold (and we didn't originally plan to use them, we planned on scooping the rice and shaping it to order—but that turned out to be a huge pain in the ass), you can shape the rice by hand into a ball or a cylinder (figure 3 tablespoons to ⅓ cup per serving) and proceed as below.

1. Light a hot fire in your grill or heat a grill pan over high heat.
2. Using a rice mold or wet hands, shape the rice into 8 cylinders (or balls, or whatever shape you like). Brush each one all over with the pork fat and sprinkle with salt. Grill the molded rice just until it's colored on one side, then very gently flip it over and mark the second side. Remove from the grill or pan and serve hot, with the miso soup.

2⅔ cups (420 grams) cooked and cooled Short-Grain Rice (recipe follows)

¼ cup (50 grams) rendered pork fat, warm

Maldon salt

short-grain rice

MAKES 4 CUPS

Japanese short-grain white rice is the only rice we make. We, like all restaurants and many home cooks, use a rice cooker to prepare it—it's just that much easier and more reliable than cooking rice on the stove. Here are directions for both methods.

1. Put the rice in a large bowl (or in the insert that fits into the rice cooker) and add enough water to submerge it by an inch. Use your fingers to stir the rice—stirring the rice like this will loosen the powdery rice starch from the grains and cloud the water. Tilt the bowl to drain the rice, using your hand to keep the rice from going down the drain with the water, and repeat until the rice no longer clouds the water.
2. If using a rice cooker, cook the rice according to the manufacturer's instructions. If cooking on the stovetop, put the rice in a medium saucepan with a lid, add the water, cover the pan, and bring to a boil over medium-high heat. Once the water boils, reduce the heat to low and cook, covered, until the rice has absorbed all the water in the pot, about 20 minutes.
3. Regardless of whether you've cooked it on the stove or in a cooker, when the rice is ready, paddle it: we use a short, wide, wooden rice paddle to do so, but any wooden spoon will work. Just stir and fluff the rice, letting the steam escape, then let it sit for another 10 minutes with the lid of the pan or the cooker slightly ajar before serving.

2 cups short-grain white rice (sometimes labeled "sushi rice")

2 cups water (if cooking on the stovetop)

cereal milk SERVES 8

The plan was to chase the miso soup course with a pre-dessert. We planned something fresh and small and cold, like a quenelle of fresh pineapple sorbet over a chewy piece of dried pineapple. Something to set the diner up for the big finish, the apple pie.

But the freezers we had when we opened Ko didn't always play nice. Sorbet needs to be kept at a certain and constant temperature, and if your freezer isn't holding one, it can melt and refreeze and the texture goes to shit.

So Tosi devised this panna cotta as a last-minute addition to the menu for nights when the sorbet wasn't up to snuff. She'd been kicking around the idea of doing something with a cereal-flavored milk for a while—when she worked at wd~50, they'd played with it—and this was the first incarnation. We were all psyched about the custard as soon as we tasted it, but then there was the question of how to elevate it to make it more than just a simple riff on a childhood flavor.

Tosi talked with Serpico about what to do and he suggested avocado as a possible pairing. If that sounds unlikely, it's only stranger then that Tosi had an avocado puree ready to go in the kitchen downstairs—it's a fruit that gets little play in the dessert world, and it was something she was toying with at the time. They plated it, ate it, agreed to add chocolate, and after a couple days of Tosi's tinkering, this dessert was born.

cereal milk custard

6 cups (265 grams) cornflakes

3 cups (710 grams) whole milk

2 cups (470 grams) heavy cream

¼ cup (30 grams) packed light brown sugar

Generous ½ teaspoon (2 grams) kosher salt

2 sheets (4 grams) gelatin

garnish

Avocado Puree (opposite)

Chocolate-Hazelnut Thing (opposite)

Caramelized Cornflakes (page 287)

1. Heat the oven to 300°F.

2. Spread out the cornflakes on a baking sheet and pop it in the oven. Toast the cereal for 12 minutes—it will deepen lightly in color and more so in flavor. Cool the cereal on the sheet for a few minutes, just until it's no longer hot to the touch.

3. Combine the milk and cream in a container large enough to accommodate them and the cornflakes. Add the warm cornflakes, stir to combine, and let steep for 40 to 45 minutes. (The finished custard will be too starchy if it steeps longer than that.)

4. Strain the milk, passing it through a fine-mesh sieve and pressing on the cornflakes with the back of a rubber spatula to extract as much liquid from them as possible. (At this point, you can discard the soggy cereal, or do like Sam Gelman and eat it.) Pass the milk through the strainer one more time as you transfer it to a microwave-safe container.

5. Add the brown sugar and salt to the milk and heat it in the microwave on low power for 1½ minutes—just long and hot enough for the sugar to dissolve easily. Give the milk a quick gentle stir to help disperse the sugar. (You can lightly warm the milk on the stove instead of doing it in the microwave, but if you do, do not whisk or overly aerate or overheat it.)

6. Bloom (soften) the gelatin in 2 cups of cold water. After 2 to 3 minutes—when it's supple and no longer crisp, with a texture Tosi calls "like a jellyfish"—remove it from the water, wring it out, and add it to the cereal milk. Stir it once or twice to melt the gelatin in the milk.

7. Divide the milk among eight 5- to 6-ounce ramekins, or use a silicone mold—the molds we use at Ko, which look like soft plastic ice cube trays, shape the custard into 3-inch-long by 1-inch-wide rectangles. Put the cereal milk in the refrigerator to set, about 30 minutes. Then, if you're serving the custard out of the containers you chilled it in, cover them and reserve until ready to serve. If you're using silicone molds, put them in the freezer for an hour or so, and the custard blocks will pop out just like ice cubes. Store them in the refrigerator until ready to use. (Also, note that these custards can be frozen for at least a few weeks once set. Defrost them, still covered, in the fridge, on a rimmed tray lined with wax paper—not parchment paper, which will stick to the custards.)

8. To serve, plop a large dollop—a couple of tablespoons—of avocado puree just off the center of eight large white plates, then use the back of the spoon to drag some of it across each plate. Put a cereal milk custard down in the avocado trail, lean a chip of chocolate-hazelnut thing up against it, and scatter caramelized cornflakes on the plate with restraint.

avocado puree

MAKES ABOUT ¾ CUP

Prepare the puree as close as possible to the time you intend to serve it.

1. Chill the avocado until cold, or for up to 5 hours.

2. Combine the avocado, citric acid, salt, and sugar in a blender. Blend until smooth, then pass the puree through a tamis or strainer into a small bowl and reserve, with a piece of plastic wrap pressed up against the exposed surface of the puree, until ready to serve.

1 ripe Hass avocado, halved, pitted, and peeled

Pinch of citric acid

Pinch of kosher salt

Pinch of sugar

chocolate-hazelnut thing

SERVES 8

1. Combine the praline paste, gianduja, oil, salt, chocolate, and corn syrup in a microwave-safe container and stir to combine. Microwave the mixture for 10 seconds, then stir it up, and repeat four or five more times, until the mixture is fluid and homogeneous, with just the finest, tiniest amount of grit in it from the nut content. (Alternatively, you can do this in a heatproof bowl set over a saucepan of a couple of inches of simmering water.)

2. Spread the mixture out in a ¼-inch-thick layer (if it's any thinner than that, it's too thin) on a Silpat-lined baking sheet, and scatter the chocolate puddle with the caramelized cornflakes. Freeze it to set, which should take about 20 minutes (though you can leave it in the freezer longer).

3. Grab the frozen piece of chocolate-hazelnut thing from the freezer and break it into random, uneven pieces. Store them in a sealed container in the freezer until ready to use, or for up to a few weeks—by which point you will have probably snacked them out of existence.

¼ cup (55 grams) Praline Paste (page 286) or store-bought praline paste

⅓ cup (55 grams) gianduja

¼ teaspoon (1 gram) grapeseed or other neutral oil

Pinch of kosher salt

1 tablespoon (10 grams) smallish pieces bittersweet chocolate, ideally in the 70% to 72% cacao range

½ teaspoon (5 grams) light corn syrup

2 tablespoons Caramelized Cornflakes (page 287)

praline paste

MAKES ABOUT 1 CUP

A few things about praline paste: It can be purchased if you don't want to make it. Homemade praline paste is like soigné (and trans-fat-free) Nutella and is good on anything, even fingers, so double or triple the recipe at will. And the Chocolate-Hazelnut Thing (page 285) only requires ¼ cup, so there will be leftovers in any case.

½ cup (70 grams) whole hazelnuts

½ cup (100 grams) sugar

Tiny pinch of kosher salt

1. Heat the oven to 400°F.

2. Spread out the hazelnuts on a rimmed baking sheet and toast them in the oven for 10 to 15 minutes, until they're warmed through and aromatic. Remove from the oven and let cool.

3. Put the sugar in a heavy-bottomed pot over medium-low heat. Leave it alone and let it start to caramelize around the edges of the pan before you begin to stir it with a heatproof spatula or wooden spoon. Patiently and attentively shepherd the sugar into a state of delicious caramelization: stir it slowly and constantly, until it's medium amber—like the color of Grade B maple syrup—and is very fluid.

4. Put the hazelnuts into a food processor or blender, add the caramel and salt, and process for 3 to 5 minutes, scraping down the hot sweet mush from the sides of the bowl as often as necessary until it comes together into a smooth, even paste. Store the praline paste in the refrigerator for weeks, if not months, until ready to use.

caramelized cornflakes

MAKES ABOUT ¾ CUP

1. Heat the oven to 275°F.

2. Put the cornflakes in a large mixing bowl and crush them with your hands. Seven or eight squeezes should be sufficient; you want crumbles, not powder.

3. Stir together the milk powder, sugar, and salt in a small bowl. Add the butter to the cornflakes and sprinkle the sugar mixture over them. Toss and stir to coat the cereal evenly.

4. Spread out the cereal on a baking sheet lined with parchment paper (or a Silpat, if you have one) and bake for 20 minutes, or until the milk powder and sugar have started to caramelize and turn a satisfying deep golden color. Remove from the oven and let cool. The flakes will keep, in a sealed container at room temperature, for at least a week.

¾ cup (60 grams) cornflakes

3 tablespoons (12 grams) nonfat dry milk powder

1 tablespoon (12 grams) sugar

½ teaspoon (1 gram) kosher salt

3½ tablespoons (45 grams) unsalted butter, melted

fried apple pie SERVES 6

Fried apple pie. Who doesn't have a memory of searing the skin off his tongue when eagerly biting into a too-hot McDonald's apple pie?

The concept and motivation behind this dish were simple, but Tosi did the work to complicate and elevate it. She took it as a challenge to combine apples and miso—a somewhat popular combination with pastry chefs in New York—and do it in a new way. That was how the miso butterscotch came about. The butterscotch is delicious on its own and adds a salty note to the dessert that keeps the pie grounded.

Coming up with a dough that would fry well and that would hold together was another hurdle. Tosi came up with this dough, which is the opposite of any good pastry dough—it's overworked, tough like wonton dough, not tender, not flaky. (If you try to deep-fry a classic buttery pastry dough, it'll fall to pieces.) So this is a specially designed dough that deep-fries nicely—the cornstarch and low proportion of fat help with that—and it's very easy to handle and work with because it's not delicate in the slightest.

And then there are the apples. The technique here seems fussy because it is, but the payoff in the pie is big. Preparing the apples two ways means that some of them are tender soft while others still have crunch to them, and the pectin adds that oozy pie texture to the junk the apples are suspended in. It's perfect.

apple pie

1¾ cups (250 grams) all-purpose flour, plus more for rolling the dough

3 tablespoons (15 grams) cornstarch

3 tablespoons (45 grams) sugar

Scant 1 teaspoon (3 grams) kosher salt

2½ tablespoons (37 grams) cold unsalted butter, cut into pieces

1 tablespoon plus 2 teaspoons (25 grams) vegetable shortening or pork fat

½ teaspoon (2 grams) white, apple cider, or rice wine vinegar

1¼ cups (125 grams) water

Apple Pie Filling (page 292)

Grapeseed or other neutral oil or rendered pork fat for deep-frying

garnish

Cinnamon Dust (page 293)

Miso Butterscotch (page 293)

Sour Cream Ice Cream (page 293)

1. Make the dough: Combine the flour, cornstarch, sugar, and salt in the bowl of a stand mixer fitted with the paddle attachment. Turn the machine on to low and beat for 10 to 15 seconds to mix them together. Add the butter and shortening and beat on medium-low speed for about 3 minutes, until the dough looks like clumpy sand—it should still be shy of the gravelly/pellet stage.

2. Add the vinegar to the water and then, with the mixer running on medium-low speed, add the liquid to the coalescing dough a few table-spoons at a time: this dough will be much wetter and more overworked than you'd ever want a traditional pie or tart dough to be. It should take about 2 minutes of mixing for it to come together into a dough; mix it for a couple of additional minutes once it does. Take the gummy dough out of the mixer, shape it into a flat, thick square or rectangle, wrap it in plastic, and refrigerate it for at least an hour. Freeze apple pie dough for up to 2 weeks if you are not going to use it the day you make it. Defrost in the refrigerator before proceeding.

3. Bring the dough back up to almost room temperature; it will be shiny and greasy, not a pretty pastry dough. Tosi uses a scale to measure the amount of dough she needs for forming the pies and you should too. You need 6 tops and 6 bottoms. For the bottoms, grab off 50-gram (golf ball–sized) pieces of dough and on a lightly floured surface roll into rectangles that measure 6 by 3½ inches; for the tops, roll out 30-gram (Ping Pong ball–sized) nuggets of dough into rectangles that measure 5½ by 4 inches. Both should be just more than an ⅛ inch thick.

4. Generously flour the molds. Press each of the larger bottom rectangles into a 4½ by 2½ by ¾-inch mold (failing a rectangular mold, you could substitute fluted mini-tart pans with removable bottoms, in which case, you'd need to roll the dough out into circles to fit your pans), making sure the dough is flush against the fluted sides and the bottom, with a very slight excess of dough hanging over the edges. Put ⅓ cup (75 grams) apple filling in each one, and use the back of a spoon to smooth it out. Tap each mold against the counter to make sure the apples shimmy their jellied selves into the corners of the mold; there should be some clearance between the top of the apple mush and the rim of each mold. Dip a pastry brush in a bowl of cold water and moisten the edges of the dough in the molds, then gently lay the other rectangles of dough over the molds, crimping the tops and bottoms of the dough together all the way around.

5. Freeze the pies in the molds for 30 minutes, just enough time for the dough to firm up and release itself from the mold. Pop the pies out of the molds, transfer them to a rimmed baking sheet, wrap it in plastic, and freeze the pies until frozen solid, at least a few hours. You can keep the pies frozen for weeks before proceeding.

6. When you're ready to serve the dessert, heat a quart or two of oil to between 350° and 370°F in a large pot with high sides. Set up a cooling rack for the pies to drain on after they're fried. Put the cinnamon dust in a small sieve to use to dust the pies with later, and set it on a plate. Turn the oven to 250°F—it doesn't need to preheat; it just needs to be warm. Set a cooling rack over a baking sheet and put it in the oven, to keep the just-fried pies hot until ready to serve.

7. When the oil reaches temperature, use a slotted spoon to lower a frozen pie into the hot oil (frying them one at a time is the most advisable course of action). The oil will bubble and hiss a bit when the pie goes in, but the bubbling should subside as it sinks to the bottom of the pot. After a couple of minutes, the pie will become more buoyant, and in 4 to 6 minutes, it should be taking on a good auburn color—getting a good brown on the pie makes it more delicious and is a good visual indication that the inside will be appropriately piping hot. When it's browned and bobbing up near the surface of the oil, scoop it out of the pot and transfer it to the cooling rack to drain (actually, for the first 4 pies, transfer to the rack in the oven to drain and stay hot). After a minute or so, once the pie has shaken off the searing heat of the fryer, dust the top of it generously with cinnamon dust. Fry the rest of the pies. (Don't worry if a pie leaks or develops a crack—we wouldn't serve a pie like that at Ko, but we've eaten a few of those rejects, and they just have an extra deep-fried flavor to them.)

8. To plate the apple pies, plop down a very generous tablespoon of miso butterscotch slightly off the center of each of six wide white plates. Use the back of the spoon to schmear the butterscotch across the plate. Arrange a fried pie on the plate perpendicular to the butterscotch schmear. Scoop out a quenelle or ball of sour cream ice cream and arrange it on the plate. Serve at once.

apple pie filling
MAKES ENOUGH FILLING FOR 6 FRIED APPLE PIES

The filling for the apple pies is a mix of an apple compote and an apple jelly. The jelly turns into the hot gooey ooze that makes the pies so appealing; the compote has the chunky, comforty texture of apple pie.

compote

2 small Empire apples, peeled, cored, and roughly chopped

¼ cup plus 2 tablespoons (65 grams) packed light brown sugar

⅓ cup (65 grams) apple cider

1 cinnamon stick

Pinch of kosher salt

Juice of ½ lemon

jelly

1¼ teaspoons (4 grams) pectin crystals

¼ cup plus 1 tablespoon (50 grams) packed light brown sugar

Large pinch of ground cinnamon

Scant 1 cup (190 grams) apple cider

2 Fuji apples, peeled, cored, and chopped

1. Make the compote: Combine the Empire apples, brown sugar, apple cider, and cinnamon stick in a medium saucepan and slowly bring to a boil over medium heat. As soon as the mixture boils, remove the apples with a slotted spoon and transfer them to a mixing bowl (leave the cinnamon stick in the pan).

2. Turn the heat up under the pan and reduce the cooking liquid by half. Add the reduced cooking liquid to the apples, season them with the salt and lemon juice, and set aside to cool.

3. Make the jelly: Combine the pectin, brown sugar, cinnamon, and apple cider in a small saucepan and bring to a boil over high heat. Meanwhile, put the chopped Fuji apples in a bowl large enough to accommodate them and the contents of the pan.

4. When the syrup boils, pour it over the apples and stir to combine, then cool the mixture to room temperature. Put the bowl in the refrigerator to chill so the pectin can set and the jelly will gel.

5. Add the jelly to the compote and stir to blend well. Store in the refrigerator until ready to use, up to 1 week.

cinnamon dust

MAKES ABOUT 2 TABLESPOONS

Combine the sugar, cinnamon, and salt in a spice grinder and process for a minute to turn it from a granulated mix into a dust. Covered and stored away from the light, it keeps indefinitely.

Heaping 2 tablespoons (30 grams) sugar

1 teaspoon (3 grams) ground cinnamon

¼ teaspoon (1 gram) kosher salt

miso butterscotch

MAKES 1 CUP

1. Heat the oven to 400°F.
2. Spread the miso in a thin, even layer on a Silpat-lined baking sheet and pop it into the oven for 20 to 30 minutes. The miso should be on the blackened side of browned and should have an incredibly appetizing burnt smell to it.
3. Let the miso cool briefly, so it's easier to handle, then scrape it into a blender jar. Add the brown sugar, mirin, vinegar, and butter and blend until the mixture is homogeneous and smooth. Scrape the mixture into a bowl and store, covered, in the refrigerator for weeks, if not months.

¼ cup plus 2 tablespoons (100 grams) shiro (white) miso

¼ cup plus 2 tablespoons (65 grams) packed light brown sugar

¼ cup plus 1 tablespoon (67 grams) mirin

Splash of sherry vinegar

4 tablespoons (½ stick; 58 grams) unsalted butter, at room temperature

sour cream ice cream

MAKES 1 QUART

1. Combine the sugar and water in a small saucepan and bring to a simmer, stirring until the sugar dissolves. Remove from the heat and let the sugar syrup cool completely.
2. Whisk the sour cream in a large bowl until smooth. Gradually whisk in the sugar syrup, lime zest, and juice. Refrigerate until cold.
3. Transfer to an ice cream maker and freeze according to the manufacturer's instructions.

1 cup (200 grams) sugar

¾ cup (50 grams) water

1 pint (454 grams) sour cream

Grated zest of ½ lime

3 tablespoons (37 grams) fresh lime juice

sources

My answer about sources—about what ingredients are and where to get them—is pretty simple: Google it. What's a dried scallop? Google it. Where can I buy Kewpie mayonnaise? Google it. We Google for information all the time at the restaurants. And while you can't trust everything you read on the Internet, you can find a lot of helpful information there.

The most important ingredients to worry about getting your hands on are fresh top-quality meat, fish, shellfish, and vegetables. Whatever kind of local market you have access to—be it seasonal or year-round, as sprawling as the one in Santa Monica (where I've seen four kinds of Asian pears) or as modest as the one I saw in Madisonville, Tennessee (where the live country music was awesome)—is the place to start. Cook with vegetables in their seasons if you can afford to. The results will be better.

Meat is trickier. Old-school butcher shops and fancy supermarkets like Whole Foods are often your best bets, though meat available at farmers' markets, even if it comes at a premium, is worth checking out (and may very well be the best option). Niman Ranch (nimanranch.com) is well set-up to sell its meat online, and we buy enough bellies and shoulders from them to vouch for it.

Fish is the trickiest: quality fish shops are few and far between, especially as you get farther away from the coasts. Developing a relationship with your local fishmonger will pay off greater dividends in the end.

The good news is that shellfish ships well: live clams and mussels should be easy to find. Many oyster-growing operations will mail you a few dozen of their oysters; check oysterguide.com (overseen by Rowan Jacobson, who wrote an excellent inlet-by-inlet guide to America's oysters) for leads, or just get the name of the oyster and grower the next time you have a great oyster at a restaurant, then Google and call them up. Jonah crab claws are available through mainelobsterdirect.com.

Then there are plenty of specific ingredients we call for—foodstuffs made by artisans that we don't think there's any substitute for. Allan Benton's bacon and ham fall into that category; his bacon is just some of the best stuff out there. Get Allan's products at bentonshams.com or call the smoke-

house at (423) 442-5003 and you might get him on the other end of the line. Anson Mills sells grits and more through ansonmills.com; Burgers' smoked jowls are at smokehouse.com.

Beyond that, there's the arsenal of Korean, Chinese, Vietnamese, and Japanese products that we use. Hoisin sauce and sriracha (the one in the green-topped bottle with the rooster on it) are widely available. Usukuchi soy sauce (we like the Yamasa brand), fresh noodles, rice wine vinegar, Asian sesame oil, fish sauce (we like the Squid brand), Kewpie mayonnaise, and dried shiitake mushrooms are sold at almost every well-stocked Asian grocery store and certainly at Japanese and Korean markets. Some supermarkets carry all of those ingredients.

For yuzu products, mirin, seaweeds like nori and konbu, katsuo-bushi, furikake, and shichimi togarashi you may need to seek out a Japanese market or, if there isn't one in your area, head to the internet. Mitsuwa, which has eight stores in the United States, has a website (mitsuwa.com) from which you can order many Japanese ingredients.

Salted shrimp, kochukaru, ssämjang (and anything that ends with -jang), rice cakes, and other Korean ingredients are stocked at any self-respecting Korean supermarket (by which I don't mean stores owned by Koreans, but stores catering to a Korean clientele). H Mart has stores in a dozen states and a well-stocked website (hmart.com).

Toban jan, Chinese sausage, dried shrimp, dried scallops, and packaged fried shallots (cousins of the canned fried onions used in a million American households for Thanksgiving casseroles) are all easily acquired in any Chinatown or Chinese grocery.

Getting to the more esoteric end of things, meat glue, as well as many harder-to-find spices (like Sichuan peppercorns), can be purchased from Le Sanctuaire (le-sanctuaire.com), a fancy chef's- and spice-supply operation in southern California. The alkaline salts for alkaline noodles are available through bio-world.com. Pastry supplies, like the molds for making the fried apple pies from Ko, are available through nycake.com, the online home of New York Cake Supplies in Chelsea.

ssäm bar

noodle bar

ko

milk bar

acknowledgments

dave chang

Thank you to the Momofuku family past and present for contributing so much:

Noodle Bar: Quino Baca, thank you for being instrumental in our survival early on and believing when no one else did. We wouldn't be here without you. May the Brooklyn Star live long and prosper! Tim Maslow, Scott Garfinkel, Kevin Pemoulie, Johanna Ware, Pedro Dominguez, Eugene Lee, Zipa Acosta.

Ssäm Bar: Tien Ho will always have the last laugh. Josh Kleinman, Francis Derby, Sean Gray, Anacleto. Jude, Tex, and Gabe, can't believe how much you guys have grown. Cory Lane, for teaching us what service means.

Ko: Peter Serpico, six years and counting down, chef. Sam Gelman, thanks for believing. Mitch Bates, Ryan Miller, and Johnny Leach, you guys make Ko run. Nadia Gan-Baca, Emily 1 & 2, and Christina Turley.

Milk Bar & Bakery: Christina Tosi, thank you for teaching us the impossible about sugar consumption! Marian Mar, for putting up with my stupid antics. James "Funky Flex" Mark, Sarah Buck, and Tosi #1, #2 & #3.

Papercut: Drew Salmon das boot (team shake & bake). EunJean Song, there isn't anyone with more integrity than you. Alex Magnan-Wheelock—if Antoinette only knew how talented you are. Sue Chan, Ling Koh Hsu. Josh Corey.

To everyone who visits our restaurants: we are eternally grateful.

To the Craft Restaurant NYC BOH version 1.2: Tom Colicchio, Marco Canora, Jonathan Benno, Akhtar Nawab, James Tracey, Damon Wise, Karen DeMasco, Dan Sauer, Liz Chapman, Brian Sernatinger, Ed Higgins, Stacey Meyer, PJ Knollmeueller, Jen Redmen, and Ed Carew. I am forever indebted to all of you.

Special thanks to the kitchen crew of wd~50, especially Wylie Dufresne for sharing the fire, Hearth and Terroir restaurants, Johnny Iuzzini, Nils Noren, Dave Arnold, Adam Perry Lang, Jean-Georges Vongerichten, Eric Ripert, Daniel Boulud, The French Laundry and Per Se teams, Ken Friedman, April Bloomfield and the Spotted Pig crew, Mario Batali and Co., Alice Waters and Chez Panisse, Michel Bras, Ferran Adrià, Juan Mari and Elena Arzak, Andoni Aduriz and Mugaritz, René Redzepi and Noma, Fred & David and the Joe Beef crew, Paul Kahan, Chris Cosentino and Incanto, Michael Anthony and Gramercy Tavern, Andrew Carmellini, Don and Chika, José Andrés. Big shout-out to Sam Beall and the Blackberry Farm family. Thank you to NYC for everything.

Allan Benton, Tony Bourdain, Harold McGee. All-Clad, Hobart, Philip Preston at PolyScience, Alto-Shaam, Viking Range Corporation, Le Sanctuaire, SOS Chefs, Johnny Magazino and Primizie Foods, George Kao and New York Mutual Trading Co., Paulette and Chef Eberhard at Satur Farms, Hilly Acres Farm, Paul Willis of Niman Ranch, George Faison and Doug Rodda at Debragga & Spitler, Pat La Frieda, Piccinini Brothers, Heritage Foods, Izzy Yanay and Michael Ginor at Hudson Valley Foie Gras, Nevia and Yuno's Farm, Suzie and family at Cherry Lane Farms, Rick Bishop and Mountain Sweet Berry Farm, Tim Starck and Eckerton Hill Farm. Pierless Fish, Father's Fish, Hong Seafood.

Andrea Petrini, Sébastien Demorand, Luc Dubanchet, and the whole Omnivore team. Swee and Hiro, Carolyn Richmond, Andy Peskoe, Gary Levy, Tim Quinlan, Hassan Chaudry, Chris Stevenson, Will Egan, Marc Salafia, and everyone from Trin, thank you so much for the early support!

Thanks to Erika and Richard for introducing us to MomoGabri = Gabriele Stabile. In Korean, "Mark Ibold" translates to "runs with black pepper."

Thanks to Kim Witherspoon and team for being excellent bodyguards.

To my family: JC, Mom, Yong, Jhoon, Esther—I never say I love you guys enough.

Thanks to Rica Allannic, Marysarah Quinn, and the entire Clarkson Potter team.

Finally, Peter Meehan—no one knows the Momo story better than you. Thank you for giving me the awesome.

peter meehan

First and foremost thanks go to my book people, photographer Gabriele Stabile and male hand model Mark Ibold: you guys rule. Thank you for your hard and remarkable work and for keeping this thing fun when it threatened to stray elsewhere. I owe you forever.

At Momofuku, particular thanks go to Scott Garfinkel, Tien Ho, Sam Gelman, Christina Tosi, and the Papercut ladies for the hours worked in service of this book—it wouldn't have happened without your input and dedication. And to everybody FOH and BOH who has had to put up with me through this process. Sorry about that.

At Clarkson Potter, we owe the greatest debt to Rica Allannic, who was patient and understanding and borderline beatific and who may or may not still be traumatized by the experience. Thanks to Marysarah Quinn, who might be owed even more apologies than thanks, but whose fortitude was heroic to the end. Also to Ashley Phillips, Kate Tyler, Courtney Greenhalgh, Donna Passannante, Christine Tanigawa, Joan Denman, Jill Flaxman, Doris Cooper, Lauren Shakely, and Jenny Frost.

Thanks to Wylie and Allan and Dave Arnold and Uncle Choi for agreeing to appear in these pages and taking the time to let us bother you. Thanks to Duane Sorenson and Hillary Liberman, Lee Ranaldo and Leah Singer, Vicki Farrell and MI, and Jim Meehan for lending us your good looks. To Joshua David Stein for the dragons. Next time.

Love to Bob and Miki for letting me make a mess of your country kitchen and sorry about surprising you with the pig head that one time. Thanks to the offices of Leventhal, Kludt & Steele for desk space around the holidays. Love and thanks to all my friends who had to eat the test food or, more often, listen to me bitch during the time it took to pull this together.

A blanket thanks to anybody who got trampled in the process of making this book whom we forgot to thank here: see, we really are the assholes you guessed we were.

Love to Hannah and Oscar, for always and forever.

Oh yeah, thanks to Chang, you ornery, difficult, occasionally inspiring fucking weirdo. Thanks for letting me in.

index